Relevance of Ambedkar's Ideology

Relevance of Ambedkar's Ideology

Kanta Kataria

RAWAT PUBLICATIONS
Jaipur • New Delhi • Bangalore • Hyderabad • Guwahati • Kolkata

ISBN 978-81-316-0720-6

The publication of the work was financially supported by the Jai Narain Vyas University, Jodhpur under the UGC Scheme. The responsibility for the facts stated/expressed and conclusions reached are entirely that of the author and the University accepts no responsibility for them.

Published by
Prem Rawat for **Rawat Publications**
Satyam Apts, Sector 3, Jawahar Nagar, Jaipur 302 004 (India)
Phone: 0141 265 1748/7006 Fax: 0141 265 1748
E-mail: info@rawatbooks.com
Website: www.rawatbooks.com

New Delhi Office
4858/24, Ansari Road, Daryaganj, New Delhi 110 002
Phone: 011 2326 3290

Also at *Bangalore, Hyderabad, Guwahati* and *Kolkata*

Typeset by Rawat Computers, Jaipur
Printed at Chaman Enterprises, New Delhi

Contents

Foreword

Dr B.R. Ambedkar was one of the most significant makers of modern India. His work was qualitatively different from that of his predecessors. He at once stood for social liberation, economic emancipation and political advancement of the downtrodden millions – a task never undertaken by any high caste Hindu leader with so much vigour and force. He was indeed a social rebel who raised the banner of revolt against the iniquitous caste-ridden society. He roused the frozen conscience of the depressed people and brought new consciousness among them. He urged them that their social liberation must be ensured in this very life and that too as their legitimate right as free citizens.

In addition to the abolition of untouchability, Dr Ambedkar's contribution towards the making of the Indian Constitution was enormous. As the Chairman of the Drafting Committee he was one of the architects, who designed and built the remarkable edifice of our Constitution. Further, Dr Ambedkar's conversion to Buddhism gave a new life to Buddhism in India. As such, he combined in himself the role of a social reformer, a political leader, a constitutionalist and a spiritual guide of the untouchables. He, therefore, played a unique role in shaping the mind, the political outlook of his community and the transformation of society in modern India.

Though Dr Ambedkar occupies an exalted position in shaping the destiny of 20th century India, very few scholars in the field of modern Indian social and political thought have been able to capture the essence of his ideology and, the extent to which it is relevant in building a vibrant and harmonious social order. Connected with this particular context of Ambedkar's ideology, Professor Kanta Kataria's present work is highly significant – definitely greater than any other work in the related field.

Professor Kanta Kataria is a scholar of eminence in Political Science, possessing a good specialization in modern Indian social and political thought. More than two decades back, she secured the doctoral degree on the dissertation titled, 'Political Ideas of M.N. Roy,' and recently, she had been awarded the degree of D. Litt. in Political Science by J.N. Vyas University, Jodhpur on the thesis titled 'Dr B.R. Ambedkar: Ideology and Its Relevance Today'. This post-doctoral research work of Professor Kanta Kataria is, in my opinion, an outstanding contribution to the existing knowledge on Ambedkar. Its impcrtance is on account of a combination of three factors. First, she has been able to grasp the essence of Ambedkar's ideology and has evaluated it in a critical tone, free from bias. Second, she has demonstrated that in the present day situation in India, where caste is being polarized and social tensions are on the rise, the ideology of Ambedkar, if adopted, either partially or wholly, can usher in a new social revolution. And lastly, being an authentic and reliable work, it provides useful clues toward minimizing frictions in society in a better way instead of searching for their solutions in the mirages of supernatural forces.

I am really happy to state that Prof. Kanta Kataria, being one of the most distinguished scholars, especially in the Ambedkarian studies, has indeed produced an impressive work – brilliant both in language and scholarship. I am hopeful that her work would be acclaimed as a masterpiece about Ambedkar's ideology and its relevance. For the researchers and general readers, the work would be worthwhile and interesting.

I should not fail to congratulate Prof. Kanta Kataria for producing a magnificent work of scholarship on Dr Ambedkar's ideology and its relevance.

Professor L.S. Rathore
Emeritus Professor in Political Science
and Former Vice Chancellor, Jodhpur University

Preface

Among all the social and political thinkers of the 20th century in India, B.R. Ambedkar occupies a highly significant place. It is generally believed that his contributions are threefold: (i) the principal architect of the Constitution of India; (ii) the revival of Buddhism; and (iii) the abolition of untouchability in our country. Though these achievements are remarkably substantial, but I strongly feel that they do not reveal the complete picture of his contributions.

Let me say that the basic contribution of Ambedkar, and the one which is more enduring and more durable, is his *ideology* which continues to have its relevance, even today. Discarding the infallibility of the *Vedas, Manusmriti,* scriptures and theology, he emerges as a supreme stalwart of a new socio-political ideology, rooted in rationality, and aiming towards social transformation and reconstruction. Like the thinkers of the age of enlightenment, he believes in the power of reason and advocates that the social order be guided by it. Rationality is the criterion or standard by which all things are to be judged. It is only through the employment of reason that a new and progressive society can be built, and its divergent fractions can be woven in one thread. His rationalistic approach to understand the problems of society and to unify it is quite reliable. The application of critical reason, critical analysis and scientific temper to dissect religion, politics and society are not only fundamental in his ideology, but also equally trustworthy.

Ambedkar places Man at the centre of his ideology, and its sole concern is the all-round development of Man. He believes that solving human problems with the help of reason is more reliable than adhering to religious dogmas and beliefs. He thus exalts Man and reduces the importance of God in his life. His concern for Man and rationality makes his ideology perennially relevant.

There are other features of his ideology which are clearly reflected in the Constitution of India. The most significant one is his concept of social justice which is a holistic one embracing the liberal ideas of liberty, equality and fraternity. His social justice is meant to strengthen the bases of social justice, social democracy and social humanism, thereby to enhance the dignity of Man.

Being a social rebel, Ambedkar is against customary morality and glaring inequalities which clog the wheels of progress. He pleads modern morality, based on the recognition of rationality, Man and social justice. He feels that customary morality is harmful for the advancement of Man; rational morality can alone liberate him.

Further, Ambedkar regards that the teachings and doctrines of Buddha are highly relevant for a new social and political revolution. His ideology based on Buddhism sets standard for a moral life for an individual to follow. His advocacy of a social order based on the doctrines of love, wisdom and virtue should not be neglected.

Ambedkar ideology is a quest towards the creation of a just, coherent and ideal society, free from the tendencies of exploitation and oppression. His ultimate aim is the liberation of Man and the establishment of a new social order through constitutional means.

The present work is an attempt to reassert the relevance of Ambedkar's ideology to the existing situation in our country. His ideology is a viable one to resolve the conflicts and controversies that prevail in our society; and thereby to usher in a vibrant social order, social solidarity and nation-building.

Kanta Kataria

Acknowledgements

It gives me great pleasure to write this acknowledgement as a sign of gratitude to my teachers and family members who have been supportive and encouraged me, directly or indirectly, towards the completion of this research project.

I am most grateful to my research advisor, Professor P.S. Bhati, Emeritus Professor in Political Science, former Head, Department of Political Science, J.N. Vyas University, Jodhpur; and former Director, Ambedkar Study Centre (UGC), Jodhpur, for help and guidance towards the completion of this research study. I am deeply indebted to Professor P.S. Bhati for valuable guidance.

To my respected teacher, Professor L.S. Rathore, Emeritus Professor in Political Science and former Vice Chancellor, J.N. Vyas University, Jodhpur, I am equally indebted for encouragement, help and guidance, in the absence of which this research study could not have been possible. Further, Prof. Rathore deserves special thanks and gratitude for writing a brief 'Foreword' to this work.

I am also thankful to Professor Madalsa Ujjwal, former Head of the Department of Political Science, for all the support and encouragement. I am grateful to my colleagues for their co-operation.

I should not miss to extend my sense of gratefulness to my family members who have maintained a congenial atmosphere throughout the course of my research study. My husband Dr M.L. Kataria, Principal Specialist, Medicine, Bhopalgarh (Jodhpur), has been a profound source of inspiration. His contribution is much more impressive than he would ever realize. My sons, Anurag and Abhishek, too have helped me in their own way.

Here, I should not forget to remember my father, Late Shri Khuba Ramji, Retd. Security Commissioner (RPF), and my mother Smt. Leelawati for their blessings throughout my research study. I also extend gratitude to my father-in-law; mother-in-law and my beloved sisters for the encouragement they have given to me all the time, constantly and repeatedly. I should not forget to mention my thanks to Dr H.R. Goyal, R.C.H.O., Jodhpur, whose collection of literature on Babasaheb Ambedkar have been of great benefit to me.

I am indebted to several authors and academicians whose works I have used in writing this thesis. They have been duly acknowledged.

I am also thankful to Shri Pranit Rawat of Rawat Publications and his associates for bringing out this book in its present form in the shortest possible time.

I do hope that this work on Ambedkar would certainly evoke an interest in the readers and researchers and inspire them to further undertake research, or to ponder over, Ambedkar's contribution to the cause of nation-building and social cohesion.

Kanta Kataria

1

B.R. Ambedkar: A Biographical Sketch

The history of modern India is very unique in the sense that it had produced political activists who were also original thinkers. The striking thing about Indian freedom struggle is the combination of 'political activism and theoretical reflection'. The persons who manufactured freedom and cast a spell on national awakening in the 20th century also wrote most authentically about the country. In his recently published edited work, *Makers of Modern India*, Ramachandra Guha writes:

> The country's leading politicians were its leading political thinkers. This is especially true of the trinity of Mohandas K. Gandhi, Jawaharlal Nehru and B.R. Ambedkar. The first was the father of Indian nationalism who, between the 1920s and 1940s, forged a popular, countrywide movement against British colonial rule. The second was the architect of the modern Indian nation-state, serving as prime minister from the nation's birth in August 1947 until his death in May 1964. The third was the great leader of country's oppressed castes, who also oversaw, as the country's first law minister, the drafting of the Indian Constitution, which came into effect on 26 January 1950. But even as they fought and struggled, led and governed, Gandhi, Nehru and Ambedkar wrote at great length about the world they saw and shaped.[1]

The trinity as mentioned above not only threw themselves heart and soul into the freedom struggle of the country, but they also were creative thinkers of great wisdom and depth. To quote Guha again:

> Gandhi's *Collected Works*, published by the Government of India between 1958 and 1994, run into more than ninety volumes. More than fifty volumes of Nehru's *Selected Works* have so far been published by a trust erected in his name. In the 1980s the government of Ambedkar's home state, Maharashtra, published sixteen volumes of his writings, each volume sometimes is exceeding a thousand pages. Although many of the entries in these collected or selected works are routine letters or speeches, others represent extended essays on subjects such as national identity, democracy, religious culture and social justice. Indians in general (and Indian writers in particular) tend to be prolix and verbose, but in these instances at least quantity has not necessarily been at odds with quality.[2]

The *Writings and Speeches* of Ambedkar when published, got a mixed reception both from the public as well as the press. His admirers hailed the volumes as a valuable addition to the literature on the social problems and politics of India. But Ambedkar was not popular with the press. He was treated, to use his own words, 'as a snake in the grass'. Instead of reviewing the volumes, some of the newspapers set about criticizing his life, work and ideology. Though Ambedkar was misunderstood, he was far ahead of his time.

What is striking in modern India is that at the moments of crisis, the country did not fail to produce 'thinker-activists', or 'thinker-politicians'. These 'thinker-activists' were both men of vision and men of action. The most unusual thing is that when these men were in the thick of political action, they were capable of producing theoretical writings on the Indian society and politics. Of course, there was a great deal of diversity in their ideas. This was on account of the diversities of people, religion, culture and graded inequalities. During the freedom struggle, the Gandhian tradition was more powerful but gradually after independence of the country, its impact frittered away considerably. The tradition of Nehru was more dominant during the first two decades of independence, but after his death in 1964, it slowly withered away. The only thinker-activist whose relevance has lasted longer, even gradually improved and getting stronger, day-by-day, is B.R. Ambedkar.

The relevance of Gandhi and Nehru are suffering eclipses in the present day India; whereas Ambedkar continues to attract attention because of the vitality of his ideology, that is pragmatic, rationalistic and far-sighted, meant to transform and reconstruct society in an organic whole. To the believer, it presents, first, a system of ultimate ends that embody the meaning of life and absolute standards by which to judge events and actions; and secondly, a guide to those ends which implies a plan of salvation for the downtrodden and to promote the unity of society. His ideology promises paradise for the oppressed and fraternity for all. Taken in this sense, we may call Ambedkar's ideology as a great one – greatness here is linked to vitality.

Ambedkar was a true leader, master and in a way prophet also. His prophetic statements and utterances of wisdom attract friends and foes alike from all parts of the world. While the great men of yesterday are being dwarfed into insignificant non-entities, the stature of Ambedkar is gaining in height and strength.

A Multidimensional Personality

Ambedkar was a prominent figure in the history of socio-political evolution of India. He was one of the illustrious figures who played a significant part in the annals of modern India; at a time when changing trends and conditions were making an important impression on the life and social structure of the nation. He was one of those who helped to accelerate the process of social change in the country, a process which had enabled, hundreds of thousands, even millions, to look forward to a happier and better life.

Ambedkar was one of India's leading citizens, a great social reformer and a valiant upholder of human rights. His deep erudition and experience in fields such as law, economics, sociology, labour and politics had enabled him to make an impressive contribution in the world of literature.

Ambedkar's contribution to the cause of removal of untouchability was immense. He played a leading role in the emancipation of social injustice and for the upliftment of the deprived. He was the first person to raise the voice of the untouchables at the Round Table Conferences in 1930 and 1932. What he did and what he achieved for the untouchables had no parallel in the history of the country. Nobody in the whole history of India had achieved so much for so many, with so little resources in spite of stubborn opposition from millions of his own countrymen. According to him, human life was free. He was free to take his decisions independently resting on his intellect. He believed in:

> Be a light unto yourself. And you can be a light unto yourself; when you go beyond the body, the mind, the heart. Find the centre of your being and suddenly there is light. It is already there, it is already burning bright. It is your very being; you just have to discover it.[3]

The above words of Gautam Buddha formed the central idea in the spiritual ideology of Ambedkar. He advised the untouchables to take inspiration from the teachings of Gautam Buddha, which would help them in their emancipation.

Ambedkar was the builder of modern India. He fought relentlessly to establish a society based on the democratic ideals of liberty, equality and fraternity. He endeavoured to build a new social order, based on social emancipation and economic prosperity. His message was: awake, arise and stop not till the goal is achieved. His advice to the downtrodden was: 'Struggle'. He observed:

> Lost rights are never gained again, by begging, and by appeal to the conscience of the usurpers, but by relentless struggle. Goats are used for sacrificial offerings not lions. Untouchability was such an abominable strain that it would not matter much even if some lives were sacrificed to wash it out. Dragging on life somehow, or to live like a crow for a thousand years is not the only and worthy way to live in this world. Life can be ennobled and immortalized by sacrificing for a lasting good such as the cause of truth, a vow, honour or country.[4]

Ambedkar was a pragmatist to the core. He believed that in the absence of economic and social justice, political freedom would not bring about either social solidarity, or national integration. He believed that the first step towards the attainment of social solidarity and nation-building was the liquidation of the hierarchical structuring of Indian society on democratic principles. He upheld the rights of men and constitutional remedies for making them real and effective. He cherished the goal of an ideal democracy. An ideal democracy could be realized through right kind of leadership.

Ambedkar was a great constitutionalist. He rendered a remarkable service to the drafting of the Indian Constitution. As chairman of the Drafting Committee, he demonstrated his worth and capability in the framing of India's Constitution. In the Constituent Assembly, he stood like a tower of strength, defending, guiding, explaining and clarifying the various provisions of the draft Constitution. He completed the task of framing the Indian Constitution in a commendable way. Appreciating the services of Ambedkar, Rajendra Prasad, President of the Constituent Assembly, had said:

> Sitting in the chair and watching the proceedings from day to day I have realized as nobody else could have with what zeal and devotion the members of the Drafting Committee and especially its Chairman, Dr Ambedkar, in spite of his indifferent health, have worked. We could never make a decision which was or could be ever so right as when we put him on Drafting Committee and made him its Chairman. He has not only justified his selection but has added lustre to the work which he has done.[5]

The outstanding ability with which Ambedkar piloted the draft Constitution showed his unique mastery over the constitutional problems. His work in the Constituent Assembly was one of his greatest contributions in the history of modern India.

Ambedkar was a great scholar-activist in the field of religion. He had studied almost all the religions of the world. He was not anti-religion, but he believed in finding out what a true religion ought to be. He measured every religion from the angle of rationality. He came to the conclusion that most of the religions which had influenced human civilization are dogmatic, narrow and sectarian in their outlook. They depended on miracles, wizardry and witchcraft for their existence. They are afraid of reason and hate scientific analysis and independent interpretation. The history of religion, according to Ambedkar, is replete with barbarism and inhumanity of man against man. He believed that religion during the early years of its formation might have been revolutionary institution but with the passage of time it turned out to be a reactionary force which enslaved man and dwarfed his intellect. Being a keen student of Marxism and a great admirer of philosophers like John Dewey, Bertrand Russell, Charles Darwin, Voltaire and free thinkers like G.B. Shaw and Sidney and Beatrice Webbs, Ambedkar believed that these theistic religions were crumbling like houses of cards before the onslaught of science, technology and communism.

Ambedkar held that the major religions of the world are not free from inequality. The Sikhism proclaims spiritual equality, but outside the Gurudwaras they are just as bad as any orthodox Hindu. Christianity and Islam did not appeal to Ambedkar because they lack rationality. So far as Hinduism was concerned, he believed that it glorified ignorance and preached inequality. He said:

> Hinduism is a senile old body which suffered in all its joints from old age and disease and holds no hope for the suffering humanity much less for the downtrodden masses of India for whose appalling poverty and miserable condition it is directly responsible.[6]

After dissecting all the major religions of the world, Ambedkar came to the conclusion that 'there is one religion which can satisfy all needs of man in this scientific age and soothe his tired nerves. It is Buddhism, the religion of reason and religion of morality'. The most significant feature of Buddhism was that it did not soil its history with the blood of innocent people for the propagation of the creed. It did not endeavour to raise its mansions and palaces on the ruins of others. It made advances with the help of persuasion, reason, renunciation, self-sacrifice and service. As such, Ambedkar tried to revive the orthodox (original) Buddhism after purifying it by removing all the dirt and garbage which had accumulated during the centuries. This was Ambedkar's true religion.

A true religion should purify our minds. It should help a man to acquire good qualities. Good character is an integral part of a true religion. He said:

> A true religion checks bad behaviour. A bullock-cart has two wheels, two bullocks but only one driver. The wheels have to be lubricated from time to time so that they run smoothly. Religion is like the axis of the bullock-cart, it is the axis of the chariot of life. There can be no stability without religion.[7]

As such, Ambedkar was not anti-religion; but an advocate of a true religion.

Ambedkar was an eminent scholar of law. He had a tremendous respect for the rule of law, constitutional methods and legal structures. He favoured the uniform code of laws. In the Constituent Assembly, he said:

> We have a uniform criminal code, law of the transfer of property, Negotiable Instruments Act. This would prove that this country has practically a civil code, uniform in its content and applicable to the whole of the country. The only province the civil law has not been able to invade so far is marriage and succession.[8]

The Hindu Code Bill, which Ambedkar introduced in the Provisional Parliament, was meant to strengthen the codification of Hindu laws on vital fields, such as, marriage, divorce, inheritance, guardianship and adoption. His knowledge of laws and legal systems was profound.

Ambedkar was an ardent champion of social justice. He held that the proper implementation of social justice could usher in an era of development for all. Development would be meaningful if the state could reach out to the most neglected and the poorest in society – the dalits and the untouchables – and treat them as equals, thus removing the psychological divide created and perpetuated through wrong ideas and practices in our society. A just society could be built on social justice; that is, the removal of socio-economic disparities and inequalities.

Ambedkar was a believer in the unity of society. He organized the depressed classes to work in unison with others, so that no wall might be created between the different classes of the society. According to Ambedkar:

> The downtrodden people should get accustomed to work in unison with others. The most vital need of the day is to create among the mass of the people a sense of common nationality ... the feeling that they are Indians first and Indians last.[9]

As a 'thinker-activist', Ambedkar occupies a high position in the history of modern India. Apart from being an outstanding social and political thinker, he was a dauntless activist in the field of politics. In January 1919, he gave evidence before the South Borough Reforms (Franchise) Committee, claiming political rights for the depressed classes of India. In 1920, he brought out a Marathi fortnightly, the *Mooknayak* (Leader of the Dumb). In 1924, he started an organization in Bombay, named the *Bahishkrit Hitkarni Sabha* for the moral and material progress of the untouchables. Between 1925 and 1930, he set up four boarding houses in the Bombay Presidency for untouchable students.

Another Marathi fortnightly, the *Bahishkrit Bharat* and a weekly, *Janata* were started by him in April and November 1930, respectively. In September 1927, he started the *Samaj Samata Sangh* for preaching social equality among the untouchables and the caste Hindus. As an organ of this body, he started another paper, *Samata*, in March 1929.

Not content with mere preaching and writing to secure social justice for the dalits, Ambedkar took to the path of agitation. In December 1927, he led a *satyagraha* to establish the civic right of the untouchables to draw water from a public tank, 'Chavadar Talen', at Mahad in district Kolaba. The caste Hindus claimed the tank as a private property and a prolonged litigation followed.

Ambedkar led another *satyagraha* in March 1930 to establish the right of the untouchables to enter the famous temple of Kalaram at Nasik. The *satyagraha* was withdrawn in March 1934. During this period, he introduced several bills for the welfare of the peasants, workers and the untouchables. They were, however, not passed because of the opposition of the orthodox sections of the society.

In October 1936, Ambedkar founded Independent Labour Party of India which captured all the seats in the legislature of Bombay Presidency (1937) reserved for the scheduled castes. In April 1942, Ambedkar formed the Scheduled Castes Federation as an All-India political party. In July 1945, he founded the 'People's Education Society,' to promote the interests of the scheduled castes. This society started a number of colleges in the Bombay Presidency for scheduled caste students.

Ambedkar, thus, was a buoyant and dynamic activist. He was tall and stout. At home he put on simple Indian dress, but in public he was always in immaculate western dress.

This was the multidimensional personality of Ambedkar. He was a relentless critic of the caste-based society. As an emancipation of the untouchables and a liberator of the social injustice, he had no parallel. Indeed, he was a great social reformer. He was an advocate of true religion. His was a versatile legal brain. In addition, he was an outstanding constitutionalist, whose achievements in framing and piloting the Indian Constitution and in preparing the Hindu Code Bill were unique. He was a dauntless champion of social justice. He led numerous *satyagrahas* for asserting the rights of the untouchables. Apart from being a social activist and a champion of the cause of the downtrodden, Ambedkar was a prolific writer and a thinker (discussed in third chapter). Among the 'thinker-activists' of the period, Ambedkar stood on a high pedestal in the history of modern India.

With this sketchy introduction of Ambedkar, it is desirable to present his biographical sketch in brief.

Repudiated the Infallibility of the *Vedas*

In the 19th century, especially after the beginning of British Crown's rule, there had occurred important social movements, aiming towards the revival of India's past glory. Revivalism was the key feature in the ideas of the social reformers. The social reformers wanted to model the life of the nation on the basis of past scriptures like the *Vedas*, the *Upanishads*, the *Gita* and the *Puranas*. They advocated the revival of the old pietistic and religious cultures of India. A new humanist and cosmopolitan interpretation began to be put upon the old writings. Ambedkar did not believe in the revival of past glories and Vedantic tradition. He cast aside the infallibility of the *Vedas*.

The main reform movements were the *Brahmo Samaj*, the *Arya Samaj* and the Vivekananda movement. These movements manifested their faith in moral and spiritual awakening of India, based on Vedantic tradition, in one form or the other. They opposed narrow caste loyalties, untouchability and pleaded for the upliftment of women. They, however, had an immense faith in the infallibility of the *Vedas*.

One of the earliest movements was *Brahmo Samaj* that was started by Raja Ram Mohan Roy (1772–1833) in the second quarter (1828) of the 19th century. Revolting against the social stagnation, Ram Mohan Roy believed in the goodness of the Almighty power and the metaphysical spiritual monism of the *Upanishad*. He advocated social reforms – widow remarriage, abolition of *Sati* system, etc. He was hostile to sectarianism, superstition and idolatry. His was a catholic approach to religions truths. He, however, did not repudiate the traditional Hindu belief of the *Vedas* being coeval with creation. He formulated a discipline of spiritual culture which had affinities with Vedantism.[10]

The *Arya Samaj* was founded by Swami Dayanand Saraswati (1824–1883) in 1875. He was a Vedic scholar and a social reformer. He was a prophet of perfect Vedism. He wanted to solve the problems of life in accordance with Vedic canons. He said that the *Vedas* contained eternal, pure and pristine knowledge given to humanity at the primordial hour of creation. He claimed to find, in the ancient code of Vedic wisdom, the words of God himself and hence justified his rocklike faith in the *Vedas.*[11] He believed that the theory of four *Varnas* based on a psychological and occupational criterion, may provide a good solution of many social and functional conflicts. The criterion of *Varna*-belongingness is not truth but the psychological capacity to perform a particular function. He thus pleaded for an occupationally stratified social system. His slogan was, 'Go back to the Vedas'. He sung the glories of ancient India. His programme of action was based on Vedic idealism. He accepted the *Vedas* as the fount of scientific and metaphysical knowledge. He felt the supreme urgency of the emancipation of the depressed and fallen sections of Indian society, but he was also intensely keen to spread the pure faith of the *Vedas.* He was categorical that *Varna* should be determined by one's qualities, actions and psychological propensities, but he did not visualize an equalitarian society rid of all artificial social distinctions of *Varnas.*

Swami Vivekananda (1863–1902), wanted a radical reconstruction of society. He condemned the iniquities of the caste system and untouchability. He started a crusade for the betterment of the conditions of the fallen, the sinner, the suppressed and the poverty-stricken. But he too was a metaphysician of the Vedantic school. He was one of the great interpreters of the Vedantic philosophy in modern times.

Though the social reformers of the 19th century had interpreted the *Vedas* according to their mode of rationality, they did not renounce them. They had a tremendous faith in the *Vedas* and the Vedantic tradition. This was the nature of sociological thought that dominated the scene, when Ambedkar made an advent in the field in the first quarter of the 20th century.

The most striking thing about Ambedkar and that which formed the basis of his ideology was that he discarded the Vedantic tradition of the 19th century in toto. He repudiated the *Vedas* and the *Varna* system. He did not believe in theism. The central concern of his ideology was Man; and the key method to evaluate any phenomenon was rationality. Instead of *Vedic* canons, man and rationality were the main features in Ambedkar's ideology. No one would be able to grasp the meaning of Ambedkar's ideology, if these two key elements are ignored or set aside.

A Biographical Sketch

Bhimrao Ramji Ambedkar was born on 14 April 1891 at Mhow, near Indore. His father, Ramji Maloji Sakpal, a Mahar[12] by caste, was an instructor in the local military school. He was a Kabirpanthi devotee. He hailed from a village, Ambad (Ambavade), in Madangad taluk of Ratangiri district of erstwhile Bombay Presidency (now Maharashtra). Being a Kabirpanthi, Ramji Sakpal was deeply attached to the devotional and mystical Varkari[13] sect. He admired Jyotirao Phule for reforms brought amongst the lower classes in that region in the second half of the 19th century.

Bhimabai,[14] the mother of Ambedkar belonged to a Murabadkar, a Mahar Kabirpanthi family which had served the British army for generations. Ambedkar was the fourteenth child of his parents. He lost his mother at the age of five (1896).

Ambedkar married Ramabai in 1905 when he was fourteen and she was nine. She was from a poor Mahar family and illiterate. She died in 1935. Ambedkar married a second time, Sharda Kabir (later named Savita) in 1948. She was from a Saraswat Brahmin family of Bombay.

By 1896, Ramji Sakpal, the father of Ambedkar had moved to Satara after retirement from the Army where he got re-employment. The family shifted shortly to Bombay, living in lower Parel, a textile labour colony. Ramji put his son in the Elphinstone High School, where from Ambedkar passed his matriculation examination (1907).

Ambedkar passed his B.A. from Elphinstone College (1912). He joined the armed forces as a Lieutenant of the Baroda state after his B.A., for which he had got financial assistance from the state of Baroda. He returned to Bombay within two weeks as his father passed away. He got one of the two scholarships for backward caste students set up to study abroad by the

Baroda state and joined the Columbia University (USA) in 1913. At Columbia University, he had great teachers like John Dewey, Edwin Seligman and others. Here, Ambedkar sharpened his mind, learning and vision. He took his M.A. in Economics in 1915 and Ph.D. in 1916. His dissertation for M.A. was 'Administration and Finance of East India Company'. He submitted his Ph.D. on 'National Dividend: A Historical and Analytical Study' to the University. In May 1916, he presented a paper on 'Caste in India: Their Mechanism, Genesis and Development' at the Anthropology Seminar of Dr A.A. Goldenweizer. The paper was later published in *Indian Antiquity* (May 1917, Vol. XLI).

In October 1916, Ambedkar moved to London School of Economics and Political Science with an introductory letter written in glowing terms and favour by Edwin Seligman to Sidney Webb, the social economist. Ambedkar was greatly influenced by the Fabianism of Sidney and Beatrice Webbs and came to appreciate the role of the state in social progress. He also joined the Grey's Inn for Bar-at-Law. Thus, he was working for his M.Sc. in Economics and was also preparing for the Bar.

But in 1917, he had to discontinue his studies on the expiry of his scholarship and returned to India. He had to serve the Baroda state under the obligation of the scholarship. At Baroda, Ambedkar faced disgraceful treatment from colleagues and subordinates and even by peons. He was treated like a leper. He stayed in a Parsee rest house in disguise where also a group of Parsees arrived one day menacingly armed with sticks and he was made to vacate the guest house with a relaxation of eight hours. Hindus or Muslims, none was prepared to give him a place to stay in the city. His note to the Maharaja came to the *Dewan* who expressed helplessness. Tired and hungry, humiliated in agony. Ambedkar sat under a tree and wept. His academic achievements, literacy and education had little to deliver.[15] For Ambedkar the experience was bitter reminder of untouchability – practiced in the Indian society and he, therefore, resolved to fight throughout his life to mitigate and root out the evil from the Indian society.

Ambedkar returned to Bombay disheartened and did not have a regular job till he was appointed in Sydenham College of

Commerce and Economics as a temporary professor. He served at Sydenham College from 1918 to 1920. Having saved some money and with financial assistance from some of his friends, and a loan from the Maharaja of Kolhapur, he went to England again in 1920 to complete his studies. He obtained the M.Sc. degree in 1921 and was awarded the D.Sc. degree in 1923. In the same year he was also called to the Bar and joined the legal profession.

Besides his academic pursuits, Ambedkar made submissions before the Southborough Committee in January 1919, which was enquiring into the franchise issue for the Montagu-Chelmsford Reforms (1919) pleading for a separate electorate for the depressed classes on lines of one granted to the Muslims.

After obtaining Bar-at-Law in 1923, Ambedkar started legal practice at the Bombay High Court in June 1924; and from that time onwards till his death, he played an active role as social worker, politician, writer, jurist and an educationist.

In addition to his legal practice, Ambedkar also taught part-time at Batliboi Accountancy Training Institute, Bombay, from January 1925 to March 1928. He became Professor of Law in Government Law College, Bombay, from June 1928 to March 1929; and later on was appointed its Principal (1935–1938).

Ambedkar was not confined to mere studies, teaching and scholasticism. In 1920, he started a Marathi fortnightly, the *Mooknayak*; in April 1927, he started another Marathi fortnightly, the *Bahishkrit Bharat*; and in November 1930, a weekly the *Janata* was started. The organizations like *Bahishkrit Hitkarni Sabha, Samaj Samata Sangh,* etc. preaching social equality among the untouchables and the caste Hindus, were started by him in the third decade of the 20th century.

In December 1927, the Mahad non-violent *satyagraha* at the 'Chavadar Tank' was launched to assert the right to have access to the tanks and wells used by all. During the *Mahad satyagraha*, the *Manusmriti* was criticized and publicly burnt by Ambedkar and his followers on 25 December 1927. Stating the significance of *Mahad satyagraha*, Ambedkar said:

> Gentlemen! You will understand from this the significance of the struggle we have begun. Do not let yourselves suppose that the Satyagraha Committee had invited you to Mahad merely to drink the water of the *Chavadar* Lake of Mahad. It is not as if drinking the water of the *Chavadar* Lake makes us immortal. We have survived well enough all these days without drinking it. We are not going to the *Chavadar* Lake merely to drink its water. We are going to the Lake to assert that we too are human beings like others. It must be clear that this meeting has been called to set up the norm of equality.[16]

During this year (1927), Ambedkar was appointed a member of the Legislative Assembly for five years and was re-nominated in 1932 for a further period of five years.

In 1928, a Commission headed by John Simon came to India to examine the question of constitutional reforms. The Simon-seven were all Englishmen. The Congress boycotted its proceedings. The reason of boycott was that its members were all white.

Ambedkar, who appeared before the Commission, on behalf of the depressed classes, argued that the depressed classes be treated as 'a distinct, independent minority' – as separate from the Hindus, as the Muslims already were. 'He also advocated direct action for the fulfillment of their rights, launching *satyagrahas* to all untouchables to drink water from tanks and to enter temples from which they were excluded. There was determined opposition by the upper castes; leading Ambedkar to conclude that reform would come only through the purposive action of the state. He thus asked, to begin with, for greater representation for the depressed classes at all levels of public service'.[17]

The other important events where Ambedkar created a significant mark in Indian politics were the Round Table Conferences. He was nominated as a delegate to the three Round Table Conferences held in London and served on some of the Committees till 1934. The first Round Table Conference was held from 12 November 1930 to 19 January 1931. The purpose of RTC (Round Table Conference) was to enable Indian political leaders to come to an agreement for the purpose of drafting a Constitution for the future set up in India.

This Conference consisted of 89 members. Of these, 16 represented the British parties, 20 representatives were of princely states of India, and 53 members were from British India. At the first Conference, the Congress did not participate; but later on at the second Conference M.K. Gandhi joined it. Untouchables of India were represented by B.R. Ambedkar and Roy Bahadur T. Srinivasan.

The Round Table Conference was significant in the sense that it was the first time in the history of the British Empire that an untouchable rose to speak in the capacity of a representative of the classes which had been considered 'low, backward, unintelligent, inefficient, untouchable of varying degrees and despicable'.[18] He was none else than Ambedkar, who possessed the highest academic qualifications, intelligence and character which had put many a saint to shame.

Pleading for the political rights of the depressed classes, Ambedkar said that their position in India was between that of 'the serf and the slave'. They were leading a life of enforced servility, full of discrimination and inequality. He pleaded that the bureaucratic form of government in India should be replaced by a government which should be a government of the people, by the people and for the people. He stated that the depressed classes had welcomed the British as their deliverers from age long tyranny and oppression by the orthodox Hindus, but the British failed to fulfill their obligations towards the depressed classes. He said:

> When we compare our present position with the one which it was our lot to bear in Indian society of the pre-British days, we find that, instead of marching on, we are only marking time. Before the British, we were in the loathsome condition due to our untouchability. Has the British Government done anything to remove it? Before the British, we could not enter the temple. Can we enter now? Before the British, we were denied entering into the Police Force. Does the British Government admit us in the Force? ... The British, who have

> held so large a sway over us for such a long time, have done some good we cheerfully acknowledge. But there is certainly, no fundamental change in our position.[19]

Ambedkar continued that the British Government had accepted the social arrangements as it found them and preserved them faithfully in the manner of the Chinese tailor who, when given an old coat as a pattern produced with pride an exact replica, rents patches and all. He frankly stated:

> Our wrongs have remained as open sores and they have not been righted although 150 years of British rule have rolled away.[20]

Ambedkar did not accuse the British. He found that they were quite incompetent to tackle the problems of depressed classes, because of the fear of resistance from upper classes and landed aristocracy. Explaining the reason, why the British were indifferent to the problems of depressed classes, Ambedkar stated:

> The reason why it does not intervene is because it is afraid that its intervention to amend the existing code of social and economic life, will give rise to resistance.[21]

He felt that such a government which was afraid to amend the social and economic code was of little or no value. He pleaded that, in fact, nobody could remove the grievances of depressed classes, unless they get political power in their hands. No share of this politics power could evidently 'come to us so long as the British Government remains as it is'. He held that the problem of the depressed classes would never be solved unless they 'get political power in their own hands'. At every successive step taken by the British Government to widen the scope of representative government the depressed classes had been systematically left out. No thought was given to their claim for political power. He, therefore, pleaded that the settlement of the problem of depressed classes 'must be a part of the general political settlement and must not be left over to shifting sands of the sympathy and goodwill of the rulers of the future'.[22] The depressed classes would regard it as the greatest betrayal on the part of the British Government if it were 'to leave us to the mercy of those who have taken no interest in our welfare and whose prosperity and greatness is founded on our ruination and degradation'.[23] The whole exercise of Ambedkar was meant to demonstrate the creation of separate electorate for the depressed classes in the Provincial Assemblies in the proposed Constitution of India.

In the second Round Table Conference held in September 1931, M.K. Gandhi participated in its deliberations as the sole representative of the Congress. He was opposed to the grant of separate electorate to the depressed classes. However, the British Prime Minister, Ramsay MacDonald in his Communal Award, dated 4 August 1932, granted separate electorate in selected areas where the depressed classes were most numerous.[24] These special depressed classes constituencies were meant for a limited time of 20 years. According to Ambedkar, 'the communal award gave the untouchable two benefits: (i) a fixed quota of seats to be elected by a separate electorate of untouchables; (ii) a double vote, one to be used through separate electorates and the other to be used in general electorates.[25]

What was most disturbing to Gandhi was that the British Government awarded separate electorate for untouchables! He, therefore, went on a fast to protest. To save his life, a compromise was reached with Ambedkar (known as the Poona Pact, 1932) whereby a joint electorate would remain for Hindus, but with greater seats for the depressed classes. Instead of separate electorate, more seats were given to the depressed classes. Here, Ambedkar proved that he was a hard negotiator and still harder to compromise with his thoughts and beliefs.[26] Having signed the Agreement, Ambedkar never forgave himself. It gave the untouchables 'more seats, less rights and no power'. Commenting on this Agreement between Gandhi-Ambedkar at Poona, Bhagwan Das wrote:

> Like Dronacharya of the Mahabharata and Ramachandra of the Ramayana, a Mahatma of the 20th century had deprived the trusting untouchables of what their ablest liberator had

achieved through his intelligent, honest, courageous and able advocacy of their cause.[27]

Why did Ambedkar sign the Poona Pact? This was made clear by him in the speech dated 27 October 1951, that he delivered at Jalandhar. He said:

> In the Round Table Conference, I posed this question for the first time and asked for separate electorate for the untouchables of India as was granted to the Muslims, the Sikhs, Christians and other minorities. I could not secure support from my countrymen in the Round Table Conference in favour of the legitimate demand for separate electorates for the depressed classes of India but I won the political rights for my people. What happened afterwards is known to every body in this country. Suffice to say, that Gandhi started his fast unto death in order to deprive us of the political rights which we had won for the first time in the history of modern India. Gandhiji was not in favour of the untouchables having political rights for fear of ambitions growing in their mind. He wanted them to depend on the mercy of the benevolent master – the caste Hindus. Trusting the words of Gandhiji and the assurances given by other Hindu leaders, we sacrificed our rights to save his life.[28]

Ambedkar criticized Gandhi's role in the Second Round Table Conference. He had challenged his claims to represent the untouchables and charged him with entering into a 'mean deal' with Muslims in order to get rejected the demand of the untouchables for separate electorate.[29] Though Ambedkar wanted to have separate electorate for the depressed classes, he had to withdraw the demand reluctantly in Poona Pact in order to save the life of Mahatma Gandhi. However, through the 1930s and 1940s, he wrote a series of tracts excoriating Gandhi and Gandhism.

Ambedkar could not reconcile himself to this political compromise (Poona Pact) which did not eliminate the social stigma attached to the untouchables. As such, on 13 October 1935, he made an announcement in a public meeting at Yeola, District Nasik, that the untouchables would leave the Hindu fold altogether and accept some other religion, as he felt that within the Hindu fold they would never get social equality. At Yeola, he explained the futility of agitation like the entry to the Kalarama temple that was lingering on in courts for five years and decided that no more time and energy be wasted in such agitations.[30] He vowed that 'though he was born a Hindu, he would not die a Hindu'. This happened in 1956 with Ambedkar adopting Buddhism as his faith along with a million of his followers. Ambedkar was aware that conversion was not the solution. In all religions, the untouchable converts will have to strive for equality and freedom.[31]

Ambedkar was invited to the Zat-Pat-Todak Mandal, Lahore, to their annual conference. However, he did not agree to modify his speech and, therefore, did not address the Conference. But he published his speech in a book form, *The Annihilation of Caste* advocating inter-caste marriages, kinship and not merely inter-dining and worship in temples.[32]

In 1936, Ambedkar formed the Independent Labour Party to fight the elections mandated under the new Government of India Act of 1935. In later years the party changed its name twice, becoming, first, the Scheduled Caste Federation and later, the Republican Party of India.

In June 1942, Ambedkar was nominated to the Viceroy's Executive Council, 'the first untouchable to be distinguished'. 'This set him even more firmly in opposition to the Congress which, in August of the same year, started its Quit India Movement.[33] He remained as Labour Member in the Viceroy's Executive Council till July 1946. As a Labour Member, he continued the work for the betterment of the scheduled castes in services. He also took keen interest in the Damodar Valley and the Mahanadi Projects.

In 1945, Ambedkar founded the Peoples' Education Society which started a number of colleges in the Bombay Presidency for scheduled caste students.

Ambedkar got elected from Bengal in 1946 to the Constituent Assembly. On account of the partition of India, he lost that seat; as such, he was elected to the Constituent

Assembly in July 1947 from Bombay. He joined the Nehru Cabinet as Law Minister in August 1947. He was appointed Chairman of Drafting Committee of the Constitution on 19 August 1947. As Chairman of the Drafting Committee he piloted the draft successfully, winning encomium from all. He proved himself worthy of the task and confidence reposed in him and the Indian Constitution was adopted on 26 November 1949, and India became a Republic under this Constitution on the 26 January 1950. About Ambedkar's role in the framing of the Constitution, Ramachandra Guha, writes:

> As the thirteen volumes of the proceedings of the Constituent-Assembly demonstrate, Ambedkar handled criticism with tact and authority. He also made some quite brilliant speeches on the significance of the Constitution for the future of democracy.[34]

Apart, from piloting the Constitution of India through a sometimes 'fractious' assembly, Ambedkar made one other important contribution as Law Minister. According to Ramachandra Guha:

> This was to oversee the drafting of a new law that would, for the first time, allow Hindu women to choose their marriage partners, to divorce them if necessary and to inherit a fair share of ancestral property. These reforms only came into effect after Ambedkar resigned from the cabinet in 1951. But he was their principal architect, as he was of the constitution itself.[35]

Ambedkar lost his election to the Parliament in February 1952, but was nominated by the Bombay Legislature to the Council of States (Rajya Sabha) in May 1952. He also lost his second election to the Parliament in 1953.

Ambedkar participated in the World Buddhist Congress, in Ceylon (1950), Burma (1954) and Nepal (1956). In 1955, he founded the *Bharatiya Buddha Mahasabha* for the spread of Buddhism. On 14 October 1956, he embraced Buddhism at Nagpur along with his followers. He passed away on 6 December 1956. In 1957, 'Buddha and his Dhamma' was published posthumously. The 'Bharat Ratna', the highest civilian honour of India was conferred upon Ambedkar in 1990 posthumously.

The Columbia University conferred upon its alumnus B.R. Ambedkar the degree of the Doctor of Laws (LL.D.) in 1952. The citation read:

> Dr Ambedkar is a framer of the Constitution, Member of the Cabinet and of the Council of States, one of India's leading citizens, a great social reformer and a valiant upholder of human rights.[36]

Again, the Columbia University honoured him in 2010 by setting up a chair in Constitutional Law in the name of Dr Ambedkar.

A Nation-Builder

Ambedkar played varied roles in the Indian public life. Starting as leader of the untouchables, he rose to be a great nation-builder. From a practicing lawyer, he elevated himself to the enviable position of the principal architect of India's Constitution.

The main contributions of Ambedkar were: (i) the liberation of the untouchables; (ii) the drafting of the Constitution of India; and (iii) the revival of Buddhism in the land of its origin.

Ambedkar was an iconoclast who did not hesitate to criticize ruthlessly the beliefs, customs and ideas of Hinduism that led to the creation of the *Varna* system and graded inequalities in the society. He was equally a crusader for the forgotten rights of the untouchables, and to achieve them he carried out a long and determined struggle. He fought valiantly for achieving human rights for the depressed classes and then for political rights with reservation in legislature together with share in the administration.

Ambedkar had undertaken the task of removing untouchability and establishing equality earnestly. He said:

> This is a struggle in order to raise ourselves; hence we are bound to undertake it, so as to remove the obstacles to our

> progress. We all know how at every turn, untouchability muddies and soils our whole existence.[37]

He further stated:

> Untouchability is not a simple matter; it is the matter of all our poverty and lowliness and it has brought us to the abject state we are in today. If we want to raise ourselves out of it, we must undertake this task. We cannot be saved in any other way. It is a task not for our benefit alone; it is also for the benefit of the nation.[38]

He believed that there could be no real social revolution without ending untouchability. But this social revolution, he held, should be accomplished peacefully. He said to his opponents:

> Please do not oppose us. Put away the orthodox scriptures. Follow justice. And we assure you that we shall carry out our programme peacefully.[39]

Ambedkar thus brought determination to assert the rights of the untouchables. He refused to be treated any longer as lower than criminals, or even to be patronized by sanctimonious political bosses, climbers and bounders. He resolved to assert their rights as Indians to enter all walks of life, to advance in every possible direction, to carve out their own destiny to fight for social, educational and economic equality with higher castes. And in this prolonged battle for the rights of the untouchables, despite all sorts of humiliations and indignities, Ambedkar emerged out successfully. This was one of his foremost contributions.

The second important contribution of Ambedkar was that he was the principal architect in the drafting of the Indian Constitution. The framing of the Constitution was a gigantic task in which he displayed his wisdom, skill and authority in an amazing way that surprised his critics and adversaries. Many of the members of the Constituent Assembly, including its President, Rajendra Prasad, had showered praises upon Ambedkar for completing a highly difficult task in a meticulous way. Even his critics in the Constituent Assembly, one of them was Jaspat Rai Kapur, had to admit:

> I had started with a prejudice against Dr Ambedkar for I had felt very sure many years ago when Mahatma Gandhi was undergoing fast against grant of separate electorate to the scheduled castes and I had read in the newspapers the news that when he had been invited to see Mahatma Gandhi to discuss the question, he once said that for a day or two he was not free because he had to attend to some professional engagements. I felt very sorry then. I do not know how far it is correct. But even if it was so the great work that he has done during these years (in the Constituent Assembly) has washed away that particular sin or any other sins which he may have committed. I have developed an admiration and also affection for Dr Ambedkar for the very useful work and the very patriotic work which he has done. His very first speech in this Assembly had dispelled all my doubts and fears in relation to him and today I may say that I consider him to be one of the best patriots of this country. I have always found him to bring to bear upon the subject a very constructive approach.[40]

In fact, Ambedkar's work in the Constituent Assembly was acclaimed as the greatest patriotic service to the country. A thoroughly upright person and a man with a keen jurist sense, a proud and irreconcilable heart, a great learner, Ambedkar approached the whole matter of the framing of India's Constitution in the right spirit, full of co-operation and friendliness. He put a profound impress upon the drafting of India's Constitution. In its framing 'moral vision, political skill, legal acumen: were all brought together by him'.[41]

And lastly, the greatest service that Ambedkar did is the revival of Buddhism in the land of its origin. He dug up Buddhism from the grave where it had been lying buried for well over 2000 years and gave it new life and strength. He brought the message of Buddha to the downtrodden masses. He was in a sense, the greatest revivalist of Buddhism in India. He was disillusioned with Hinduism, Sikhism, Islam and Christianity. He regarded them as dogmatic and sectarian in outlook. He considered that Buddhism could save mankind from destruction and ruination. He was not only the interpreter of Buddha's message but he raised that message from the abysmal dens and lived up to it in his life. All in all, he was a true prophet of the revival of Buddhism in modern India. In a broadcast in May 1956, Ambedkar said:

> I prefer Buddhism because it gives three principles in combination which no other religion does. Buddhism teaches *Prajna* (understanding as against superstitions and supernaturalism), *Karuna* (love), and *Samata* (equality). He preferred Buddha in comparison to Marx, because the former alone could provide liberty, equality and fraternity. Marx emphasized equality, but failed to provide liberty and fraternity.[42]

Ambedkar thus was a great nation-builder. He had 'multiple agendas as well as multiple careers'. He was, at various times, 'a lawyer, teacher, legislator, educational organizer, party builder and cabinet minister. Through all these roles and assignments he continued to be a prolific writer. He published important books on many topics, including federalism, theology and philosophy, finance, language, constitutionalism and, not least, the sociology, politics and history of the caste system'.[43]

Dhananjay Keer, the biographer of Ambedkar has summed up his contribution as a nation builder in the following words:

> What did Ambedkar achieve for the untouchables? The story of the past life of the Scheduled Caste Hindus was pitch dark ... it was for the first time in the history of the past twenty-five hundred years that the sun of a better future arose on their horizon. Ambedkar, the son of their soil, their kith and kin, focused the world's attention on their civil, social and political rights and liberties; made untouchability a burning topic of the day, raised it to an international importance, and gave it a global publicity. His ceaseless hard struggle and his merciless hammer forced an opening for them, and inaugurated an era of light and liberty. He awakened in them a sense of human dignity, a feeling of self-respect and a burning hatred of untouchability that was worse than slavery. He pulled them out of slough and exorcized despondency and despair from their minds. He infused courage and new life

> into their demoralized and dehumanized cells. He gave them their soul and reimbued them with a spirit which enabled them to voice their grievances, and to stand for justice, equality and liberty. Before the rise of their leadership they were treated worse than animals. His heroic struggle raised them to political equality with other communities in India ...[44]

There cannot be a better description than this about Ambedkar's transformative role towards the liberation of the depressed people and the building of the nation.

Ambedkar was a great crusader for the rights of the downtrodden and weaker sections of Indian society. Through his speeches and writings, organized social struggles and movements he tried to create self-respect among lower castes and the untouchables so that they could fight for social justice and be able to undo the indignities heaped on them for the past many centuries. He 'tried to liberate people from the clutches of religious scriptures and outworn traditions. He organized the low castes, infused in them the spirit to fight and reassert themselves, and secured for them the status of human beings'.[45] Thus, he was a great nation-builder, who ushered in peaceful social revolution towards the transformation of Indian society.

Jawaharlal Nehru's assessment of Ambedkar was that though he was 'one of the architects of our Constitution'; and took 'greater care and trouble over constitution making'; he was mainly 'a symbol of revolt against all the oppressive features of Hindu society'. He rebelled against something against which 'all ought to rebel and we have, in fact, rebelled in various degrees'. While paying a tribute to Ambedkar in Parliament on 6 December 1956, Nehru said:

> When I think of Dr Ambedkar, many things come to my mind, because he was a highly controversial figure. He was not a person of soft speech. But, behind all that was this powerful reaction and an act of rebellion against something that repressed our society for so long. Fortunately, that rebellion had the support ... of Parliament ... Anyhow, Dr Ambedkar, as I said, became prominent in his own way and a most prominent symbol of that rebellion .... He was a prominent

champion of the oppressed and depressed in India and one who took such an important part in our activities .... He was a very leading and prominent personality, who has left his mark in our public affairs, and on the Indian scene.[46]

Ambedkar had a remarkable and fascinating career. As a teacher, as an economist and as a labour and political leader, he rendered significant services, but the greatest one was that he brought a new awakening and gave the oppressed a sense of social significance and confidence. Had Ambedkar not been there, perhaps, India would not have been what it is today!

In some respects, the iron and bitterness that had entered his soul was on account of the treatment meted out to the untouchables at that period of time. His deep anguish against the caste Hindus was understandable. However, there is no doubt that starting from the humblest beginning; Ambedkar became a great national leader and a nation-builder. His name is writ large on the scroll of Indian history as one of the great makers of modern India.

Notes

1. Ramachandra Guha (ed): *Makers of Modern India* (New Delhi, Penguin Books India, 2010), p. 1.
2. Ibid., pp. 1–2.
3. M.G. Chitkara: *Dr. Ambedkar and Social Justice* (New Delhi, APH Publishing Corporation, 2002), p. 199.
4. Ibid., p. 197.
5. Bhagwan Das (ed): *Thus Spoke Ambedkar*, Vol. 2 (Jalandhar, Buddhist Publishing House, 1968), p. 25.
6. Ibid., p. 29.
7. M.G. Chitkara, p. 208.
8. Ibid., p. 204.
9. Ibid., p. 217.
10. Sitamath Tattvabhushana: *The Philosophy of Brahmoism* (Madras, Higginbotham & Co., 1909), pp. 6–7.

11. V.P. Varma: *Modern Indian Political Thought* (Agra, Lakshmi Narain Agarwal, 1978), p. 41.
12. It is said that '*Mahar*' is a corrupted form of 'Maha + Ari', meaning 'the great enemy, and the name 'Maharashtra' is supposed to have come down from 'Mahar + Rashtra'. (Dhananjay Keer: *Dr. Ambedkar: Life and Mission*, p. 8; S.R. Sharma: *Life and Works of Dr. B.R. Ambedkar*, pp. 2–3, 261)
13. The 'Varkaris are devotees of Lord Vitthal of Pandharpur, situated on the right bank of the Bhima river. The Varakaris follow the traditions of the ancient saint poets of Maharashtra and may be a Vaishnava, shaiva or a smarta. Devotees living nearby visit the temple twice a month on two '*ekadashis*,' the eleventh days of the lunar months'. (Valerian Rodrigues: *The Essential Writings of B.R. Ambedkar*, New Delhi, Oxford University Press, 2002, p. 7.)
14. Bhimbai, also of Mahar origin, came from the family of Murabadkars, named after the village, Murabad in Thane district of the Bombay state. (Dhananjay Keer, op. cit. p. 9; Valerian Rodrigues, op. cit. p. 7)
15. S.R. Shrama: *Life and Works of Dr. Ambedkar* (Jaipur, Book Enclave, 2006), pp. 14–15.
16. Ramachandra Guha, op. cit. pp. 208–209.
17. Ibid., p. 206.
18. Bhagwan Das (ed): *Thus Spoke Ambedkar*, Vol. 1 (Jalandhar, Buddhist Publishing House, 1963), p. 17.
19. Ibid., pp. 20–21.
20. Ibid., p. 21.
21. Ibid., p. 22.
22. Ibid., p. 25.
23. Ibid., p. 34.
24. A.C. Banerjee: *Indian Constitutional Documents*, Vol. III (Calcutta, A. Mukherjee & Co., 1949), p. 202.
25. Yogesh Chadha: *Rediscovering Gandhi* (London, Arrow Books, 1988), pp. 327–328.
26. Dhananjay Keer, op. cit. pp. 403–404.
27. Bhagwan Das (ed): *Thus Spoke Ambedkar*, Vol. 1, p. 39.
28. Ibid., pp. 40–41.
29. V.P. Varma, op. cit. p. 569.

30. Yogesh Chadha, op. cit. pp. 310–311.
31. S.R. Sharma, op. cit. pp. 59–61.
32. Ibid., p. 63.
33. Ramachandra Guha, op. cit. p. 206.
34. Ibid., p. 313.
35. Ibid., pp. 313–314.
36. M.G. Chitkara, op. cit., p. 193.
37. Ramachandra Guha, op. cit., p. 211.
38. Ibid., p. 212.
39. Ibid.
40. Bhagwan Das, Vol. 2, op. cit. p. 26.
41. Ramachandra Guha: *India After Gandhi* (London, Picador, 2008), p. 107.
42. Dr Babasaheb Ambedkar: *Writings and Speeches*, Vol. 3, 1987, p. 462.
43. Ramchandra Guha (ed): *Makers of Modern India*, p. 207.
44. Dhananjay Keer, op. cit. p. 207.
45. Mohammed Shabbir (ed): *Ambedkar on Law, Constitution and Social Justice* (Jaipur, Rawat Publications, 2005), p. 300.
46. Dr Babasaheb Ambedkar: *Writings and Speeches*, Vol. 15 (1997), pp. 976–78.

2

Influences

Vision in the leadership may spring from its original thinking or may be derived from an outside source. Vision, however, is generally expressed as the inner voice, the insight or the intuition in a leader, which helps in visualizing. Kouzes and Posner have defined intuition as the bringing together of knowledge and experience to produce new insights. Vision may not necessarily be a pure conception of the leader, but the leader is one who chooses the images and articulates it into a vision and focuses attention of the people on it. Where from Ambedkar's vision sprang? What were the sources of his vision?

All that is great in men come through labour, 'You have no idea of my suffering and labour, and you would have been wiped out' said Ambedkar to one journalist. His early life was full of painful experiences, sometimes disgracing, barring some exceptions. His life, ideas, ideals and vision were a projection of various influences. It is true that the thoughts cannot be independent of others. They emerge either as a reaction or response to the nature, situation, person or thought. In other words they grow dialectally. Besides stories from the Mahabharata and Ramayana, which he heard with rapt attention in his childhood, the life of Buddha, the teaching of Kabir and the struggle of Phule contributed tremendously to the building of his personality. These personalities gave him soul force and Western education gave him his weapons. But by the combination of idealism and practical life, by knowledge and experience, Ambedkar belonged to the race of Ranade, Bhandarkar, Tilak and Telang who unfurled the Indian flag of learning in the world of learning and research.

Ambedkar's hold over his people was unshakeable. One striking feature about Ambedkar was his marvellous combination of obstinacy and resilience and his ability to seize an opportunity by the forelock which succeeds in politics. It was resilience and not expediency that made him shed his obstinacy without compromising his stand or conscience. He was shrewd enough to know that dawn does not come twice to awaken a man. He had the gift of catching the ball as it bounced.

Ambedkar did not accept the *Geeta,* at all; to him it was an irresponsible book on ethics, a compromise of all errors. He believed in the necessity of religion but preferred to evaluate every religion from the angle of rationality. Rationality occupied a central place in his political ideology. He also formulated his concept of a true religion. He believed in God in the sense that some unknown power might be influencing human destiny. This faith in God, he, however, unified; since he took an active interest in the revival of Buddhism. To him, Man is the measure of all things. The revival of Man is the key feature in Ambedkar's ideology. This idea of the importance of Man, he probably derived from the classical Greek thought and the Age of Enlightenment. He is a symbol of protest against the old decadent social order and a protagonist of a new social order based on liberty, equality and fraternity. The main objective of his life-mission was to emancipate his brethren from the thraldom of untouchability and casteism and integrate them with the main stream. In this task he had to follow the foot prints of Lord Buddha, Mahatma Kabir and Jyotiba Phule.

Ambedkar's philosophy was the outcome of a number of influences. The formative period of his life was full of impacts and influences. These influences were many and varied, ranging from personal sufferings to the impacts of social reformers. It should not be forgotten that apart from an amalgam of influences, Ambedkar had his own individuality, grounded in philosophical thought. His political philosophy developed out of his unbending struggle for the freedom of servile humanity. He had revolted against orthodoxy and traditionalism and developed a sort of political philosophy, which is best reflected in the Preamble of India's Constitution.

His ideas reflect in the events, experiences and the acts of his life. He did not write it in an air-conditioned room as most of the academicians do, but his philosophies evolved out of his active life. Some of the primary influences on Ambedkar were that of Kabir, Ramji Sakpal, Jyotirao Phule, M.G. Ranade and Lord Buddha, while the secondary influences were that of Karl Marx, J.S. Mill and John Dewey. The following are some of the main influences which moulded the tone and spirit of his ideology.

Ramji Sakpal

The first and foremost influence on Ambedkar was that of his father, Ramji Sakpal, who, despite extremely limited resources, took a great care to provide education to his son; and guided him to learn the English language. His influence on Ambedkar was in the field of religion and values. Ambedkar derived from his father his painstaking spirit, his forceful mental energy and the intense interest in the welfare of his society.

There is a legend associated with the birth of Ambedkar which is connected with the symbolic interpretation of the dreams dreamt by the mother of the Great Buddha when he was in pre-natal stage. About Bhim Rao's birth, D.C. Ahir quite correctly observed that at the time of Ambedkar's birth, his parents were residing at Mhow near Indore, in Madhya Pradesh, where Ramji Sakpal was serving as Headmaster in the Army School. As in case of Lord Buddha, a prophecy had also been made prior to the birth of Ambedkar that he would be a great man.

It is said that one of the uncles of Ramji Sakpal, who had turned a *Sanyasi*, once came to Mhow, along with some other hermits. Ramji Sakpal happened to meet him and entreated the *Sanyasi* to bless his house with a visit. The *Sanyasi* declined to visit the house. However, he conferred on Ramji Sakpal a boon that a boy would be born in the family who would leave his mark on history. This boon took effect at Mhow on Tuesday 14 April 1891; on a very auspicious day indeed as Lord Buddha is also said to have been born on 14 April (*Vaisakha Purnima*) in 623 BC or 2,579 years ago.[1]

Ambedkar was born in a lower middle class Mahar (Hindu untouchable) community. His grandfather, Maloji Sakpal, was a Haveldar in the Bombay Army of the East India Company. He was a gallant soldier, and earned 19 medals during his military career. He had two children: Ramji Sakpal (Ambedkar's father) and daughter Mira Bai. Like his father, Ramji Sakpal, also joined the Army. He belonged to the Konkan region of the Bombay Presidency. He was an enlightened person who worked hard and attained proficiency in English language. Later, he obtained a Diploma in teaching from the Army Normal School in Poona. Subsequently, he was appointed as a teacher in the Army. He had served as Headmaster for 14 years and secured the rank of Subedar-Major in the Army. Ambedkar's mother, Bhima Bai came from a rich family of Murbad village in Thana District of Maharashtra. Her father and her six uncles were all Subedar Majors in the Army.

Here, we can see two common features of the families of Ambedkar's parents. One is, both belonged to soldier class and secondly, both belonged to Kabir cult, which did not believe in differences based on caste and birth. With this family background, along with untouchability (Mahar) tag attached, was born their fourteenth and the last child Bhimrao Ambedkar. But out of 14 children only five survived – two daughters, Manjula and Tulsi and three sons, Balaram, Anandrao and Bhimrao. Within two years of Ambedkar's birth, Ramji Sakpal had retired from the military and the family moved to Satara and then onto Bombay. Ambedkar, later on, in his life once proudly called himself as the 'Choudwa Ratna' (14th jewel), because he was the 14th child of his parents.

The Bhakti Movement in Maharashtra had impressed Ambedkar's family to imbibe its spiritual content. The biographer of Ambedkar, Dhananjay Keer, has observed, 'Ramji Sakpal lived a very industrious and intensely religious life. He offered prayers and devotion to God, morning and evening. The children joined in his devotions. The sweet devotional lyrics and spiritual hymns of devotion flowed from his mouth like a water from a fountain. It was a very rigid observance and a slight deviation from it on the part of the children incurred his displeasure. It was at times easy to evade or hurry through the hymns in the morning under the show and bustle of study, but in the evening it was a very stern affair. Then the chain of sweet songs of God would go on in a choir. This compulsory routine continued till their father's death'.[2]

Ramji Sakpal not only imparted education to his son but also taught some values to him. He was hard working man, deeply religious. Ramji read and recited to his children the great national epics, the Ramayana and the Mahabharata, the two unfailing sources of divine inspiration, the motive force, which have nurtured and moulded the lives of great men in India in every generation. Ramji Sakpal also sang the spiritual songs from the Marathi saint – poets like Moropant, Mukteshwar and Tukaram. His children derived immense benefits from these songs. Constant recitals, recitations and exposition of these songs helped develop a taste in his children and provided them with a certain toning and command of the language in their early age. Perhaps, the religious atmosphere which Ambedkar had imbibed early in his childhood made him to dedicate and struggle for a just cause later in his life with utmost sincerity and whole-heartedness. Though it (devotional readings) made him a deeply religious man, but at the same time he could rationalize the meaning of religion. His rationalism convinced him that religion is necessary for one's life. He said, 'without religion society will perish'. Ambedkar made a deep study of the various religions and developed a firm belief in the necessity of religion. He held that religion had a direct connection with heart and laws of reason.

Bhim's father was not merely after the spiritual development of his children. He cared also for the worldly betterment of his sons. Though a man of ordinary means and little influence, Bhim's father ungrudgingly supplied him with new books, borrowing money from his two married daughters on most of the occasions and at times even pawning their ornaments, which he had given them as marriage gifts and redeeming them after he received his monthly pension which was a meagre sum of rupees fifty. It was his ardent desire that his son should become a man of letters and light.[3]

Ramji Sakpal had obtained a mastery of the Marathi language and could easily teach his pupils and children how to use the appropriate words. He had also studied English and could teach his sons translation books with ease and confidence. Arithmetic was another subject of his liking. For the benefit of his sons he had a ready note book which served as a key to the arithmetic by Gopal Krishna Gokhale.[4] In fact, Ambedkar received an opportunity for, and encouragement in, the education through Ramji Sakpal.

Ramji Sakpal inculcated into the mind of Ambedkar that though Karna and Dhronacharya were of humble origin, but they rose to great heights by hard work and dedication. 'This deep conviction that was put into the heart of young Ambedkar could have been the beginning of the success story of Bhimrao Ramji Ambedkar. His efforts to acquire recognition by learning and achieving looks like a repetition of the story of Karna and the latter part of his life sounds like the position that Dhronacharya held, wielding authority and evoking awe and inspiration'.[5] One could thus locate the roots of 'the tremendous self-respect, confidence and religiosity of Ambedkar in the training he received in his family'.[6]

Ramji took active interest in his son's educational career. Ambedkar stated:

> It was my father who taught me how to find out a good English word for equivalent Marathi word and how to use it in the right place. I feel that I do possess some fame for writing and speaking good English. But my father in the manner in which no other teacher has ever taught me has taught how to use the right word in the right place so that it would carry the greatest weight. He always used to ask me words at random contained in Tarkhadkar's book and thus test my knowledge of English language. Similarly, idioms and how to use the right language style has also been taught by my father.[7]

Ambedkar stated that his father had great desire to see his son excel in academics. He became perfect in English by the blessings of his father. His interest in religion, attitude towards social and political problems, reading habits, etc. can be traced back to his father.

Ramji Sakpal's one outstanding characteristic was that he was a confirmed teetotaller and never touched meat. He was also a Spartan. In his youth he was a good cricketer and played football well. Cheerful and courageous in society, he took keen interest in religious and theological discussions. He was a friend and admirer of Mahatma Phule, a great social reformer of the period. Taking inspiration from him, Ramji Sakpal, was actively involved in social affairs. This is borne out of the fact that he had tried to petition the British Government to rescind their orders for banning the recruitment of Mahars in the army. He approached for help, and thus came into contact with, M.G. Ranade, another great social reformer. Ramji Sakpal's inclination towards social reform were mainly inspired through his contacts with Mahatma Phule and M.G. Ranade.

Ramji Sakpal breathed his last on 2 February 1913, the saddest day in Bhim's life. Subedar Ramji Maloji Sakpal was industrious, abstemious, devotional and aspiring to the end of his life. He died ripe in age but poor in wealth, for he had run into debt, but exemplary in character and unconscious of his great legacy to his clan, country and humanity. Having infused in his son strength of will to resist worldly temptations and a depth of spirituality very seldom found in his son's contemporaries, he left him behind to fight the battle of life and to break the world to his way.[8] Such family tree was bound to bear fruit of enduring sweetness. No wonder then that Bhim derived from his father his painstaking spirit, his forceful mental energy and the intense interest, in the welfare of his society.

Teachers

The next were the influences of teachers on Ambedkar. During Ambedkar's school days it is learnt that only a few teachers encouraged him towards his studies. The orthodox Hindu society did not encourage or create a favourable environment for the untouchables to acquire knowledge and get them educated. They were denied admission to schools and if admitted they were allowed on one condition that they would not sit with other students in common. Further, they were denied to learn Sanskrit because the Vedic text prohibits untouchables to learn or to hear Sanskrit. It was at the school that Ambedkar had the first experience of untouchability. Under these circumstances, the role of few teachers in Ambedkar's schooling is worth mentioning.

Bhim's schooling began at Dapoli. At Satara he completed his primary education and began his high school career. One day at Satara he went to school in soaking rains. The teacher by name Pendse, who was a Brahmin, was moved by the site of Bhim and he at once asked his son to take Bhim to his residence, give him a hot bath and a piece of cloth to cover his body and to hang up his wet clothes to dry.[9] This incident had a profound effect on young Bhim's mind.

There was another Brahmin teacher in the Satara High School whose surname was Ambedkar. He loved Bhim very much. He dropped daily a part of his meal into the hands of Bhim during the recess. This teacher changed the surname of Bhim Rao Ambavadekar to his own surname Ambedkar in the school records. Ambedkar gratefully remembered this teacher who treated him kindly during his school days. Later in life, when he was on the eve of departure for the first session of the Round Table Conference, Ambedkar received a letter of hearty congratulations from the same teacher, which he had treasured with pride and pleasure. Well has it been said that one good word can warm three winters.[10]

Ambedkar passed his Matriculation examination in 1907 from Elphinstone High School, Bombay, which was a great achievement for an untouchable. To commemorate this success, his community in fact arranged a function to honour him under the Presidentship of S.K. Bole, who was a well known social reformer. At this function, Krishnaji Arjun Keluskar who was an assistant teacher at Wilson High School, a social reformer and a

Marathi author was also present. It is interesting to note that Keluskar met Ambedkar in the Churmi Road garden where he used to go in the evenings. Charmed by the young studious student, Keluskar introduced himself to Ambedkar and enquired about him and his family. On knowing his background Keluskar began to help him in his studies. Keluskar in this function presented his new book, *Life of Gautam Buddha* which inspired Ambedkar greatly and eventually helped him for his conversion. Keluskar was also responsible in getting a monthly scholarship of twenty five rupees from Maharaja of Baroda, Sri Sayajirao Gaekwad. This helped Bhimrao to complete his graduation in 1912. It was Keluskar who was able to secure a scholarship for Ambedkar by the same Maharaja for higher studies in America. Accordingly in July 1913, he joined Columbia University, New York, America. After the death of Ramji Sakpal, Keluskar stood for the intellectual development of Ambedkar as a guardian.

Ambedkar was inspired by Muller at Elphinstone College, who used to give him clothes and lend books. However, his education received more encouragement in foreign countries rather than in the own home land, Ambedkar was inspired by the new academic atmosphere which greatly helped his faculty to grow.

Ambedkar was greatly enamoured by Edwin S.A. Seligman in Columbia University. He was his teacher for Public Finance.[11] Ambedkar took to Seligman as a duck takes to water and ran after the professor from class to class with his special permission to attend his classes.[12] This professor, who was fond of dog-earing the pages of the book in hand while teaching, taught well and guided his students with affection, and thus produced a lasting effect upon Ambedkar. When asked by Ambedkar as to the methods of research, he advised him to go on earnestly so that he might evolve his own method. This started the *Dnyana Yandnya*. For eighteen hours a day went on the endless digging for knowledge and this continued for months together. At last after two long years of toil, success came with tremendous gusto. Ambedkar obtained his M.A. degree in 1915 for his thesis 'Ancient Indian Commerce'.

Ambedkar was working simultaneously on another thesis. It was the 'National Dividend of India: A Historical and Analytical Study'. Columbia University awarded him the degree of Doctor of Philosophy for this dissertation. In the introductory note of Ambedkar's thesis, Seligman remarked, 'Nowhere, to my knowledge, has such a detailed study of the underlying principles been made'.

John Dewey was another teacher of Ambedkar at Columbia University. He was an exponent of the philosophy of instrumentalism. His was a pragmatic approach towards the problems of humanity. The pragmatism of John Dewey had an influence on Ambedkar. He was attracted towards realism. The practical rather than merely academic politics engaged his attention. In addition to pragmatism, John Dewey's integral rather than piecemeal approach, had an influence on Ambedkar.

In his essays on caste, Ambedkar had referred to John Dewey, his teacher, 'whom I owe so much'. By quoting the views of John Dewey he had tried to suggest the worship of the past in every respect is harmful for the reconstruction of the society. Almost all thinkers and leaders of India were children of the liberal tradition of thought of England; but Ambedkar was the only leader who received inspiration from America. He acknowledged the debt to John Dewey. A.M. Rajasekhariah, writes:

'Of all the professors in the University, Dr Ambedkar was influenced much by John Dewey'.[13]

It is said that he took down every word that the great teacher uttered in his teaching. Ambedkar used to tell his friends that if Dewey died, I could reproduce every lecture verbatim.[14]

The philosophy of John Dewey is based on pragmatism; and it is often called instrumentalism. It is a tendency and movement rather than a philosophy. It is an attitude and habit of thought – a habit of looking forward to results rather than backward to first principles. Everything is to be judged by its fruits, by its consequences. Reality is found in the flow of experience. Life is a series of problems to be solved, a succession of real struggles with real difficulties, the spirit of pragmatism is the spirit of youth, adventure and experimentation. It is a forward looking philosophy of hope and promise. Instrumentalism shows how knowledge has arisen in the evolutionary movement and points out the function of intelligence. Looking at from the above angle can very well conclude that Ambedkar's views and thinking of social problems was fundamentally based on instrumentalism. Ambedkar's philosophy of education struck roots in Dewey's Pragmatic Theory of Education which stands as the means of social continuity of life. This made Ambedkar to establish Peoples Education Society for the spread of education in India.

Dewey's philosophy led Ambedkar towards a critical analysis of the concrete problems facing humanity. Dewey's pragmatic approach convinced him that any philosophy, which sought after a way out from the troubles in which humanity was taught most, be dynamic and pragmatic. He criticized the old philosophers who advocated idealism and other utopian and prescriptive ideals. Ambedkar also criticized the ancient philosophers of India like Kapil, Manu, and religious scriptures known as *Vedas, Upanishads,* once he even burnt *Manusmriti*. Dewey's Method of inquiry, which indicated a way to deal with painful situations, influenced him. He was also impressed by Dewey's activist epistemology and the idea of a realistic school of political philosophers and therefore he paid attention to practical rather than merely academic politics. Politics is nothing, if not realistic. Before passing judgement on any scheme of politics, it is essential that one must consider the ground plans. The ground plan means the social structure of a community to which the political plan is sought to be applied.

Dewey's integral approach provided the basis for systematic analysis of problems relating to politics, economics, sociology, religion and history. There is a thread running through these problems, which calls for an integral rather than a piecemeal approach. This integral approach enabled Ambedkar to find that society is equally, if not more, aggressive and tyrannical than the government. Thus Ambedkar was very much influenced by Dewey's political philosophy and overall integral approach.

Ambedkar no doubt owed his success to his teachers whose ideas, dedication and inspiration helped him look at life afresh. His academic pursuit in the USA was indeed very satisfactory. One can quote Blake Clark's words:

> Under the stimulating influence of the University's greats John Dewey, Charles Beard, Boas, Seligman, Monroe and others, he became absorbed in ancient and modern history, anthropology, sociology, psychology and economics and signed up course after course. When he finished, he had more than double the number of credits usually required for his Degree.[15]

After remarkable success at Columbia University, Ambedkar turned his attention at the London School of Economics and Political Science for the study of Economics and the Grays Inn for Law. His admission into the prestigious institution was greatly facilitated by the introductory letters given by his Columbia Professor, R.A. Seligman to Professors Edwin Cannan and Sydney Webb. Ambedkar was of the view that the sympathy and the keen interest of Professor Cannan in his academic pursuits placed him under obligation which he can never repay.[16]

Ambedkar's exposure abroad, particularly his interaction with the famous professors in the USA and England and his own diligence, contributed in a significant way to his greatness.

Indian Social Reformers

Ambedkar was greatly inspired by the ideas of Indian social reformers. Indian society was rigid and conservative during his time and the social reformers had naturally an important role in the Indian society. Ambedkar was greatly influenced by Lord Buddha, Mahatma Jyotirao Phule[17], Kabir and Dalit Saints like Nandnar, Ravidas and Chokhamela.

Jyotirao Phule

Phule, a social thinker of Maharashtra, who did considerable work for the removal of social ills of the Hindu society, had influenced Ambedkar. Phule's field of social work related to the problems of untouchability, abolition of Sati, upliftment of women in society, abolition of child marriage, etc. His one of the important social reforms was the education of women and *Shudras*. He believed that with the dissemination of knowledge, light would come to them. He stated that it was their ignorance due to which their low condition had continued. He had started a low caste Girls School at Poona in 1848. Another similar school was opened by him in 1851. These reforms carried out by Phule had a strong impact on Ambedkar, who cultivated the philosophy that all men are equal by birth but social evils made one man superior over another man. He wanted to provide opportunities to the suppressed to raise themselves socially, economically and politically. Phule views that *Manusmriti* had bound the *Shudra*'s hand and foot; unless they revolted against it, they would never be able to shake off the shackles of bondage. Ambedkar had a similar view point, which he derived from Phule.

According to Ambedkar, laws of *Manusmriti* governed the lives of the Hindus in every village. Their low social, economic and political status and degradation were due to the injunctions of the *Manusmriti*. Ambedkar burnt the *Manusmriti* on 25 December 1927. It was a very important landmark in Ambedkar's career as social reformer. On this burning of *Manusmriti*, Ambedkar's biographer writes; 'This act was one of the greatest sacrilegious blows ever since in days of Luther upon the egoistic bigots, custom-managers and no-changers on earth .... It was a red-letter day in the annals of India as it was on this day that Ambedkar burnt the old *Smritis* and demanded a new one in order to reshape the Hindu code governing the life of so vast people'.[18] Ambedkar dedicated his book *Who Were the Shudras*? to the memory of Phule as 'The Greatest Shudra of Modern India who made the lower classes of Hindus conscious of their slavery to the higher classes and who preached the gospel that for India social democracy was more vital than independence from foreign rule'.[19] In short, Phule's work in the arena of social reforms provided a great inspiration to Ambedkar, who was essentially a man of action. He once said that 'the battle is a matter of joy for me'. More than once, he told his people: 'Lost rights are never regained by begging and by appeals to the conscience of the usurpers, but by relentless struggle'. Many of Ambedkar's arguments regarding the origin of untouchability, the role of Brahmins can be traced to Phule. Thus Ambedkar was very much influenced by Phule on social and political reforms in India. This influence was one of the inspirations to Ambedkar to become a great socio-political thinker of modern India.

M.G. Ranade

Mahadev Govind Ranade also influenced Ambedkar. Ranade had given precedence to social, economic, and religious reforms over political reform. Ambedkar admired the logic and wisdom of Ranade. He also stressed that social reforms in order to be lasting must precede political reform.

Ranade had the sincerity of a social reformer. About him, Ambedkar in his book *Ranade, Gandhi and Jinnah*, wrote:

> He was great not merely by the standards of his time, but he was great measured by any standard.

Ranade realized that the downfall of the Hindu society was due to certain weaknesses in its social system. Social reform, therefore, became the dominant purpose of his life. Ambedkar held him in high respect. The three postulates of Ranade's political philosophy had a remarkable influence on Ambedkar. First, Ranade had never before him an imaginary ideal; his ideal was a practical one. Second, in politics, sentiment and temperament of the people are more important than intellect and theory. Third, in political negotiations, the rule must be what is possible. Ambedkar regarded these three postulates of Ranade as 'the right one'.

Ambedkar agreed with the terms of the Poona Pact due to the above mentioned political philosophy. By accepting the terms of Poona Pact, he could save the life of Gandhi and also the lives of millions of untouchables. Ambedkar said:

> As to me, it is no exaggeration to say that no man was placed in a greater and grower dilemma than I was then. It was

> baffling situation. I had to make a choice between two different alternatives. There was before me the duty, which I owed as a part of common humanity, to save Gandhi from sure death. There was before me the problem of saving for the untouchables the political rights, which the prime minister had given them. I responded to the call of humanity and saved the life of Mr Gandhi by agreeing to alter the Communal Award in a manner satisfactory to Mr Gandhi. This agreement is known as the Poona Pact.

During Ranade's time, there was another school in Maharashtra, who gave precedence to political reforms over social reforms. Its prominent exponent was B.R. Tilak. Ambedkar did not like the arguments propounded in favour of political reforms first, and social reforms to be pursued later on. Ambedkar remarked that the 'political' school never realized that democracy was not a form of government; it was essentially a form of society.[20] It involves two things – the first is an attitude of mind, an attitude of respect and equality towards fellow human being. The second is a social organization free from rigid social barriers. He argued that Ranade's opponents never realized the fact that 'Democracy is incompatible and inconsistent with isolation and exclusiveness, resulting in the distinction between the privileged and unprivileged'. He aimed at creating a real social democracy, without which there could be no sure and stable politics. He warned his opponents against playing the part of liberal in politics and social conservatives. He said:

> You cannot be liberal in politics and conservative in religion. The heart and head must go together.[21]

Once when Ambedkar was invited by the Deccan Sabha of Poona to deliver an address on the 101st birthday of late Justice Mahadev Govind Ranade on 18 January 1940, he appreciated Ranade's mode of living as a social reformer but at the same time exposed the weakness of Ranade's philosophy which according to him was responsible for the failure of the Liberal Party in India.[22] Ambedkar said that Ranade belonged to the classes. He was born and bred among them. He never became a man of masses. This aversion to mass çontact is the legacy of Ranade. There is another legacy of Ranade to the Liberal Party and that relates to the false faith in the driving force of principles and policies.

Lord Buddha

Buddha is the founder of Buddhism. Buddha is one of the three Gurus of Ambedkar, the other two being Jyotiba Phule and Kabir. The teachings of Buddha had profoundly influenced Ambedkar's mind. It was the Buddha's influence that entirely shaped the personal, social and moral philosophies of Ambedkar. He preferred Buddhism, because it gave us three principles in combination, which no other religion did. Buddhism taught *Prajna* (understanding as against superstition and supernaturalism), *Karuna* (love) and *Samata* (equality). Ambedkar in his book *Annihilation of Caste* begins with the words of Lord Buddha, 'Know Truth as Truth and Untruth as Untruth'. According to G.S. Lokhande, 'Buddha's doctrines of *Arnicas* (Transistorizes) and *Annatta* (Egolessness) exercised a profound influenced on Dr Ambedkar'.[23] It was the teachings of Buddha which imbibed Ambedkar to follow his faith upholding the basic principles of Buddhism namely Equality, Justice, Non-violence and Truthfulness. Buddha gave him mental and metaphysical satisfaction and showed the way leading to the emancipation of the untouchables, by resorting to the path of mass conversion.[24]

Buddha's emphasis on the recognition of the mind as the centre of everything and that mind is the fountain of all good and evil that arises within and befalls us from without, led Ambedkar to affirm that cleaning of the mind is the essence of religion. The untouchability was not a by-product of blood or race inferiority. He ceaselessly strove to raise the mental stature of the downtrodden masses by encouraging them to have faith and hope in their creative potentialities. Once he said:

> What struck me most was that my community still continues to accept a position, of humiliation only because caste Hindu persists in dominating over them. You must rely on your

> strength, shake off the notion that you are in any way inferior to any community.

He laid great emphasis on the individual as the centre of all doctrines and activities. He appreciated Buddha's belief in men's capacity to work out his salvation without extraneous aid.

Buddha's doctrines of egalitarianism and humanism; and his faith in the capacity of man to shape his own destiny, exercised a lasting influence on Ambedkar. Keluskar had presented a book on Lord Buddha to Ambedkar, when Ambedkar passed matriculation in 1907. The book left an indelible mark on Ambedkar's mind. Ambedkar later on said:

> The Buddha's *Dhamma* (religion) had nothing to do with God and soul. His *Dhamma* had nothing to do with life after death. Nor has his *Dhamma* any concern with rituals and ceremonies. The centre of his *Dhamma* is man and the relation of man to man in his life on earth. This was his first postulate. His second postulate was that men are living in sorrow, in misery and poverty. The world is full of sufferings and that how to remove the suffering from the world is the only purpose of *Dhamma*. The recognition of the existence of suffering and to show the way to overcome the suffering is the foundation and the basis of his *Dhamma*.

The Buddha's religion is not a revelation. It was discovered by man for man. His message to the people was the message of man to man. The moral order in the human society rests on man and nobody else. In it, morality has been given the place of God. *Dhamma* rejected the infallibility of the *Vedas, Moksha* (salvation) of the soul, efficacy of rites, *Chaturvarna, Iswara* (God), soul, *Karma* and transmigration of the soul. *Dhamma* accepted the law of cause and effect. It preached social equality and stood for pulling down of all social barriers. It was for these reasons that Ambedkar was attracted towards Buddhism. He held Buddha in high esteem for the way in which they had struggled to remove the stain of untouchability.

Ambedkar had once said that Kabir was his second *guru*. Kabir's poems elegantly expressed in imaginative terms; the rational and secular ıdeas of Buddha. The third *guru* Phule inspired him to strive for anti-Brahmanism and amelioration of the masses, their education and economic uplift; the impact of the first *guru*, combined with that of second and third *gurus* left a deep mark on the growth of Ambedkar's ideas.

Lala Lajpat Rai

Ambedkar was very close to Lala Lajpat Rai. After his exile from India, Lalaji was in the United States of America from 1913 to 1916. He was radical in political affairs and simultaneously a confirmed social reformer. Ambedkar was confirmed about his integrity. Lalaji thought that the caste Hindus must try honestly to educate the untouchables and raise them to elevated positions in society and for this Ambedkar revered him most.

Ambedkar was studying in Columbia University. He was very regular and used to sit in the library in a particular place. Lalaji used to go to that library. He saw that an Indian student was studying very regularly and seriously. Lalaji enquired about this youth. When he came to know that Ambedkar was an untouchable by birth, he tried to win over and persuade him to the political, if not the Gaiter movement. Lalaji's efforts to win over Ambedkar failed. In September 1916, Lalaji called a conference of Indian students studying in America but Ambedkar did not attend.

Lalaji was caned by the police when he was leading the demonstration against the Simon Commission in Lahore on 30 October 1928, and he succumbed on 17 November. When Ambedkar read this he burst into tears and in a public meeting condemned the police atrocities. He wrote an article in *Bahishkrit Bharat* in which he said, 'Lalaji was honest, selfless, and ready to sacrifice for what he undertook. He did not separate politics and social reform'. Ambedkar praised all his precious qualities as a national leader, a social reformer, an educationist and a journalist. Though Lalaji's sympathetic attitude towards the upliftment of the untouchables was regarded as honest, still Ambedkar regarded it as insufficient for the uplift of untouchables.[25]

Bal Gangadhar Tilak

Bal Gangadhar Tilak and his friends were not in favour of giving precedence to social reforms against political reforms but at the same time they were helpful towards depressed classes. Ambedkar called them politically progressive and socially conservative.

Tilak had rejected even to sign on the resolution against untouchability. Tilak's student, G.S. Khapre used to say in his campaign against Ambedkar that 'the men who are working to uplift the untouchables they themselves are fallen'.

Ambedkar's bitter reaction was expressed in his *Bahishkrit Bharat* about the behaviour of Tilak and his students towards the depressed classes. He wrote:

> Had Lokmanya Tilak been born among untouchables then he would not sound the slogan of 'Freedom is my birth right' but his first slogan would have been 'the end of untouchability is my birth right.[26]

Western Political Thinkers

Karl Marx

Ambedkar had a thorough study of Karl Marx, the great socialist thinker of the 19th century. He appreciated the theory of class struggle as propounded by Karl Marx. He was aware of the ruthless exploitation of the poor going on all over the world. While pointing out the difference between class and caste he observed that the downtrodden people in India were the last to be hired and the first to be fired.

Ambedkar believed that those who were under the fetters of slavery could themselves remove their slavery; those on whom exploitation is imposed should unite with the realization of being slaves and revolt against it. But he differed from Marx on one point that the suffering is not only due to economic exploitation but also due to social exploitation.

Ambedkar knew from history that injustice is not removed till the sufferer himself does away with it by his own exertions and actions. He said:

> As long as the conscience of a slave does not burn with hatred for his slavery there is no hope for his salvation .... The social reform is a thorny path. People may sprinkle rose water on the roads of political liberators and orators. But reverse is the fate of those who launch a ruthless attack to liberate society from its ills, superstitions, outworn traditions and evil customs. For Ambedkar, man is something more than god. He did not believe in god. He wrote: 'You must abolish your slavery yourself. Do not depend for its abolition, upon god or superman'.[27]

The view of Karl Marx on socialism had a great influence on Ambedkar. So he started the struggle for human equality.

All in all, Ambedkar rejected the Marxian philosophy as 'deficient'. Marxism can give equality, but not liberty and fraternity. Equality will be of no value without fraternity and liberty.

J.S. Mill

J.S. Mill also influenced Ambedkar. The idea of the importance of individual's initiative and personal responsibility, Ambedkar had derived from J.S. Mill's argument that unless men are free to form and maintain their own opinions, they could not develop that mental well-being on which every body depends. Freedom of thought is absolutely indispensable although freedom of action may be limited. Ambedkar held that the actions of an individual must not become a nuisance to other members of the society.

Ambedkar was greatly impressed by the philosophy of democracy of J.S. Mill. Mill's views on 'Majority' and 'Minority' had a lasting effect on Ambedkar's philosophy. His struggle to safeguard the interest of the minority against the communal majority in India was based on J.S. Mill's analysis of parliamentary democracy in which the rights of the minorities has to be protected. Ambedkar studied extensively, the works of J.S. Mill to support his arguments. Ambedkar agreed with Mill when he said that those interested in the maintenance of democracy should not 'lay their liberties at the feet of even a great man, or to trust him with powers which enable to subvert their institutions'. Ambedkar wanted the successful working of democracy as suggested by Mill. Ambedkar's criticisms on hero-worship can be seen in his books, *What Congress and Gandhi Have Done to the Untouchables* and *Mr Gandhi and the Emancipation of the Untouchables.* For Ambedkar, hero-worship prevents the successful working of democracy.

Edmund Burke

Burke was an 18th century political philosopher. Ambedkar was greatly influenced by his thought. He had highly appreciated Burke's line of thinking on various issues. Burke's views on the moral regeneration of society greatly influenced Ambedkar. According to Burke, mere enactment of law to tax the American Colonies was not of any avail since the whole body of people was determined to overthrow it. Ambedkar applied the same logic and same thought to Indian society. The social conscience of the caste Hindus in India were not prepared to recognize the untouchables as their equals in matters of social status. Therefore, the mere law of removal of untouchability will prove to be of no practical value.

If one reads the volumes of *Writings and Speeches of Ambedkar*, one can find Burke's influence on Ambedkar. Once by following Burke, Ambedkar said in the Constituent Assembly, 'rights are protected by the social and moral conscience of a society. But if the fundamental rights are opposed by the community, no law, no parliament and no judiciary can guarantee these rights'. Then Ambedkar questioned the use of fundamental rights to the untouchables. He quotes again Burke, 'there is no method found for punishing the multitude'.

Ambedkar considered Edmund Burke as the 'greatest teacher of political philosophy'. Ambedkar had great admiration for Burke for his role in the impeachment of Lord Warren Hastings. Burke, according to Ambedkar, espoused the cause of the oppressed and strained all his nerves to redress their wrongs and punish their offender. He saw in Burke a great fighter against oppression and exploitation and very readily borrowed ideas which fitted his own framework of social injustice in India.

Extensive and Wide Reading

Ambedkar was a versatile reader. He loved the company of books. There are not many who had the same passion for reading as Ambedkar. At London, he often spent from 8 a.m. to 5 pm in the pursuit of knowledge in the libraries. He was a regular visitor to the Indian Office Library, the London University Library and other city libraries. At his house '*Rajagriha*', Ambedkar maintained a very good library. His collection of books was enormous. His extensive reading of history had given him proper perception to tackle the social and political problems of India. Ambedkar studied the history of slavery in Rome, the condition of Negroes in America and Jews in Germany. It would be useful to know the indigenous books and the foreign books which helped Ambedkar to mould his character and personality and gave him ideas to stand up to the challenge of social inequality and injustice in India.

K.S. Thankre's *Gramanyacha Itihas*, Marathi publication published in 1892[28] gives information regarding performing *Upnayana*. Ambedkar used this book to mention that the 'Brahmins exclusive right to perform the *Upnayana* and the support of the Brahmins for the performance of *Upnayana* need not be based on religious grounds'. It could be purchased by money. For instance, Shivaji got the support of the Brahmin Gangabhat on payment of money. Ambedkar was interested in reading some of the excellent Marathi dramas written by Gadkari. From London, he used to write letters to Shivtarkar to send some excellent Marathi drama of Gadkari.[29]

Ambedkar's proficiency in Sanskrit made him to have wide knowledge about Hinduism. The original texts of Hinduism were all in Sanskrit. Ambedkar studied *Mahabharata, Ramayana, Upanishads, Manusmritis* and other religious texts. Due to vast reading he could assess the drawbacks of Hinduism and could build his own theories. His books on *Castes in India*,

Annihilation of Caste, *Philosophy in Hinduism*, *Who Were the Shudras?*, *Revolution and Counter Revolution in Ancient India*, *Riddles in Hinduism* speak of his wide knowledge which Ambedkar had derived from the original Hindu Religious texts. Ambedkar had studied great deal of literature on religious, social, political and economic life of India. Hopkins's *The Great Epic of India*, Vincent Smith's *Early History of India*, C.V. Vaidya's *The Riddle of the Ramayana* and *History of Medieval India*, P.T. Srinivasa Iyengar's *Life in Ancient India in the Age of Mantras*, Abbe Dubois's *Hindu Manners and Customs* and D.S. Triveda's *The Original Home of the Aryans* were some of the great books which Ambedkar read with great interest and delight which contributed in no mean way to the development of his own ideas.

Buhler's *Laws of Manu*, Oldenberg's *Life of Buddha* and C.F. Oldham's *Life of Napolean*, Sloane's *The Sun and the Serpent*, Jeanyee Wong's *Buddha: His Life and Teachings*, Kautilya's *Arthashastra*, Jaiswal's *Hindu Polity*, Wilson's *Vishnu Purana* and *Rigveda*. Senart's *Castes in India*, Webber's *The Hindu Social System* and Ketkar's *History of Caste in India* were all read by Ambedkar along with many other literary works.

Since Ambedkar was exposed to western countries, he was attracted by western liberal doctrines and traditions. Ambedkar had thoroughly read books written by liberal writers like, Walter Bagehot, James Bryce, Jennings, Pendleton Herring, L.T. Hobhouse, John Shore, A.B. Hart, H.J. Laski, Dicey and many others. Ambedkar had wide knowledge about parliamentary form of democracy. This was possible due to his extensive reading of the writings of experts on democracy. It was his wide reading which made him to understand democracy in a meaningful way. He said that to his knowledge no one had explained the relationship of the king and his ministers in a responsible government better than Macaulay.[30]

Books were a constant company and Ambedkar managed to read books even when he was totally involved in public life. His very extensive reading helped him to speak and write with authority and confidence on the political, economic, social and religious problems of India.

Experiences

The bitter experiences Ambedkar had in his own country and the pleasant time he had outside helped him to compare the social status of individuals which in turn shaped his personality. His experience made him raise the slogan 'Educate, Organize and Agitate' to liberate the oppressed and restore their deprived rights. Ambedkar was exposed to two particular trends of experience – one was his own experience which was a very important part of his life and personality and the other was the experience of others which he learnt as a sensitive reader and a shrewd observer.

Ambedkar's first realization of his being an untouchable came about when he was hardly 9 years old. While on his way to Goregaon from Satara along with his brother and sister's son, he had to suffer the indignity of going without water and food because of his low caste. The harrowing experience of the cart ride and the denial of water by the toll collector and the improper shelter to his caste had indelible impression[31] on Ambedkar's young mind.

Ambedkar was fully aware that untouchables were subjected to certain indignities and discriminations. For instance, he knew that he could not sit in the midst of his classmates in the school and could not drink water without the assistance of the high caste. At home, he knew no washermen would wash the clothes of an untouchable and no barber would entertain an untouchable.

Ambedkar's experience at Baroda, while in job had a tremendous impact on him. As he was educated by the Baroda State, he was bound to serve the State according to the contract. At the railway station of Baroda, no one came to receive him. He managed to stay at a Parsi's Inn on condition that he should enter himself as a Parsi in the register,[32] but it was on 11th day of his stay in the Inn, that the owner came and gave Ambedkar an ultimatum to leave the Inn by the evening. Ambedkar cursed all and wept bitterly for being deprived of his precious possession namely his shelter. The Baroda State did not come to his rescue by providing him either State bungalow or his two friends one Hindu and another a Christian allowed him to stay with them. It was then that he learnt a 'person who is untouchable to Hindu is also an untouchable to Parsi'.[33]

Another bitter experience occurred in 1934 at Daultabad, the historical city. Ambedkar and his friends washed their faces and legs on the pavement with the water from the tank near the fort. The Mohammedans came shouting 'the *Dheds* (meaning untouchables) have polluted the tank'[34] and abused with filthy language. Ambedkar asked one of the young Muslims in the crowds if an untouchable converted to Islam could use the tank. The Muslim was unable to answer this query. This incident proved that untouchability was seeped in the Indian social system affecting all.

Ambedkar had also learnt of other's experiences through book's narrations, complaints, etc. which had a tremendous impact on him. The harrowing tales of ill-treatment because of one's low caste made Ambedkar to throw himself in the struggle for the emancipation of the deprived people of the society. The tragic case of the wife of an untouchable school teacher in a village Kathiwar shocked Ambedkar. The woman had just delivered and was not feeling very well but the doctor refused to treat the patient because of her being at the untouchable colony, only when the patient was brought outside the untouchable colony then the doctor gave his thermometer to a Muslim and this Muslim gave it to the teacher who gave it to his wife and then it was returned by same process. The doctor looking at the thermometer said that the patient was suffering from pneumonia. Although doctor sent medicine he refused to see her later though the fee was paid. The woman and her child died. This inhuman attitude of the doctor towards the untouchable was greatly criticized by Ambedkar. According to Ambedkar, 'the Hindu would prefer to be inhuman rather than touch untouchable'.[35]

All the above episodes are bitter reminders of the inhuman treatment meted out to the untouchables and a very sensitive Ambedkar could not have been a mere witness. He found himself launching agitations like the Mahad agitation to allow untouchables to drink water from public tanks and the agitation of temple entry.

Visits

Ambedkar never dreamt of going abroad because of his family's living conditions but due to his hard work in studies he got a great opportunity to go abroad for higher education under the royal patronage of Maharaja of Baroda Sri Sayaji Rao Gaekwad.

Ambedkar stayed in America from 1913 to 1917, and got his M.A. and Ph.D. degrees from Columbia University. The life in America changed Ambedkar's mind. Here he breathed the air of liberty, equality and fraternity. One can agree with Dhananjay Keer's remark that 'life at Columbia University was a revelation'[36] to Ambedkar. Around this time Ambedkar began to entertain new ideas of social reform against the background of untouchability in India. Dhananjay Keer is of the opinion that Ambedkar, while in America must have been deeply impressed with two things. First, was the Constitution of USA. and more so the 14th amendment to that Constitution which declares the freedom of Negroes. The second was the life of Booker T. Washington. He was a great reformer and educator of the Negro race in America and was the founder and president of the Tuskegee Institute which disseminated among the Negroes, the doctrine of education of the head, heart and hand, and thus broke the shackles of bondage which had crushed the Negroes for ages physically, mentally and spiritually,[37] and no doubt Ambedkar must have been an admirer of such a great man as was his vogue towards all original thinkers and reformers.

For emancipation of the Negroes in America the 14th amendment could not have been of much use. After the end of civil war in America the White had not shown generosity towards the Negroes despite the fact that much blood had been shed by them for maintaining the unity of nation. Ambedkar was aware of the trends. In fact, his study and understanding of American history and the Civil War of 1860 between the South and North America had strengthened his belief that real emancipation is possible only when there is a change of heart.

Ambedkar was, on the other hand, greatly impressed by the views of William Garrison of America who worked sincerely for the emancipation of Negro slaves and fought for their civil liberty. Garrison through his newspaper 'Liberator' created public opinion in favour of liberating the Negroes. Ambedkar inspired by Garrison's experiment and started his own newspapers, *Bahishkrit Bharat, Mooknayak* and *Janata* to awaken the untouchables towards their emancipation. In 1917, Ambedkar was doing his master degree in economics but he was attracted by the academic atmosphere and excellence of Oxford University, London which was the most reputed centre of higher education. His stay at Oxford happened to be the most formative years of his academic life. While abroad, Ambedkar came under the lasting influence of Edmund Burke, J.S. Mill, Voltaire and many other liberal thinkers.

Company

Ambedkar always kept very good company. Though he was born as an untouchable, he had many friends outside his caste. He had Brahmins who admired him for his role towards social equality. It was his friends, who helped him during personal financial crisis, Naval Bhathena, a Parsi, was a life-long friend who readily helped Ambedkar with finances whenever he was in need. S.K. Bole and Krishnaji Arjun Keluskar were his well wishers. His Highness, Maharaja Sir Sayajirao Gaekwad and Maharaja Sri Shahu of Kolhapur were Ambedkar's benefactors. S.N. Shivtarkar who stood by Ambedkar for over twenty years in his great war against untouchability depended on him for guidance. Chimanlal Harilal Setalvad, G.K. Nariman,. R.P. Paranjpye and B.G. Kher were his good friends who worked for Bahishkrit Hitakarini Sabha. Sorendranath Tipnis, Subhedar Savadkar and Anantrao Chitre used to take care in arranging Ambedkar's Programmes. Savarkar used to whole heartedly support Ambedkar's struggle. Pamjabrao Desmukh, G.A. Gavai and Krishnaji, S. Kadam took active part with Ambedkar during his social struggle.

Ambedkar had many Brahmin associates and friends. It is thus evident that he did not hate Brahmins but was opposed to

Brahmanism. Ambedkar's friend Dastur Bode, who was well versed in the Indo-Iranian literature, helped Ambedkar in his literary pursuits. Ambedkar got the information relating to the meaning of 'Varna' occurring in Indo-Iranian literature from Dastur Bode. Bhaskarrao Kadrekar was the editor of Ambedkar's weekly *Janata* and Ambedkar tried to help an aged Keluskar, one of his well wishers, by submitting a representation to Maharaja of Baroda to grant a monthly pension. S.M. Mate, a social reformer devoted to the cause of the education for the untouchables worked with Ambedkar in giving education to the depressed class people of the society.

The intellectual company of Ambedkar was also very good. K.A. Ezekiel, in the field of journalism supported Ambedkar and his movements. S.S. Rege, librarian of the Sidharatha College was given the responsibility of publishing the books of Ambedkar. Rattu was Ambedkar's private secretary who had the opportunity to share his life with Ambedkar till his master's death. Shakaranand Shastri, M.B. Niyogi former Chief Justice of the Nagpur High Court, M.B. Chitnis and B.H. Varale were Ambedkar's good associates who later embraced Buddhism with Ambedkar. In the Constituent Assembly, Ambedkar had the company of such stalwarts like K.T. Shah, Pandit Lakshmikant Maitra and T.T. Krishmanachari along with others.

The company that Ambedkar kept was some measure of his own personality and character. All his friends, associates and followers had a great deal to do with the mental outlook of Ambedkar and had contributed in no mean way to his greatness as a leader and a liberator.

Conclusion

These were some of the major formative influences which had shaped Ambedkar's ideas and aim of his life. The basic foundations of his thought started from his family, especially the impact of Ramji Sakpal on Ambedkar. His father, Ramji Sakpal, was a religious man and his influence on Ambedkar was paramount. Ambedkar regarded religion as essential in man's life, but he added that every religious dogma should be judged from the angle of rationality. He discarded the superstitions; mysticism and false-sayings as contained in religious scriptures, because they aimed towards the creation and maintenance of graded inequalities. He held that religion should be subjected to the test of rationality. No religious dogma should be accepted, unless it is rationally valid. In addition to his interest in religion, Ambedkar learnt English language from his father. This grounding in English language greatly helped Ambedkar in the development of his political ideology.

The Indian social reformers had greatly influenced Ambedkar. J.R. Phule's work in the field of social reforms, especially the ending of untouchability and women education had cast a great influence on Ambedkar. The ideology of Ranade that social reforms must precede political reforms fascinated Ambedkar. Ambedkar developed his *Dhamma* from the teachings of Lord Buddha and Kabir, who believed in a casteless society based on fraternity.

While Ambedkar was pursuing his higher studies at the Columbia University, the two teachers who influenced him the most were Professors Seligman and Dewey; the latter's ideology of pragmatism had left a deep impression on Ambedkar.

Ambedkar admired Marx's concern for the exploited class, though he characterized Marxian philosophy as 'deficient'. J.S. Mill's ideas of individual initiative and freedom had left an indelible mark on Ambedkar.

Though the above social reformers and thinkers had influenced Ambedkar, in one way or the other; the most enduring influence on Ambedkar came through his own bitter experiences and struggles that he waged for the liberation of the downtrodden and the building of a just society. The beauty of Ambedkar lay in the fact that he fused together the above ideas in a harmonious whole, clearly stating his goals and visions; to be attained on the basis of rationality and logic. His entire ideology revolved around Man and the ending of exploitation, especially the shackles of bondage of the untouchables, and providing them social justice.

Notes

1. D.C. Ahir: *The Legacy of Dr. Ambedkar* (New Delhi, B.R. Publication, 1990), p. 2.
2. Dhananjay Keer: *Dr. Ambedkar, Life and Mission* (Bombay, Popular Prakashan, 1971), p. 10.
3. Ibid. p. 17.
4. Keer, Ibid. p. 11.
5. Ramachandra and Sangh Mittra: *The Ambedkar Era* (New Delhi, Commonwealth Publishers, 2003), p. 2.
6. M.L. Ranga (ed): *B.R. Ambedkar: Life, Work, and Relevance* (New Delhi, Manohar Publishers, 2000), p. 16.
7. K.S. Bharti: *Foundation of Ambedkar Thought* (Nagpur, Datta Son Publication, 1990), p. 14.
8. Keer, op. cit. p. 25.
9. Ibid. p. 14.
10. Ibid.
11. Dinkar Khabade: *Dr. Ambedkar and Western Thinkers* (Pune, Usha Wagh, Sugava Prakashana, 1989), p. 34.
12. Ibid. p. 35.
13. A.M. Rajasekharaiah, *The Quest for Social Justice* Ist edition (New Delhi, Uppal Publishing House, 1989), p. 10.
14. Dinkar Khabade, op. cit. p. 42.
15. A.M. Rajasekharaiah, op. cit. pp. 9–10.
16. Dr Babasaheb Ambedkar *Writings and Speeches*, Vol. 6, (Mumbai, Govt. of Maharashtra, 1989), p. 330.
17. Dr Ambedkar has spelled Phule as Fule in his book *Who Were the Shudras*?
18. Keer, op. cit. p. 101.
19. Dr Babasaheb Ambedkar *Writings and Speeches*, Vol. 7 (Mumbai, Govt. of Maharashtra, 1990), p. 9.
20. B.R. Ambedkar: *Ranade Gandhi and Jinnah* (Bombay, Thacker and Co. Ltd., 1943), p. 38.
21. S.N. Mandal: *Dr. Ambedkar: His Thoughts and Observation*, (New Delhi, National Publishing House, 2004), p. 22.
22. Babasaheb Ambedkar *Writing and Speeches*, Vol. 1 (Mumbai, Govt. of Maharashtra, 1979), pp. 211–240.

23. G.S. Lokhanda: *Bhimrao Ramji Ambedkar: A Study in Social Democracy*, II Revised Edition, (New Delhi, Intellectual Publishing House, 1982), pp. 3–9.
24. W.N. Kuber: *Builders of Modern India* (B.R. Ambedkar, Publications Division, Ministry of Information and Broadcasting, Government of India, 1990), p. 20.
25. M.L. Ranga (ed.): *B.R. Ambedkar: Life, Work and Relevance*, (New Delhi, Manohar Publishers, 2000), p. 53.
26. S.R. Bakshi (ed.): *Social Ideology of Dr. B.R. Ambedkar (*New Delhi, Deep and Deep Publication, 2001), p. 204.
27. K.S. Bharathi: *Foundation of Ambedkar Thought* (Nagpur, Datta and Son Publication, 1990), p. 14.
28. Dr Babasaheb Ambedkar *Writings and Speeches*, Vol. 7, (Mumbai, Government of Maharashtra, 1990), p. 184.
29. Keer, op. cit. p. 47.
30. Dr Babasaheb Ambedkar *Writings and Speeches*, Vol. I, 1979, p. 324.
31. Dr Babasaheb Ambedkar *Writings and Speeches*, Vol. 12, 1993, p. 665.
32. Dr Babasaheb Ambedkar *Writings and Speeches*, Vol. 12, p. 676.
33. Dr Babasaheb Ambedkar *Writings and Speeches*, Vol. 12, p. 678.
34. Dr Babasaheb Ambedkar *Writings and Speeches*, Vol. 12, p. 684.
35. Dr Babasaheb Ambedkar *Writings and Speeches*, Vol. 12 p. 687.
36. Keer, op. cit. p. 27.
37. Ibid. p. 31.

3

His Works

B.R. Ambedkar was a scholar of eminence and one of the most learned men and a voracious reader. He owned the biggest personal library in Asia. Lord Casey, one time Governor General of India, observed that he was the fountain-head of wisdom and knowledge. His scholarly abilities were recognized by all. Edward Thompson in his 'Enlist India for Freedom' writes,

> If anything by Dr Ambedkar comes your way, read it, and you will understand why he often makes orthodox Hindus, hopping mad. He is one of the dozen most astonishing men in India.[1]

An American, Vincent Shean, who had known Ambedkar for a number of years, in his *Nehru: The Years of Power*, says,

> ... In the torrential flood of his talk there came up great chunks and whirling avatars of learning. He may not have been the greatest Sanskrit scholars but he could plaster a text with dozens of references to early Hindu authorities.[2]

In a similar tone, an Indian scholar, Trilochan Singh, writes,

> Above all, Dr Ambedkar is a philosopher. Those who read his books cannot be failed to be impressed with steadfastness with which he pursues truth; and only those who have dispassionately read his books can form a true estimate of the greatness of the man.[3]

Such a great imprint Ambedkar, the scholar, has left on his contemporaries.

An Indian scholar, T.K. Tope says:

> 'Dr Ambedkar's erudition and learning were no doubt great ... the generations to come may not remember the political achievements of Dr Ambedkar, but they will remember his lofty achievements in the field of scholarship and learning. Ambedkar the political leader, Ambedkar the social revolutionary, Ambedkar the modern exponent of Buddhism, may be forgotten, but Ambedkar the scholar, will be immortal'.[4]

Ambedkar was one of the greatest painstaking scholars of his time. He had knack for research, and whichever subject he touched upon, he acquitted himself extremely well. Neither he read for amusement nor wrote for amusement, because he was a man with a mission and seeker of truth. He said, 'What instructs me amuses me'. He had used his intellect and wisdom to create, 'Such instructive literature which is perennial source of inspiration and guidance to scholars and others alike'.

Ambedkar had thirst for knowledge; his passion for books and his erudition were unique. He acquired the highest degrees of three famous English and American Universities. He was a voracious reader and knew seven languages. Ambedkar built his bungalow 'Rajgriha' (Buddha's Palace) to suit the requirement of a good library. He stayed, took his meals and even slept in that library. His library contained up-to-date books on various subjects. There was one separate division on political biographies. He purchased books even sacrificing his daily needs. When in New York, he bought about 2,000 old books. At the time of Second Round Table Conference he purchased books in London and sent them to India in 32 boxes. Books were his greatest friends. He said, 'For a man like me who was socially boycotted, these books took me to their hearts'. He described his love for books as the love of a lover for his beloved. Pandit Madan Mohan Malaviya expressed his desire to purchase his collection for Banaras Hindu University for two lakh rupees but he refused. In fact, his fondness for books was phenomenal.[5]

Ambedkar's personal library was so big and enormous that the visitors were taken aback, and in their bewilderment they used to ask whether he had read all these books. But Ambedkar who was so intimate with his books that from a distance he could recognize any book and tell its gist, which feat often added to the bewilderment of his guests.

When Ambedkar had started his studies afresh in London (1920–1923), he joined several libraries, such as, the London University General Library, Goldsmith's Library of Economics Literature, the British Museum Library and the India Office Library. In those libraries he used to sit throughout the day even without a break for lunch, because he could not afford lunch. He resolutely avoided all kinds of diversions, such as excursions, theatres and restaurants.

At its special convocation on 15 June 1952, Columbia University conferred the degree of LL.D. (honoris causa) on him. The citation said, 'the degree is being conferred in recognition of the work done by him in connection with the drafting of India's Constitution'. Columbia University hailed Ambedkar as 'one of India's leading citizens, a great reformer and a valiant upholder of human rights'.

In 1953, Osmania University conferred the LL.D. degree on Ambedkar. In the citation he was described as 'a person of great eminence, high attainment and distinguished service, one of the ablest lawyers, prominent legislator and a champion of the backward and downtrodden people of India'.

Ambedkar's original aspiration was to become a professor and lead the life of a student; but he was thrown into the vortex of politics. He was a Professor of Economics in Sydenham College, Bombay. In June 1935, he became the Principle of the Government Law College, Bombay, and he occupied that position till his resignation in 1938. His lectures were illuminating though sometimes students differed with him ideologically. He outlined his concepts of an ideal professor. He said, 'He should not only be learned; he must speak in clear tone. He must be well versed. My inherent qualities were developed by men like Professor Seligman and others'.

Ambedkar was a renowned scholar, distinguished educationalist, powerful debater, authoritative constitutionalist, famous defender of the revolutionary social reformation and movement, and the fearless champion of the down trodden masses. In him, culture, wisdom, wit, humanism, instinct of reason, spirit of rationalism, reasonable ruthlessness for inequality, contempt for injustice and superstitions were harmoniously blended in right proportions. He brought about the renaissance of Buddhism in India and initiated a religious and social revolution of major significance. He was a versatile genius; his erudition and learning were no doubt great. 'He had', writes Raj Gill, 'such a multifaceted, scintillating personality that whosoever came into contact with him was dazzled'.[6]

Ambedkar's writings cover diverse subjects of human interest, such as; administration, anthropology, economics, finance, politics, religion, sociology and so on. During the period from 1916 to 1956, he wrote in English over twenty books, pamphlets and articles. His ten important books are:

1. *The Problem of the Rupee: Its Origin and its Solution*, 1923
2. *The Evolution of Provincial Finance in British India*, 1925
3. *Annihilation of Caste*, 1936
4. *Thoughts on Pakistan*, 1940
5. *Ranade, Gandhi and Jinnah*, 1943
6. *What Congress and Gandhi Have Done to the Untouchables*, 1945
7. *Who Were the Shudras?* 1946
8. *The Untouchables,* 1948
9. *Thoughts on Linguistic States*, 1955
10. *The Buddha and His Dhamma*, 1957

The Problem of Rupee

The thesis *The Problem of the Rupee: Its Origin and its Solution* for which Ambedkar was awarded a D.Sc. by the University of London in 1923, was published in the same year by a London firm (P.S. King and Company, London). The book had an introduction by Edwin Cannon, Ambedkar's illustrious teacher at the London School of Economics and Political Science. He paid glowing tributes to Ambedkar for the stimulating freshness of his views. He wrote, 'Even when I have thought him quite wrong, I have found a stimulating freshness in his views and reasons'. 'In the practical conclusion', Cannon said, 'Ambedkar was right'. This book was re-issued by Thacker and Company, Bombay, in May 1947 under the title: 'History of Indian Currency and Banking'.

Problem of the Rupee was a very useful contribution to Indian economics, and Ambedkar won laurels for this exceedingly thought-provoking work. It was an instructive treatise on a terribly controversial subject. Ambedkar tackled the problem of the rupee in all its details. He traced its history, analysed all sorts of opinions and finally gave his verdict that the problem had arisen on account of the neglect by those in power of the truth that it was the internal purchasing power of the rupee which was of primary importance and not its exchange value as has been assumed and worked upon by them. He held that 'stability of a currency in terms of gold was of importance only to the dealers in gold, but its stability in terms of commodities in general affected all. This highly important aspect of a gold currency was overlooked by our rulers during several decades'.[7] *The Economist* (London) also appreciated this work and wrote, 'It is clear and ably written book. Certainly none of the other numerous works on one or other aspect of the monetary problem have anything like the readability of this tract'.

Ambedkar deals with the problem in a very lucid and praiseworthy manner and puts-forward not merely its origin but also valuable proposals for a solution, which should be studied by bankers and those merchants whose business depends upon the exchange.

The Evolution of Provincial Finance in British India

The thesis 'National Dividend for India: A History and Analytical Study' for which Ambedkar was awarded a Ph.D. by the Columbia University, New York, in 1917, was published eight years later, in 1925, under the title *The Evolution of*

Provincial Finance in British India. In this thesis, he traced the growth of the financial arrangements from the Act of 1883 under the imperial system. Commenting on the taxation system, he strongly condemned the existing practice. The chapters on budget are very valuable in their educative and illustrative aspects with regard to their nature and enlargement of the Provincial Finances. From chapters x to xii, the book becomes eloquent, interesting and powerful in its appeal. Ambedkar bitterly exposes the British bureaucracy, denounces the designs and objects of the imperial system and also lashes out at all the reactionary forces in the country.

In the thesis, Ambedkar admits that there was some advancement in material progress, but observes that no people in the world can long remain content with the benefits of peace and order, for they are not dumb brutes. He adds that everybody knows that the whole policy of India was dictated by the interests of the English industries and English manufacturers. He concludes that in every country there have been downtrodden communities suffering from social oppressions and social injustice and yet, no country has had to be without political power on that account.

The introduction to this work was written by R.A. Seligman, Columbia University. Observing that the problem discussed by Ambedkar in his excellent dissertation was one that was arousing a growing interest in all parts of the world, the professor remarked, 'Nowhere to my knowledge has such a detailed study of the underlying principles been made'.[8]

This famous book became a companion of the Members of the Indian Legislative Councils and the Central Assembly at the time of budget discussions during the British regime, a ready reference for men in authority and a guide to students of economics. Shortly after the publication of this book, Ambedkar was called to give evidence before the Royal Commission on Indian Currency. It must have been a matter of great pleasure to Ambedkar to see every Member of a Commission holding the book in his hand.[9]

Annihilation of Caste

This was the presidential address which Ambedkar had prepared for the 1936 annual conference of the *Jat-Pat-Todak Mandal* of Lahore. The conference was ultimately cancelled by the Reception Committee on the ground that the views expressed in the address would be unbearable to the Conference. Ambedkar published in 1936 itself his undelivered address in the form of a pamphlet and 'the posthumous child of the Conference' has survived the passage of time as a great thesis on the annihilation of caste.

Ambedkar examined caste system from two angles – the drawbacks of the system and what is the way out. Indicating the weakness of caste system, Ambedkar writes pungent, but true remarks. He asserts that caste is based on the dogma of predestination[10]; it does not result in economic efficiency. It cannot and has not improved the race. It has disorganized and demoralized the Hindus.[11] Its effect on the ethics of the Hindus is simply deplorable. It has killed public spirit; and destroyed the sense of public charity. It has restricted a Hindu's loyalty; it is confined only to his caste. Virtue has become caste ridden and morality has become caste bound. Neither there is sympathy to the deserving, nor is their appreciation of the meritorious.[12] The four-tier classification of caste is most degrading; it is ridiculous and absurd. It forms 'the inner citadel of Hinduism'. It is a system which deadens, paralyses and cripples the people from helpful activities.[13] It is riddled with puzzles. It is a serious threat to the unification of India.

Ambedkar also deals with the problem: What is the way out? How can caste system be destroyed?

The destruction of caste, to him, does not mean the destruction of a physical barrier; it means a notional change. Hindus observe caste not because they are inhuman or wrong headed; but because they are deeply religious. Hence, the enemy, one must grapple with is not the people who observe caste, but the *Shastras* which teach them this religion of caste. As such, the real remedy is to destroy the belief in the sanctity of the *Shastras*. 'Make every man and woman free from the thraldom of the *Shastras*'.[14] The laws contained in *Vedas* and *Smritis* are iniquitous in that they are not the same for one class as for another. This inequality is made perpetual by *Shastras*. In order to destroy the caste system 'the sense of religious sanction behind caste and *Varna* must be destroyed'.[15] As such, Ambedkar says that 'such a religion must be destroyed and that there is nothing irreligious in working for the destruction of such a religion'.

Ambedkar, therefore, calls upon to annihilate the caste which is a great hindrance to social solidarity. The society, he says, must be based on reason and not on atrocious traditions of caste system. Mahatma Gandhi did not like Ambedkar's thesis 'the annihilation of caste', and once called him 'a challenge to Hinduism'. Perhaps it was not a challenge to Hinduism, but a challenge to the minds of the caste Hindu leaders.

Thoughts on Pakistan

Although by 1940, the idea of Pakistan was born, but the views of the Muslim League on it were nebulous. To the Hindu, the idea of Pakistan was quite repulsive. The Congress did not look it with favour and opposed it tooth and nail. At such a time, Ambedkar published his thought-provoking thesis in which he put forward his views candidly and favoured the creation of Pakistan. Written with courage, competence and confidence, *Thoughts on Pakistan* 'is a master-piece in which learning and thinking are blended and displayed at their highest order. It is entrancing in its magic, intriguing in its construction, terse in style, and provocative in its manner. It is a model in scientific propagation'.[16]

Ambedkar, in contrast to the all Indian leaders of the period, had shown clearly his thoughts and feelings about the creation of Pakistan. He raised the question whether integral India was an ideal worth fighting for. He argued that even if India remained as one integral whole it would never be an organic whole. India might in name be continued to be known as one country but in reality it would be two separate countries – Pakistan and Hindustan – joined together by a forced and artificial union. This would be specially so under the stress of the two nation theory. As it stood, the idea of unity had little hold on the Indian world of fact and reality, little charm for the common Indian, Hindu or Muslim, whose vision was bounded by the valley in which he lived. But it did appeal to the imaginative and unsophisticated minds on both sides. He wrote:

> The two-nation theory will not leave room even for the growth of that sentimental desire of unity. The spread of that virus of dualism in the body politic must some day create a mentality which is sure to call for a life and death struggle for the dissolution of this forced union. If by reason of some superior force the dissolution does not take place, one thing is sure to happen to India – namely that this continued union will go on sapping her vitality, loosening its cohesion, weakening its hold on the love and faith of her people and preventing the use, if not retarding the growth, of its moral and material resources. India will be an anemic and sickly state, ineffective, a living corpse, dead though not buried.

Ambedkar thus had clear cut views about the creation of Pakistan. He also dealt with the problem of minorities. He stated two methods of protecting the minorities. First was to provide safeguards for minorities and the second was to provide for the transfer of Hindu population from Pakistan. He had thus favoured the idea of 'exchange of population'[17] which came like a bombshell to many. What he had stated came true in 1947. Pakistan had come into existence almost on the same lines, as visualized by Ambedkar.

Ambedkar's *Thoughts on Pakistan* was re-published in 1946 under the title *Pakistan or Partition of India*. He did not hesitate to express his views frankly on the Muslim society. He distinctly observed:[18]

> The brotherhood of Islam is not the universal brotherhood of man. It is the brotherhood of Muslims for Muslims only. For non-Muslims, there is nothing but contempt and enmity. The Muslim has allegiance to a nation which is ruled by a Muslim; a land not ruled by a Muslim is his enemy. A Muslim is not attached to the country where he lives but he is more attached to the religion which he professes.

No Indian leader was as outright and straightforward as Ambedkar. Whatever he sincerely felt, he had stated it in a candid and honest manner, much to the dislike of many. Downright truthfulness was the core part of his personality.

Here, a passing reference should be made about Ambedkar's resignation from the Nehru Cabinet on 27 September 1951. In a press statement, he made clear all his differences with the Cabinet. Apart from the Cabinet's policy in regard to Hindu Code Bill, which was in contrast to Ambedkar's views; there was another important issue relating to Kashmir, where the views of Cabinet and Ambedkar were quite in contrast. Ambedkar had advocated partition of Kashmir. He said that the Hindu and the Buddhist parts should be given to India and the Muslim part to Pakistan. He said:

'The real issue to my mind is not who is in the right. But who is right. Taking that to be the main question, my view has always been that the right solution is to partition Kashmir. Give the Hindu and Buddhist part to India and the Muslim part to Pakistan as we did in the case of India. We are really not concerned with the Muslim part of Kashmir. It is a matter between the Muslims of Kashmir and Pakistan. They may decide the issue as they like. Or, if you like to divide it into three parts, the cease fire zone, the valley and the Jammu-Ladakh region and have a plebiscite only in the valley. What I am afraid of is that in the proposed plebiscite, which is to be an overall plebiscite the Hindus and Buddhists of Kashmir are likely to be dragged into Pakistan against their wishes and we may have to face the same problem as we are facing today in East Bengal'[19]

Ranade, Gandhi and Jinnah

On the occasion of Justice M.G. Ranade's 101st birthday on 18 January 1943, Ambedkar delivered a significant lecture in the Gokhale Memorial Hall, Poona. The theme of his lecture related to the concept of a great man; and on the basis of the criterion which he laid down, M.G. Ranade was considered a great man. He cited the theories of history, analysed them, and upheld the view that 'history is the biography of great men'.

Ambedkar said that there are three important views of history. The first is the famous Augustinian theory of history, according to which history is only an unfolding of a divine plan. This is theological interpretation of history which is absurd. The second is the theory of Buckle that the history is created by Geography and Physics. It has some element of truth, but that is not the whole truth. The third is the Marxian interpretation of history which argues that events in history are the result of economic forces. This too, according to Ambedkar, is a half-truth.

The basic flaw in the above theories of history is that they hold that impersonal forces are everything and that man is no factor in the making of history. These theories deny man any place in the making of history. Ambedkar emphasized that the effect of the impersonal forces depends on man; man is an important determinant or deciding agent of history. 'Flint may not exist everywhere. But where it does exist, it needs man to strike flint against flint to make fire'.

Ambedkar discusses the concept of a great man. He discards the view that military heroes – Alexander, Attila, Caesar and Tamerlane – are great men. They only dazzle their contemporaries by resounding victories. As the lion is among the deer, so they are among men. Their permanent effect on the history of mankind is very small. They leave no permanent mark on the character of society in which they live. Neither they affect society nor form leaven to transform or temper the whole.[20]

Ambedkar also analysed Carlyle's concept of a great man, who attached the condition of sincerity; that is, a great man must be a sincere man – a deep, great, genuine sincerity. But this too, according to Ambedkar is partial. Sincerity alone is not enough. There must be something more than mere sincerity in a man to make him great. 'A man may be sincere and yet he may be a fool and a fool is the very antithesis of a great man'. Ambedkar held that sincerity must be supplemented by other qualities. If it is supplemented by intellect alone, then a person is an eminent individual, but not a great man. Sincerity and intellect alone are not enough to make a great man. A great man must have something more than what a merely eminent individual has. That something more, Ambedkar calls, 'motivated by the dynamics of a social purpose'. He writes:

> A great man must be motivated by the dynamics of a social purpose and must act as the scourge and scavenger of society.

Thus a great man is he, who combines sincerity, intellect and motivation to act as scavenger of society.

According to Ambedkar, Ranade combined all the three elements, thus he was a great man by any standard. He wanted to vitalize the Hindu society to create social democracy. He wanted to invigorate the conscience of the Hindu society. He preferred to discard the moribund and morbid wrongs contained in the sacred injunctions of Hindu religion. Ranade aimed to create a real social democracy, without which there could be no sure and stable politics.

What Congress and Gandhi Have Done to the Untouchables

The above work of Ambedkar was published in 1945. In it, he exposed the myth, with facts and figures, that the Congress and Mahatma Gandhi were the benefactors of the downtrodden people. He made a critical analysis of Gandhism and warned the untouchables to beware of Gandhi and Gandhism. He said:

> In Gandhism, the common man has no hope, because it treats man as an animal and no more. It is true that man shares the constitution and functions of animals, nutritive, reproductive, etc. But these are not distinctively human functions. The distinctively human function is reason ....[21]

Reason is the prime human function, which elevates a man. This is the Descartean standpoint. All traditions and authority must be placed before the tribunal of Reason and their need and appropriateness be assessed. By it alone, he occupies the highest place in the scheme of animate existence. The conclusion that follows is that, while the ultimate goal of a brute's life is reached once his physical appetites are satisfied, the ultimate goal of man's existence is not reached unless and until he has fully cultivated his mind. In short, what divides the brute from man is culture. Ambedkar says:

> Culture is not possible for brute, but it is essential for man. That being, so, the aim of human society must be to enable every person to lead a life of culture which means the cultivation of the mind as distinguished from the satisfaction of mere physical wants.

Ambedkar argues that both for society as well as for the individual there is always a gulf between merely living and living worthily. Living worthily is a life of culture. The culture requires leisure. Leisure means the lessening of the toil. Toil can be lessened when machine takes the place of man. There is no other means of producing leisure. Machinery and modern civilization are thus indispensable for emancipating man from leading the life of a brute and for providing him with leisure and making a life of culture possible. Mahatma Gandhi condemns machinery and modern civilization, thus does not understand their purpose and the ultimate aim which human society must strive to achieve.

Gandhism, he says, may be well suited to a society which does not accept democracy as its ideal. A democratic society cannot be indifferent to machinery. A society which is indifferent to democracy and its civilization may discard machinery, but then it would provide leisure and culture for the few and a life of toil and drudgery for the many. A democratic society must assure a life of leisure and culture to each one of its citizens. The slogan of democratic society must be machinery and more machinery, civilization and more civilization. Under Gandhism, the common man must keep on toiling ceaselessly for a pittance and remain a brute. In short, 'Gandhism with its call of back to nature means back to nakedness, back to squalor, back to poverty and back to ignorance for the vast mass of the people'.[22]

Further, Gandhism insists upon class structure. It regards the class structure of society and also the income structure as sacrosanct with the consequent distinctions of rich and poor, high and low, owners and workers, as permanent parts of social organization. From the point of view of social consequences nothing can be more pernicious. Its psychological consequences would be grave; it would create slave mentality; and in the privileged classes it would create the anti-social spirit of a gang. But Gandhism does not mind these consequences in the least. Dr Ambedkar writes: 'It is not enough to say that Gandhism is not satisfied with mere class distinctions. It is not enough to say that Gandhism believes in a class structure. Gandhism stands for more than that. A class structure which is a faded, jejune, effete thing – a mere sentimentality, a mere skeleton is not what Gandhism wants. It wants class structure to function as a living faith. In this there is nothing to be surprised at. For class structure in Gandhism is not a mere accident. It is its official doctrine'.

Who Were the Shudras?

The above treatise was published by Ambedkar in 1946. He starts with the elaboration of the general proposition that the social organization of the Indo-Aryans was based on the theory of *Chaturvarnya,* which means division of society into four classes – *Brahmins* (priests), *Kshatriyas* (soldiers), *Vaishyas* (traders), and *Shudras* (menials). It would have been a very innocent principle if it meant no more than mere division of society into four classes. But what is worst is that the theory goes further and makes the principle of graded inequality. The system of graded inequality is not merely notional; it is legal and penal. Under the system of *Chaturvarnya*, the *Shudra* is not only placed at the bottom of the gradation but he is subjected to innumerable ignominies and disabilities so as to prevent him from rising above the condition fixed for him by law. Indeed until the fifth *Varna* of the untouchables came into being, the *Shudras* were in the eyes of the Hindus, the lowest of the low. This shows the nature of what might be called the problem of the *Shudras*.

Ambedkar after making an in-depth analysis answers the question: Who were the *Shudras*? The *Shudras* were not a dark skinned non-Aryan race that had been conquered by and enslaved by the fair-skinned Aryan invaders in pre-historic times. Nor they had been *Shudras* from the very beginning as the *Brahmins* maintained on the basis of the *Purusha Sukta* in the *Rig Veda*. He summarized his theory of *Shudras* in the following terms:[23]

1. The *Shudras* were one of the Aryan communities of the Solar race;
2. there was a time when the Aryan society recognized only three *Varnas*, namely, *Brahmins, Kshatriyas* and *Vaishyas*;
3. the *Shudras* were not a separate Varna but formed a part of the *Kshatriya Varna*;
4. there was continuous feud between the *Shudra* kings and the *Brahmins*;
5. as a result of the hatred towards the *Shudras*, the *Brahmins* refused to perform the *Upanayana* (sacred thread) of the *Shudras*; and
6. owing to the denial of *Upanayana*, the *Shudras* became socially degraded, fell below the rank of the *Vaishyas* and thus came to form the fourth Varna.

The Untouchables

Ambedkar's work *The Untouchables*, published in 1948, is a sequel to his treaties called *The Shudras*. He asserts that besides *Shudras*, the Hindu society has produced three social classes whose existence has not received the attention it deserves. The first is the criminal tribes, the second is the aboriginal tribes, and the third is the untouchables. The first is taught to accept crime as an approved means of earning their livelihood; the second is left to live in full bloom of their primitive barbarism; and the third is treated as an entity beyond human intercourse and whose mere touch is enough to cause pollution.

The existence of these classes is an abomination; it arouses horror and disgust. The Hindu civilization, gauged in the light of these social products, could hardly be called civilization. It is a diabolical contrivance to suppress and enslave humanity. Its proper name would be infamy – a shameful disgrace. The existence of these classes has not occurred to the mind of the Hindu. The reason is simple. The Hindu is taught that his civilization is the most ancient and most unique. That the Hindu civilization is the most ancient, one can understand and even allow. But how it is the most unique, nobody could understand. If it means the existence of such classes, then it is a unique phenomenon. The inculcation of these false beliefs in the sanity, superiority and sanctity of Hindu civilization is due entirely to the peculiar social psychology of Hindu scholars.

The Hindu scholarship is confined to the *Brahmins*. No *Brahmin* scholar has produced a Voltaire. He is only a learned man; he is not an intellectual. The *Brahmins* have not been able to produce a Voltaire, because of their vested interest. Every *Brahmin* is interested in the maintenance of Brahmanic supremacy. A Voltaire among the *Brahmins* would be a positive danger to the maintenance of a civilization which is contrived to maintain Brahmanic supremacy. The point is that the intellect of *Brahmin* scholar is severely limited by anxiety to preserve his interest. He himself would not play the part of an iconoclast even where it is necessary. And he would not allow such non-*Brahmins* as to have the capacity to do so to play it.

Ambedkar also presents his thesis on the origin of untouchability. He says, 'The origin of untouchability lies buried in a dead past which nobody knows. To make it alive is like an attempt to reclaim to history a city which has been dead since ages past and present it as it was in its original condition'. He continues, 'When could the seed of untouchability be said to have been sown? If it is not possible to fix an exact date, is it possible to fix an approximate date'. The present day untouchables, the scheduled caste, were Buddhists in the distant past and that they were dubbed as untouchables by the *Brahmins* when Buddhism declined. He considers the origin of untouchability as a result of hatred against Buddhists by the *Brahmins*. The roots of untouchability thus could be traced in the contempt and disgust which the *Brahmins* created against those who were Buddhists. 'The broken man' who embraced Buddhism hated the *Brahmins* because the Brahmins were the enemies of Buddhism. The Brahmins imposed untouchability against the 'broken man' because they would not leave Buddhism. The untouchability, he says, was born somewhere around 400 AD. 'It is born out of the struggle for supremacy between Buddhism and Brahmanism which has so completely moulded the history of India, the study of which is so woefully neglected by the students of Indian history'.[24] Untouchability is a corollary of the institution of caste, and not a separate institution. The untouchable formed the lowest stratum of Hindu society. They were in that position for centuries together. The touch or shadow or even voice of an untouchable was deemed by caste Hindus as polluting. They were born as untouchables; they lived and died as untouchables.[25] As such, he described untouchability as 'a curse', 'an excrescence of Hinduism', 'a poison', 'a snake', 'a canker', 'a hydra headed monster', 'a great blot', 'a device of Satan', 'a hideous untruth', 'Dyerism' and 'the bar-sinister'.

In addition, Ambedkar's book on *Riddles in Hinduism* published by the Government of Maharashtra in 1987, is useful for understanding the problem of untouchability. *Riddles in Hinduism* is an exposition of the beliefs propounded by what might be called Brahminic theology. It is intended for the common mass of Hindus who need to be awakened to know in what quagmire the Brahmins have placed them and to lead them on to the road of rational thinking.

Ambedkar has discussed the *Vedas* and *Upanishads* in his work 'Riddles in Hinduism'. The way in which he has accused the Brahmins at every step, gives the impression that Ambedkar hated the Brahmins. Perhaps, hate may be too harsh a word for a person who was patriot. It clearly reveals that he did not like the way the Brahmins dealt with the Hindu religion. He argues that in the *Vedas* the Brahmins have propounded a mischievous dogma – the dogma of the infallibility of the *Vedas*. He states: 'If the Hindu intellect has ceased to grow and if the Hindu Civilization and culture have become a stagnant and stinking pool, this dogma must be destroyed root and branches if India is to progress'. Ambedkar's critical evaluation of *Vedas*, of *Upanishads*, of *Manusmriti*, indicates his analysis of the origin of untouchability and its related problems. A scholar of history and political science should carefully study 'Riddles in Hinduism,' and of course, from the angle of rationality, objectivity and impartial judgement; then alone he would be able to understand the logic and depth of Ambedkar's thesis.

Thoughts on Linguistic States

Dr Ambedkar had clear-cut views about the re-organization of states on linguistic basis. He submitted a memorandum to the Linguistic Provinces Commission in 1948. In that, while acknowledging the danger to the unity of India inherent in the creation of linguistic provinces with their pride in race, language and literature developing into mentalities of being separate nations, Ambedkar saw certain definite political advantages in the reconstitution of provinces on linguistic basis. He expressed his final views on linguistic states in 1955 in his work *Thoughts on Linguistic States*. He favoured formation of unilingual states as against multi-lingual states. The former, according to him, fosters the fellow-feeling which is the foundation of a stable and democratic state; while the latter with its enforced juxtaposition of two different linguistic groups leads to faction fights for leadership and discrimination in administration – factors which are incompatible with democracy. He, however, qualified his support for unilingual states by the condition that its official language shall be Hindi and until India becomes fit for this purpose, English shall continue. He says: 'A linguistic state with its regional language as its official language may easily develop into an independent nationality. The road between an independent nationality and an independent state is very narrow. If this happens, India will cease to be a modern India we have and will become the medieval India consisting of a variety of States indulging in rivalry and warfare'.[26]

The Buddha and His Dhamma

Ambedkar's greatest work is *The Buddha and His Dhamma*. It was published in 1957, though he had seen the proofs prior to his sudden demise on 6 December 1956. It is a monumental work, neatly divided into eight books. This 'magnum opus' has come to be known as 'Buddhist Bible'. It encompasses the life and personality of the Buddha and presents an analytical exposition of the *Dhamma*. Each chapter of this work of about 600 pages is studded with short and crisp sentences. In this treatise, he has tried to re-interpret the *Dhamma* in order to show that Buddhism can amply meet the needs of the modern world. His emphasis is on the social gospel of the Buddha.

Since Ambedkar had not indicated the sources from where he had quoted the teachings of the Buddha, the readers feel a little handicapped to understand as to whether he was speaking for himself. This deficiency was rectified by venerable Bhadant Anand Dausalyayan (1905–1988) who translated it into Hindi; he also added footnotes tracing labouriously the sources of the Buddha's teachings quoted by Ambedkar.

Besides Ambedkar's monumental work, *The Buddha and His Dhamma,* he also expressed his views on Buddhism through speeches on various occasions and through articles in the *Maha Bodhi*, the premier Buddhist monthly of India.

In addition to the above mentioned ten works, there were some more important articles and pamphlets written by Ambedkar. The significant among them are:

1. *Caste in India: Their Genesis, Mechanism and Development* – This paper was read by him before the Anthropology Seminar of Dr A.A. Goldenweizer at The Columbia University, New York, USA on 9 May 1916. It was first published in Indian Antiquary, May 1917, Vol. XLI.
2. *Small Holdings in India and their Remedies* – This article was first published in the Journal of the Indian Economic Society, Vol. I, 1918.
3. *Russell and the Reconstruction of Society – Review on the 'Principles of Social Reconstruction' by the Hon'ble Bertrand Russell.* This article was first published in the *Journal of the Indian Economic Society*, Vol. I, 1918.
4. *Federation versus Freedom* – This address was delivered on 29 January 1939 at the Annual Function of the Gokhale Institute of Politics and Economics held in the Gokhale Hall, Poona. It was published as a '*Tracts for the Times*: No. 3' in 1939.
5. *Gandhi and the Emancipation of the Untouchables* – In response to the invitation of the Chairman of the Indian section of the Institute of Pacific Relation. Ambedkar wrote

a paper in August 1942 on the Problem of the Untouchables of India for the session which was due to be held in December 1942 in Canada. This paper was printed in the proceedings of the Conference. In September 1943, it was published in a book form.

6. *Communal Deadlock and a Way to Solve It* – This was an address delivered at the session of the All India Scheduled Castes Federation held in Bombay on 6 May 1945. It was published as a tract in the same year.
7. *States and Minorities: What are their Rights and How to Secure them in the Constitution of Free India* – this was a Memorandum on the Safeguards for the scheduled castes submitted to the Constituent Assembly on behalf of the All India Scheduled Castes Federation. It was published in March 1947.
8. *Maharashtra as a Linguistic Province* – This was the statement submitted to the Linguistic Provinces Commission and was published as a pamphlet in October 1948.
9. *The Buddha and the Future of His Religion* – This was the first article on Buddhism published by Dr Ambedkar in the *Maha Bodhi*, Calcutta, Vol. 58, April–May 1950.
10. *The Rise and Fall of the Hindu Woman* – This article was published by Dr Ambedkar in the *Maha Bodhi*, Calcutta, June 1951.

A Brilliant Intellectual

Ambedkar was a great scholar and writer. His was a versatile mind. His works reflect independence of thought, originality of expression, and contained significant ideas or concepts towards social change and transformation. His works reflect a vast array of qualities with which he was endowed – erudition, scholarship, imagination, logic and experience. His ideals, philosophy of life, wisdom and intellect, powerful and scintillating style, sincerity of purpose and frankness, cannot fail to convince even his adversaries. His writings covered diverse subjects of human interest, such as law, economics, finance, administration, sociology, anthropology, politics and religion.

An honest man with a clear conscience,. Ambedkar, without malice or ill-will, expounded his honest opinions on the varied dilemmas, injustices and ailments that afflict or weaken the fabric of Hindu society; and one should not fail to admire the beauty and loftiness of his scholarly treatises. He was indubitably one of the brilliant intellectuals of the twentieth century. He had planted ideas for the benefit of posterity, because he was a man with a mission and seeker of truth. His concepts of a Great Man, of rationalism, of social justice and of a true religion, especially deserve attention of the people today for removing the pests of society and for clearing the debris and lumber that has piled up during the course of centuries in the organic life of Hinduism; and thereby to revitalize the bodily organs of this great, ancient civilization.

Notes

1. D.C. Ahir: *The Legacy of Dr. Ambedkar* (Delhi, B.R. Publishing Corporation, 1990), p. 252.
2. B.K. Ahluwalia and Shashi Ahluwalia (ed), *Dr. Ambedkar and Hindu Rights,* Delhi, 1981, p. 30.
3. Hoti Lal Nim: *Thoughts on Dr. Ambedkar,* Agra, 1969, p. 72.
4. B.K. Ahluwalia and Shashi Ahluwalia, op. cit. p. 115.
5. Keynote Address by Prof. L.S. Rathore, *Dr. B.R. Ambedkar: His Works and Key Concepts*, National Post Graduate College, Lucknow.
6. L.S. Rathore, op. cit., p. 3.
7. Ibid.
8. Dhananjay Keer, *Dr. Ambedkar: Life and Mission* (Bombay, Popular Prakashan, 1992), p. 30.
9. Ibid.
10. Dr Babasaheb Ambedkar *Writings and Speeches,* Vol. 1 (Bombay, Government of Maharashtra, 1979), p. 50.
11. Ibid., p. 48.
12. Ibid., p. 56.
13. Ibid., p. 63.
14. Ibid., p. 68.

15. A.K. Narain and D.C. Ahir: *Dr. Ambedkar Buddhism and Social Change* (Delhi, D.K. Publishing House, 1994), p. 165.
16. Keer, op. cit. pp. 335–36.
17. *Pakistan or Partition of India*, Bombay, 1946, pp. 106–110
18. Ibid., p. 323.
19. S.R. Bakshi: *Stateman and Constitutionalist* (New Delhi, Anmol Publishers, 1992), p. 248.
20. Ranade, Gandhi and Jinnah, *Dr. Babasaheb Ambedkar: Writings and Speeches*, Vol. 1, 1979, pp. 213–215.
21. B.R. Ambedkar: *What Congress and Gandhi Have Done to the Untouchables*, Bombay, 1945, pp. 226–28.
22. D.C. Ahir: *The Legacy of Ambedkar*, p. 264.
23. B.R. Ambedkar: *Who Were the Shudras*? 1946, pp. 236–237.
24. B.R. Ambedkar: *The Untouchables*, 1948, Preface, p. I-III.
25. W.N. Kuber: *B.R. Ambedkar* (New Delhi, Ministry of Information and Broadcasting, 2001), p. 2.
26. Thoughts on Linguistic States, Dr. Babasaheb Ambedkar *Writings and Speeches*, Vol. 1, Bombay, 1979 p. 145.

4

The Making of the Indian Constitution

In the making of the Indian Constitution, the ideology of constitutionalism was the most significant feature in Ambedkar's political thought. He had a great faith in constitutional government. He was probably the first thinker in modern India who had propounded the notion of constitutionalism in a brilliant way. He possessed extremely versatile ideas, derived from the vast study of modern constitutions of the world. Keeping in view the peculiar conditions and circumstances of the country, he wove his ideas together in such a harmonious blend, realistic and sensible, that nobody did so before him. He, not only laid down the goals of the Constitution, but also framed elaborate structures to realize those goals. No study of the making of the Constitution would be complete, if Ambedkar's doctrine of constitutionalism is not properly unravelled.

While formulating his notion of constitutionalism, Ambedkar discarded narrow loyalties and partisan mentality; and was guided by lofty principles, which were of paramount importance at the time. First, was the interest of the country. He rose above the disputes between the Congress and Muslim League, and gave top priority to the well-being of the country. He said:

> When deciding the destinies of nations, dignities of people, dignities of leaders and dignities of parties ought to count for nothing. The destiny of the country ought to count for everything.[1]

Second, was that Ambedkar did not give any credence to communal or religious feelings that had spread in a devastating way; ravaging the sub-continent at the time of the partition of India. Though the Muslim League had boycotted the Constituent Assembly (hereinafter referred to as Con-Assembly), there were some Muslim members in it belonging to other parties or independents. That, at one time, when some Muslims members spoke in a communal tone on the floor of the Con-Assembly, Ambedkar warned them, saying:

> That the Muslim members have not yet given up the philosophy of the Muslim League which they ought to. They are repeating arguments which were valid when the Muslim League was there and the Muslim Provinces were there. They have no validity now; I can not understand why the Muslims are repeating them.[2]

Third, Ambedkar was disgusted with the existence of graded inequality and untouchability that was prevalent in the Hindu social order. He had strong feelings to reform the Hindu social system which, at the time, was full of inequities, inequalities, discrimination and other things, which conflicted with the goals of constitutionalism. He was a passionate defender of civil liberties, irrespective of caste, creed or sex. His efforts, therefore, led to the abolition of untouchability and its practise in any form.

Fourth, Ambedkar was equally concerned to provide safeguards to minorities. He was aware of the fact that in India both the minorities and the majorities had followed a wrong path. It was wrong for the majority to deny the existence of minorities. It was equally wrong for the minorities to perpetuate themselves. To the diehards who had developed a kind of fanaticism against minority protection, Ambedkar uttered two things:

> One is that minorities are an explosive force which, if it erupts, can blow up the whole fabric of the State. The other is that the minorities in India have agreed to place their existence in the hands of the majority .... They have loyally accepted the rule of the majority which is basically a communal majority and not a political majority. It is for the majority to realize its duty not to discriminate against minorities.[3]

And lastly, Ambedkar believed that there could be no right unless the Constitution provided a remedy for it. He said:

> It is the remedy that makes a right real. If there is no remedy, there is no right at all, and I am therefore not prepared to burden the Constitution with a number of pious declarations which may sound as glittering generalities but for which the Constitution makes no provision by way of a remedy. It is much better to be limited in the scope of our rights and to make them real by enunciating remedies then to have a lot of pious wishes embodied in the Constitution.[4]

The remedies that Ambedkar provided in the Constitution for the protection of rights constitute a fundamental part of his concept of constitutionalism.

Ambedkar's Entry to the Con-Assembly

The Constituent Assembly started its work of framing free India's Constitution on 9 December 1946. In all, 296 members were entitled to take part in the inaugural session. But only 207 members attended the session, the absentees were mainly the Muslim League members who had boycotted the Con-Assembly. On 11 December, the Assembly elected Rajendra Prasad as permanent Chairman/President of the Assembly.

The elections to the Con-Assembly were held in which members were elected from the Provisional Legislative Assemblies. Ambedkar, having failed to get elected from Bombay due to Congress opposition, managed to enter the Con-Assembly through the Bengal Assembly with the support of scheduled caste members. Consequent upon the partition of Bengal, Ambedkar ceased to be a member of the Con-Assembly. The Congress Party which had earlier opposed tooth and nail his entry into the Con-Assembly came forward and sponsored his candidature from Bombay. Accordingly, Ambedkar was re-elected in July 1947, from Bombay as a member of the Con-Assembly. Soon after, Prime Minister Jawaharlal Nehru invited him to join the Cabinet; he formed it on 15 August 1947, on the eve of independence. Ambedkar accepted the invitation and became India's first Law Minister.

On 29 August, the Assembly unanimously elected him as a member of the Drafting Committee which was assigned the task of framing the Constitution. Ambedkar who was a strong opponent of Congress had now become their 'friend, philosopher and guide' in the constitutional matters.

Chairman of the Drafting Committee

Ambedkar never believed that he would be made the Chairman of the Drafting Committee. He came into the Con-Assembly with no greater aspiration than to safeguard the interests of the scheduled castes. He admitted this fact in a speech that he delivered on 26 November 1949, at the completion of the Draft Constitution. He said:

> I had not the remotest idea that I would be called upon to undertake more responsible functions. I was therefore greatly surprised when the Assembly elected me to the Drafting Committee. I was more than surprised when the Drafting Committee elected me to be its Chairman.[5]

Ambedkar was grateful to the Con-Assembly and the Drafting Committee for reposing in him so much trust and confidence and to have chosen him as their instrument and given him this opportunity of serving the country. The task of the Drafting Committee was very arduous and difficult, but Ambedkar was ably supported by Sir B.N. Rau, the Constitutional Advisor to the Con-Assembly, and S.N. Mukherjee, the Chief Draftsman of the Constitution; and he thus completed the work in a most befitting manner.

Ambedkar introduced the Draft Constitution to the Con-Assembly on 4 November 1948. A brief general discussion followed, and the first reading of the Constitution was over. The second reading commenced on 15 November 1948, when the Constitution was discussed clause by clause in detail. The discussions concluded on 17 October 1949. The Con-Assembly again sat on 14 November 1949, for the third reading. This was finished on the 26 November 1949, when the Constitution was declared as passed and thereafter the President of the Assembly signed it.

Basic Philosophy

Ambedkar successfully carried out the herculean intellectual labour of preparing the Draft Constitution, in spite of his indifferent health. The Draft Constitution that was presented to the Con-Assembly revealed his idea of constitutionalism. In it, he emphatically proclaimed the ideological bases of his constitutionalism, namely, liberty, equality, fraternity, social justice and the dignity of an individual. He highlighted the rights and liberties and obligations of the people. He provided remedies in order to make rights real. He anticipated every conceivable requirement of the new polity.

Ambedkar's constitutionalism was the outcome of his revolt against all forms of oppression and exploitation. It was equally a call to preserve the structure and the spirit of the Constitution, the unity of the nation and the welfare and progress of the people that it intended to protect and advance. He was a passionate believer in democracy. He regarded social and economic democracy as the tissues and the fibres of political democracy. He wished to bring about radical changes in the economic and social life of the people without bloodshed. His belief in the constitutional methods for solving disputes was profound. He repeatedly emphasized the paramount need for the diffusion of constitutional morality in society. His vision of India and the future of the oppressed sections and minorities in the country were in line with this basic philosophy. His faith in the people of India was profound. He told the Con-Assembly:

> I know today we are divided politically, socially and economically. We are a group of warring camps, and I may even go to the extent of confessing that I am probably one of the leaders of such a camp. But, Sir, with all this, I am quite convinced that given time and circumstances nothing in the world will prevent this country from becoming one.[6]

During the making of the Constitution, Ambedkar emerged as a man of immense erudition and foresight, having an unshakable faith in constitutionalism.

A Monumental Document

The Draft Constitution was a monumental document. At the time when Ambedkar presented it to the Con-Assembly the members rose and spoke on it. Everyone eulogized the work of Ambedkar.

> Frank Anthony said that, Ambedkar had made 'a symmetrical and lucid analysis of the principles of Constitution,' and called the proposed Constitution as 'a monumental document'.[7]
>
> According to K.T. Shah, the Draft Constitution contained 'thought-provoking ideas'.[8]
>
> Pandit Lakshmi Kant Maitra congratulated Ambedkar for giving the constitutional proposals a definite shape.[9]
>
> P.S. Deshmukh said that the Draft Constitution was 'excellent and impressive'.[10]
>
> Joseph Alban D'souza characterized the Draft Constitution as a 'monumental piece of work,' that was 'comparative, selective and efficient in character right from the beginning to the end'.[11]
>
> Pandit Thakur Das Bhargava regarded the 'soul of the Constitution in the Preamble'.[12]
>
> Shibban Lal Saksena said that Ambedkar's speech on the Draft Constitution was 'a masterpiece of lucid exposition of our Constitution. I certainly think that there could not have been an abler advocacy for the Draft Constitution'.[13]

There were a number of other members of the Con-Assembly who showered praise on Ambedkar for producing a unique and monumental Draft Constitution.

Form of Government

The bedrock of Ambedkar's constitutionalism was his preference for the parliamentary form of government, because it could provide a more responsible executive. Defending his motion, in the Con-Assembly, he said:

> There is placed at the head of the Indian Union a functionary who is called the President of the Union. The title of this functionary reminds one, of the President of the United States. But beyond identity of names there is nothing in common between the forms of government prevalent in America and form of government proposed under the Draft Constitution. The American form of government is called the Presidential system of government. What the Draft Constitution proposes is the Parliamentary system![14]

Both the presidential forms of government, argued Ambedkar, were fundamentally different. Under the presidential system of America, the President is the Chief Head of the executive. The administration is vested in him. Under the Draft Constitution, the President occupies the same position as the king under the English Constitution. He is the head of the state but not of the executive. He represents the Nation but does not rule the nation. He is the symbol of the nation. His place in the administration is that of a ceremonial device on a seal by which the nation's decisions are made known. Under the American Constitution the President has under him Secretaries of different departments. In like manner the President of the Indian Union will have under him Ministers in-charge of different departments of administration. Here again, Ambedkar pointed out, that there is a fundamental difference between the two. The President of the United States is not bound to accept any advice tendered to him by any of his Secretaries. The President of the Indian Union will be generally bound by the advice of his Ministers. He can do nothing contrary to their advice nor can he do anything without their advice. The President of the United States can dismiss any Secretary at any time. The President of the Indian Union has no power to do so, so long as his Ministers command a majority in Parliament. Both systems of government, argued Ambedkar, are of course democratic and the choice between the two is not very easy.

Ambedkar believed that a democratic executive must satisfy two conditions: (1) it must be a stable executive, and (ii) it must be a responsible executive. There is no system of government which can ensure both in equal degree. The

American and the Swiss systems give more stability but less responsibility. The British system gives more responsibility but less stability. To Ambedkar, the parliamentary system of executive was preferably better than the presidential one, because it is based on more responsibility to more stability. This is an important aspect of his doctrine of constitutionalism.

Form of Constitution

In the Draft Constitution, Ambedkar proposed a federal constitution with a dual polity. The dual polity consisted of the Union at the centre and the states at the periphery, each endowed with sovereign powers to be exercised in the field assigned to them respectively by the Constitution. He also pointed out the differences between the dual polity between the American federation and the proposed Indian federation. In the USA this dual polity is followed by a dual citizenship. The proposed Indian Constitution was a dual polity with a single citizenship. There was no state citizenship. Every Indian would have the same rights of citizenship, no matter in what state he resides.

Further, the dual polity in the Draft Constitution differed from the dual polity of the USA in another respect. In the USA, the Constitutions of the Federal and the State Governments are loosely connected. This was not true in the proposed Indian Constitution. Here, the states were not given a right to frame their own Constitutions. Ambedkar states:

> The Constitution of the Union and of the States is a single frame from which neither can get out and within which they must work.[15]

In addition to, there were some other special features of the proposed Indian federation which marked it off not only from the American federation but from all other federations. All federal systems including the American are placed in a tight mould of federalism. No matter what the circumstances, it cannot change its form and shape. It can never be unitary. On the other hand, the proposed Indian federation was a peculiar one, quite different from the classical mould of federalism. In the words of Ambedkar:

> The Draft Constitution can be both unitary as well as federal according to the requirements of time and circumstances. In normal times, it is framed to work as federal system. But in times of war it is so designed as to make it work as though it was a unitary system. Once the President issues a Proclamation which he is authorized to do under the provisions of the Constitution, the whole scene can become transformed and the state becomes a unitary state.[16]

This was a novel feature in Ambedkar's concept of constitutionalism. He did not plead for a tight mould of federalism. According to the circumstances he believed in changing the form and shape of Indian federalism, according to the circumstances.

There was, yet another feature of vital significance, in Ambedkar's constitutionalism. He stated that generally speaking there were two weaknesses from which federations were alleged to suffer. One was rigidity and the other was legalism. These faults of a federal constitution have been found in a pronounced form in the Constitution of the United States of America. In assuaging the rigour of rigidity and legalism, Ambedkar followed the Australian plan on a far more extensive scale than had been done in Australia. Like the Australian Constitution, the Draft Constitution contained a long list of subjects for concurrent powers of legislation. The biggest advance made by Ambedkar over the Australian Constitution was in the matter of exclusive powers of legislation vested in Parliament. While the exclusive authority of the Australian Parliament to legislate extends only to about 3 matters, the authority of the Indian Parliament as proposed in the Draft Constitution extended to 91 matters. In this way, Ambedkar secured the greatest possible elasticity in Indian federalism, and freed it from the tangled net of rigidity. At the same time, Ambedkar did not adopt the Australian Constitution in toto. According to him:

> What is to be noted is that the Draft Constitution has added new ways of overcoming the rigidity and legalism inherent in federation which are special to it and which are not to be found elsewhere.[17]

All in all, though Ambedkar derived the idea of federalism from the American and Australian federations, he modified considerably the form and shape of Indian federalism, according to the conditions and facts that are connected with and affect a situation in the country. He made federalism fit to face any circumstances or an event in the context of the country. His federalism is not tight; it is flexible enough to meet situations and events that affect the life of India. In addition to, he provided the ways of overcoming the rigidity and legalism in the new Constitution. This is one of the key features of Ambedkar's constitutionalism.

Is the Centre too Strong?

A serious complaint was made against the Draft Constitution on the ground that it has made the Centre too strong and that there was too much centralization and the States have been reduced to municipalities. Ambedkar felt that this view was not only an exaggeration, but was also founded on a misunderstanding of what exactly the Constitution contrived to do. He elaborated the basic principle on which the relation between the Centre and the States would rest. He said:

> The basic principle of federation is that the legislative and executive authority is partitioned between the Centre and the States not by any law to be made by the Centre but by the Constitution itself. This is what Constitution does. The States under our Constitution are no way dependent upon the Centre for their legislative or executive authority. The centre and the States are co-equal in this matter. It is difficult to see how such a Constitution can be called centralism.[18]

Ambedkar continued that it might be that the Constitution has assigned to the Centre too large a field for the operation of its legislative and executive authority than is found in any other federal Constitution. It is true that the residuary powers have been given to the Centre and not to the States. But these features, argued Ambedkar, 'do not form the essence of federalism'. He said:

> The chief mark of federalism as I said lies in the partition of the legislative and executive authority between the Centre

> and the Units by the Constitution. This is the principle embodied in our Constitution. There can be no mistake about it. It is; therefore, wrong to say that the States have been placed under the Centre. The Centre cannot by its own will, alter the boundary of that partition. Nor can the Judiciary.[19]

As such, Ambedkar concluded that the charge of centralization defeating federalism was not correct.

Another charge against federalism was that the Centre has been given the power to override the States. Ambedkar was prepared to admit this charge, but there were certain consideration for giving overriding powers. These overriding powers 'do not form the normal feature of the Constitution'. Their use and operation have been expressly confined in emergencies only; and in such situations that would arise in future the overriding powers are justified. That in an emergency the interest of the Nation should be paramount. Only those who have not understood the problem could complain against providing overriding powers to the Centre.

There were two schools of thought in the Con-Assembly in this context. One said that 'the Centre is too strong; ' and the other pleaded that 'it must be made stronger'. Ambedkar tried to 'struck a balance'. He pleaded that it was difficult to prevent the Centre from being strong. He said:

> Conditions in modern world are such that centralization of powers is inevitable. One has only to consider the growth of the Federal Court in the USA which, notwithstanding the very limited powers given to it by the Constitution, has outgrown its former self and has overshadowed and eclipsed the State Governments. This is due to modern conditions. The same conditions are sure to operate on the Government of India and nothing that one can do will help to prevent it from being strong. On the other hand, we must resist the tendency to make it stronger. It can not chew more than it can digest. Its strength must be commensurate with its weight. It would be a folly to make it so strong that it may fall by its own weight.[20]

Ambedkar's theory of constitutionalism, in this context, was based on the recognition of the principle that the Centre should be neither too strong nor too weak; he followed the principle of mean or moderation in this connection.

Uniformity in the Basic Matters

An important feature of Ambedkar's constitutionalism was that he sought to forge means and methods whereby Indian federation should have uniformity in all the basic matters which are essential to maintain the unity of the country. The means contained in the Draft Constitution were mainly four: i) a single judiciary independent of the executive; ii) uniformity in fundamental rights; iii) the necessity of Directive Principles of State Policy; and iv) a common All-India Civil Service to main important posts.

Judiciary

Ambedkar's constitutionalism was based on the recognition of the independence of judiciary and its power of judicial review. He did not want to create an *Imperium in Imperio.* But at the same time, he preferred to give the judiciary ample independence so that it could act without fear or favour of the executive.

The Draft Constitution was criticized on the ground that it could produce a paradise for lawyers. This point of criticism was specially raised by T.T. Krishnamachari. Replying to this in the Con-Assembly, Ambedkar said:

> I am not prepared to say that this Constitution will not give rise to questions which will involve legal interpretation or judicial interpretation. In fact, I would like to ask Mr Krishnamachari if he can point out to me any instance of any Constitution in the world which has not been a paradise for lawyers. I would particularly ask him to refer to the vast storehouse of law reports with regard to the Constitutions of the United States, Canada and other countries. I am therefore not ashamed at all if this Constitution hereafter for purposes of interpretation is required to be taken to the Federal Court. That is the fate of every Constitution.[21]

Fundamental Rights

The most criticized part of the Draft Constitution was that which related to fundamental rights. It was said that Article 13, which defined fundamental rights was riddled with so many exceptions that the exceptions have eaten up the rights altogether. The critics called this as 'a kind of deception; ' and pleaded that fundamental rights were not fundamental rights unless they were also absolute rights.

Ambedkar clearly stated that the whole of the criticism about fundamental rights was based upon a misconception. The fundamental rights 'are the gift of the State' and 'the State can qualify them'. He reminded the critics that the fundamental rights even in America are not absolute rights. Freedom of speech and of the press, which was secured in the proposed Constitution, did not confer an absolute right to speak or publish, without responsibility, whatever one might choose, or an unrestricted and unbridled license that gave immunity for every possible use of language and prevents the punishment of those who abuse this freedom.

The object of fundamental rights, he said, was two-fold. First, that every citizen must be in a position to claim those rights. Secondly, they must be binding upon any authority.

Ambedkar's theory of constitutionalism regarded the fundamental rights as the very soul of the Constitution and the very heart of it. He was aware of the fact that there could be no right unless the Constitution provided a remedy for it. He, therefore, provided the constitutional remedies to make the rights real. He said:

> It is the remedy that makes a right real. If there is no remedy there is no right at all.

Directive Principles

The Draft Constitution also contained Directive Principles of State policy, which was a novel feature in the Constitution framed for parliamentary democracy. The critics had said that they were only 'pious declarations,' having no binding force.

Ambedkar called this criticism as 'superfluous'. He was not prepared to concede that they were useless because they had no binding force in law.

The Directive Principles, Ambedkar said, were like the Instrument of Instructions under the Act of 1935. The Directive Principles were another name for Instrument of Instructions. The only difference was that the Directives are instructions to the legislature and the executive. Whenever, 'there is a grant of power in general terms for peace, order and good government, it is necessary that it should be accompanied by instructions regulating its exercise'.[22] Ambedkar said:

> Whoever captures power will not be free to do what he likes with it, in the exercise of it; he will have to respect this Instrument of Instructions which are called Directive Principles. He cannot ignore them. He may not have to answer for their breach in a court of Law. But he will certainly have to answer for them before the electorate at election time.[23]

The intention to introduce Directive Principles in the Draft Constitution was that in future both the legislature and the executive should not merely pay lip service to these principles, but they should be made the basis of all executive and legislative action in the matter of governance of the country. Ambedkar, therefore, upheld the Directive Principles as they were necessary and of great value. He regarded the Directive Principles as 'Directives' to the legislature and the executive and they must not be evaded. The inclusion of ideals in the new Constitution, not legally binding but of immense practical importance, was a significant feature of Ambedkar's constitutionalism.

All-India Services

In all federations, there is a Federal Civil Service and a State Civil Service. Ambedkar in the Draft Constitution pleaded for a dual service but with one exception. He recognized that in every country there are certain posts in its administrative set up which are called strategic from the point of view of maintaining the standard of administration. It might not be easy to spot such posts in a large and complicated machinery of administration. But there was no doubt in his mind that the standard of administration depended upon the caliber of the civil servants who are appointed to these strategic posts. India had inherited from the past system of administration which was common to the whole of the country and known as strategic posts.

The Draft Constitution provided that without depriving the states of their right to form their own civil services there should be an All-India Service recruited on an All-India basis with common qualifications, with uniform scale of pay and the members of which alone could be appointed to these strategic posts throughout the Union.

The All-India Services were designed to promote and strengthen the unity of the country. The doctrine of constitutionalism, according to Ambedkar, should not loosen the unity of the country; it should be strong enough to keep the divisive forces under check.

Amendment of the Constitution

The provisions relating to amendment of the Constitution had come in for a virulent attack at the hands of the critics of the Draft Constitution. It was said that the provisions contained in the Draft made amendment difficult. It was proposed that the Constitution should be amended by a simple majority at least for some years.

Ambedkar repudiated the above charges because they appeared to be without foundation. He asserted that the provisions in respect of amending the Constitution were 'simplest' in comparison to other federal Constitutions of the world, such as, the American and Australian Constitutions. He stated:

> The Draft Constitution has eliminated the elaborate and difficult procedures such as a decision by a convention or a referendum. The powers of amendment are left with the Legislatures – Central and Provincial. It is only for amendments of specific matters – and they are only few – that the ratification of the State Legislature is required. All other Articles of the constitution are left to be amended by Parliament. The only

> limitation is that it shall be done by a majority of not less than two-thirds of the members of each House present and voting and the majority of the total membership of each House. It is difficult to conceive a simple method of amending the Constitution.[24]

The method of amendment of the Constitution was so devised by Ambedkar in order that the federal structure should remain fundamentally unaltered. He regarded that the amending procedure as contained in the Draft Constitution was the best that could be conceived in the circumstances of the case.

Second Chamber

The question of creating a second chamber at the Centre was discussed by the Con-Assembly. Ambedkar was not surprised at the views that were expressed in the Con-Assembly against a second chamber. He felt that the view of those who were opposed to a second chamber could be better put them in the words of Abbe Seiyes. His criticism was two-fold. He said that if the Upper House agreed with the lower one, then it was superfluous. If it did not agree with the Lower House, it was a mischievous body and 'we ought not to entertain it'.

According to Ambedkar, the first part of the criticism of Abbe Seiyes was undoubtedly valid, 'because it is so obvious'. But Ambedkar did not agree with the second part of the criticism of Abbe Seiyes. He said that even the French nations did not accept that view; they too had consistently maintained the principle of having a second chamber.

Speaking for himself, Ambedkar said:

> I cannot say that I am very strongly prepossessed in favour of a second chamber. To me, it is like the Curate's egg good only in parts. All that we are doing by this Constitution is to introduce the second chamber purely as an experimental measure.[25]

The Draft Constitution did not give the second chamber a permanent place. It did not make it a permanent part of the new Constitution. It was created purely as an experimental measure, and Ambedkar felt that there was sufficient provision in the present Article 304 for 'getting rid of the second chamber'.

Proportional Representation

An amendment was moved in the Con-Assembly aiming to prescribe that the election to the House of the People (Lower House) in the various states should be in accordance with the proportional representation by single transferable vote. Ambedkar did not think it possible to accept this amendment. There were weighty reasons for not accepting the amendment.

According to Ambedkar, proportional representation presupposes literacy on a large scale. It presupposes that every voter shall be literate at least to the extent of being in a position to know the numerical and to be in a position to mark them on a ballot paper. He said:

> I think, having regard to the extent of literacy in this country, such a presupposition would be utterly extravagant. I have not the least doubt on that point.[26]

While excluding the system of proportional representation Ambedkar mentioned another reason. The proportional representation according to him, did not suit to the form of government which the Draft Constitution laid down. The proportional representation would lead to the fragmentation of the legislature into a number of small groups. It would not permit a stable government to remain in office, because Parliament would be so divided into so many small groups that every time anything happened which displeased certain group in Parliament, they would, on that occasion, withdraw their support from the government with the result that the government losing the support of certain groups and units would fall to pieces. He emphasized that the future governments must be stable, capable of maintaining law and order. The proportional representation, therefore, would damage the stability of government and Ambedkar was hesitant to accept the proposal.

'There is Nothing New'

The critics[27] of the Draft Constitution said that:

> There is nothing new in the Draft Constitution; that half of it has been copied form the Government of India Act of 1935

> and that the rest of it has been borrowed from the Constitutions of other countries. Very little of it can claim originality.[28]

In reply to them, Ambedkar said:

> One likes to ask whether there can be anything new in a Constitution framed at this hour in the history of the world .... The only new things if there can be any, in a Constitution framed so late in the day are the variations made to remove the faults and to accommodate it to the needs of the country. The charge of producing a blind copy of the Constitutions of other countries is based, I am sure, on an inadequate study of the Constitution .... The Drafting Committee in performing its duty has not been guilty of such blind and slavish imitation as it is represented to be.[29]

As to the accusation that the Drafting Committee had produced a good part of the provisions of the Government of India Act, 1935, Ambedkar made no apologies. He frankly stated:

> There is nothing to be ashamed of in borrowing. It involves no plagiarism. Nobody holds any patent rights in the fundamental ideas of a Constitution.[30]

Ambedkar explained to the members of the Con-Assembly that the provisions taken from the Government of India Act of 1935, related mostly to the details of administration. Though he agreed that administrative details should have no place in the Constitution and that the Drafting Committee could have avoided their inclusion in the Constitution; there was a necessity which justified their inclusion. He reminded the House that the form of administration has a close connection with the form of the Constitution. The form of the administration should be appropriate to and in the same sense as the form of the Constitution. Hence, argued Ambedkar that the details of administration were taken from the Government of India Act of 1935; and there was nothing inappropriate in it. He thought it wiser not to trust the legislature to prescribe forms of administration. That was the justification for incorporating administrative details in the proposed Constitution.

Neglect of the Ancient Indian Polity

Another criticism against Ambedkar's proposed Constitution was that no part of it represented the ancient polity of India. It was said that the new Constitution should have been drafted on the ancient Hindu model of a state and that instead of incorporating Western theories the proposed Constitution should have been raised and built upon village panchayats and district panchayats.[31] Ambedkar disagreed with this view point.

Ambedkar said that those who take pride in the village communities did not care to consider what little part they had played in the affairs and destiny of the country. The village communities had survived through all vicissitudes might be a fact, but mere survival had no value. He stated:

> The question is on what plane they have survived, surely on a low, or a selfish level. I hold that these village republics have been the ruination of India .... What is the village but a sink of localism, a den of ignorance, narrow-mindedness and communalism?[32]

Ambedkar, therefore, discarded the village and adopted the individual as its unit in the new Constitution.

Constitutional Morality

Ambedkar believed that the constitutional government, in the absence of constitutional morality among the people, would be a hollow one. He felt that 'however good a Constitution may be, 'it is sure to turn out bad because those who are called to work it, happen to be a bad lot; ' lacking in constitutional morality. On the other hand, 'however, 'bad a Constitution may be, it may turn out to be good if those who are called to work it, happen to be a good lot; ' saturated with constitutional morality. Defining constitutional morality, he quoted with approval, the words of Grote, the historian of Greece, who said:

> The diffusion of Constitutional morality, not merely among the majority of any community but throughout the whole, is the indispensable condition of government at once free and peaceable; since even any powerful and obstinate minority may render the working of a free institution impracticable,

without being strong enough to conquer ascendancy for themselves.[33]

By constitutional morality Grote meant 'a paramount reverence for the forms of the Constitution, enforcing obedience to authority acting under and within these forms yet combined with the habit of open speech, of action subject only to definite legal control, and unrestrained censure of those very authorities as to all their public acts combined too with a perfect confidence in the bosom of every citizen amidst the bitterness of party contest that the forms of the Constitution will not be less sacred in the eyes of his opponents than in his own'.[34]

Ambedkar, therefore, emphasized the diffusion of the constitutional morality for the peaceful working of a democratic Constitution. He said:

> Constitutional morality is not a natural sentiment. It has to be cultivated. We must realize that our people have yet to learn it. Democracy in India is only a top-dressing on an Indian soil, which is essentially undemocratic.[35]

Constitutional morality, as such, had been a part and parcel of Ambedkar's doctrine of constitutionalism.

The Adoption of the Constitution

The Constituent Assembly met from 17 November to 26 November 1949, for the third reading of the Draft Constitution. On 17 November, Ambedkar moved: 'That the Constitution as settled by the Assembly be passed'. The motion was adopted on 26 November. It became law on the 26 January, 1950.

The members of the Con-Assembly greatly appreciated the work done by Ambedkar and his Drafting Committee. While commending the calibre and capacity of Ambedkar, V.I. Muniswamy Pillay, said:

> Coming as I do from a community that has produced Dr Ambedkar, I feel proud that his capacity has now been recognized, not only by the Harijans but by all communities that inhabit India .... Ambedkar has been able to show to the world that the Scheduled Castes are no less important but they can rise to heights and give to the world their great services.[36]

Seth Govind Das, stated that 'it has been said about Dr Ambedkar that he is the Manu of the present age. Whatever be the truth of that statement, I can say that he was quite equal to the task of constitution making that had been entrusted to him'.[37]

Pandit Thakur Das Bhargava conveyed that Ambedkar piloted this Constitution through this House by his legal acumen, the untiring industry, the consummate skill and the firmness, tempered with moderation and solved all the knotty questions that arose in connection with it. In view of the public spirit manifested by Ambedkar, he made an appeal to him in the following words:

> Dr Ambedkar, who has so far considered himself the leader of the Scheduled Castes alone, to join the Congress, he has made for himself a high position in our hearts and I do hope that he shall thereby be able to enter the circle of Congress High Command – a position which is much more significant and important than the narrow one he is occupying today.[38]

H.J. Khendekar, while appreciating the work done by the Drafting Committee, said:

> Now today, sir, we are enacting a law of Independent India under the genius of Dr Ambedkar, the Chairman of the Drafting Committee. If I may do so, sir, I call this Constitution the Mahar law, because Dr Ambedkar is a Mahar and now when we inaugurate this Constitution on the 26 January 1950 we shall have the law of Manu replaced by the law of Mahar and I hope that unlike the law of Manu under which there was never a prosperity in the country the Mahar law will make India virtually a paradise.[39]

S.M. Ghose in a very candid tone, stated:

> Manu represents a conception of Indian people – an ideal of law given for humanity. In that sense Dr Ambedkar was rightly called the Manu of the present age.[40]

Jaspat Rai Kapur stated that Ambedkar rightly deserved the praise which has been showered on him by almost every speaker. He continued:

> I have developed an admiration and also affection for Dr Ambedkar for the very useful work and the very patriotic work which he has done .... I can say that I consider him to be one of the best patriots of this country.[41]

Syamanandan Sehaya categorized Ambedkar as 'the great architect of our great Constitution,' and said:

> He deserves the gratitude not only of the Assembly but of this nation ... the masterly way in which Dr Ambedkar piloted it will ever be remembered not only by us but by the posterity with gratitude.[42]

R.V. Dhulekar said that Ambedkar performed a very great work. He always tried to understand the opponent's view and he always tried to accommodate him and he always tried to put his own views in the clearest language. He stated:

> I would not say Herculean because that is a very small word. He has performed a task worthy of the great Pandava Bhim and worthy of the name that he has – Bhim Rao Ambedkar. He has certainly justified his name – Bhim Rao – and he has performed the task with clarity of vision, clarity of thought and clarity of language.[43]

Alladi Krishnaswami Ayyar expressed high appreciation 'of the skill and ability' with which Ambedkar had piloted the Constitution and his untiring work as the Chairman of the Drafting Committee.[44]

K.M. Jedhe said that some members have called Ambedkar as the 'present Manu' – an appellation 'he does not like, for he hates Manu,' and had burnt *Manusmriti* in the huge meeting of the untouchables at Mahad in 1929. Jedhe, therefore, called the new Constitution as 'Bhim Smriti'[45]. Several other members of the Con-Assembly had spoken in a similar tone, appreciating the great task accomplished by Ambedkar.

A Solitary Dissident

Ambedkar was congratulated by all the members of the Con-Assembly for accomplishing so formidable a task in so short a time. But there was a solitary dissident – he was

Naziruddin Ahmad; who condemned the Constitution outright and called it 'positively below par'. He coined a new name for the Drafting Committee evidently to show his contempt for it. He categorized the Drafting Committee as 'A Drifting Committee'.

Ambedkar gave him a fitting reply:

> Naziruddin Ahmed calls it a Drifting Committee. He must no doubt be pleased with his hit. But he evidently does not know that there is a difference between drift without mastery and drift with mastery. If the Drafting Committee was drifting, it was never without mastery over the situation. It was not merely angling with the off chance of catching a fish. It was searching in known waters to find the fish it was after. To be in search of something better is not the same as drifting. Although Naziruddin Ahmed did not mean it as a compliment to the Drafting Committee, I take it as a compliment to the Drafting Committee.[46]

Ambedkar was glad to find that with the exception of a solitary member, there was a general consensus of appreciation from the members of the Constituent Assembly of the work done by the Drafting Committee.

Factual Information

The Con-Assembly took 2 years, 11 months and 17 days to complete the entire work of making the Constitution since it first met on the 9 December 1946. During this period the Con-Assembly altogether held 11 sessions. Out of these 11 sessions the first six were spent in passing the objectives, resolution and the consideration of the Reports of Committees on Fundamental Rights, on Union Constitution, on Union Powers, on Provincial Constitution, on Minorities and on the Scheduled Castes and Scheduled Tribes. The 7th to 11th sessions were devoted to the consideration of the Draft Constitution. These 11 sessions of the Con-Assembly had consumed 165 days. Out of these, the Assembly spent 114 days for the consideration of the Draft Constitution.

Coming to the Drafting Committee, it was elected by the Con-Assembly on 29 August 1947. It held its first meeting on 30 August. Since August 30 it sat for 141 days during which it was engaged in the preparation of the Draft Constitution. The Draft Constitution, as prepared by the Constitutional Adviser as a text for the Drafting Committee to work upon, consisted of 243 Articles and 13 Schedules. The first Draft Constitution as presented by the Drafting Committee to the Con-Assembly contained 315 Articles and 8 Schedules. At the end of the consideration stage, the number of articles in the Draft Constitution increased to 386. In its final form, the Draft Constitution contained 395 Articles and 8 Schedules.

The total number of amendments to the Draft Constitution tabled were 7,635. Of them, the total numbers of amendments actually moved in the House were 2,473. Thus, the framing of the Constitution was a formidable task ably accomplished by Ambedkar, the Drafting Committee and the Con-Assembly.

Ambedkar's Warnings

Ambedkar wished to maintain democracy not merely in form, but also in fact. What should therefore be done? He, therefore, in his last address to the Con-Assembly uttered certain wise remarks, and gave to the nation pearls of wisdom.

The first thing in his judegment was to hold fast to constitutional methods of achieving social and economic objectives. It meant the abandonment of the bloody methods of revolution. It meant the abandonment of the methods of civil disobedience, non-cooperation and *satyagraha*. When there was no way left for constitutional methods for achieving economic and social objectives, there was a great deal of justification for unconstitutional methods. But where constitutional methods were open, there could be no justification for the unconstitutional methods. These methods were nothing but 'the Grammar of Anarchy' and the sooner they were abandoned, the better for the country.

The second thing to do was to observe the caution which John Stuart Mill had given to all who were interested in the maintenance of democracy, namely, not 'to lay their liberties at the feet of even a great man or to trust him with powers which enable him to subvert their institutions'. There was nothing wrong in being grateful to great man who had rendered life-long services to the country. But there were limits to gratefulness. He quoted with approval the words of the Irish Patriot Daniel O' Connel, 'no man can be grateful at the cost of his honour, no woman can be grateful at the cost of her chastity and no nation can be grateful at the cost of its liberty'. As such, Ambedkar warned the nation that in politics hero-worship should be avoided, because 'that is a sure road to degradation and to eventual dictatorship'.

The third thing was that the country should not be content with mere political democracy. The people should make political democracy a social democracy as well. Social democracy meant a way of life which recognizes liberty, equality and fraternity as the principles of life. These principles of liberty, equality and fraternity should not be treated as separate items in a trinity. They form a union of trinity in the sense that to divorce one from the other would defeat the very purpose of democracy. He said:

> Liberty cannot be divorced from equality, equality cannot be divorced from liberty. Nor can liberty and equality be divorced from fraternity. Without equality, liberty would produce the supremacy of the few over the many. Equality without liberty would kill individual initiative. Without fraternity, liberty and equality could not become a natural course of things. It would require a constable to enforce them.[47]

Ambedkar stated that there was complete absence of two things in Indian society. One of these was equality. On the social plane, the Indian society was based on the principle of graded inequality which meant elevation for some and degradation for others. On the economic plane, wide disparities of wealth existed and many lived in abject poverty. He said 'As such, on the 26 January, 1950, India would be entering into a life of contradictions. How long the people would continue to deny equality in our social and economic life?' He stated:

> If we continue to deny it for long, we will do so only by putting our political democracy in peril. We must remove this contradiction at the earliest possible moment or else those who suffer from inequality will blow up the structure of political democracy which this Assembly has so laboriously built up. [48]

The fourth thing that he referred to was fraternity – a sense of common brotherhood of all Indians. India could never be a nation in the absence of fraternity. He had his doubts about the use of the expression: 'the Indian nation'. He uttered:

I am of opinion that in believing that we are a nation, we are cherishing a great delusion. How can people divided into several thousands of castes be a nation? The sooner we realize that we are not as yet a nation in the social and psychological sense of the word, the better for us .... The realization of this goal is going to be very difficult.[49]

Ambedkar asserted that castes were anti-national. They have brought about separation in social life. They have generated jealousy and antipathy between castes. These difficulties should be overcome, if India and its people wish to become a nation in reality. He said:

> For fraternity can be a fact only when there is a nation. Without fraternity, equality and liberty will be no deeper than coats of paint.[50]

And lastly, Ambedkar said that after 26 January 1950, in addition to the old enemies in the form of castes and creeds, the country will be going to have many political parties with diverse and opposing political creeds. Will Indians place the country above their creed or will they place creed above country? Probably, he did not know, but one thing was certain to him. He stated:

> But this much is certain that if the parties place creed above country, our independence would be put in jeopardy a second time and probably be lost for ever. This eventuality we must all resolutely guard against. We must be determined to defend our independence with the last drop of our blood.[51]

These were the reflections of Ambedkar about the tasks that lay ahead after the Draft Constitution was passed. He said that political power in this country had too long been the monopoly of a few and many were not only beasts of burden, but also beasts of prey. This monopoly had not merely deprived them of their chance of betterment, it had sapped them of life. These downtrodden classes were tired of being governed, 'they are impatient to govern themselves'. This urge for self-realization in the downtrodden should not be allowed to develop into a class struggle or class war. That would indeed be a day of disaster. Therefore, he said:

> The sooner room is made for the realization of their aspiration, the better for the few, the better for the country, the better for the maintenance for its independence and the better for the continuance of its democratic structure. This can only be done by the establishment of equality and fraternity in all spheres of life.[52]

'If after independence things go wrong', asserted Ambedkar, 'we would have nobody to blame except ourselves'. There was great danger of things going wrong. Times were fast changing. People were being moved by new ideologies.

. Ambedkar felt that the new Constitution is good enough to start with. It is workable; it is flexible and it is strong enough to hold the country together both in peace time and war time. However, if things go wrong under the new Constitution, 'the reason will not be that we had a bad Constitution, what we will have to say is, that Man was vile'.[53]

The truth of the matter is that the people of India have to learn the arts of democracy. The lessons of democracy are not taught in any book, but they have got to be developed. It all depends upon the character of the people, their integrity and love for democratic principles and zeal to pursue and follow them. The Constitution does not depend upon the cold letters, however beautifully or brilliantly printed in a book; it depends for its growth and development upon the character of the nation. The seeds of Constitution can germinate and bloom, if the people of India sincerely follow the wise remarks or the pearls of wisdom expounded by Ambedkar, the principal architect of the Constitution of India.

In fact, Ambedkar had laid the foundation of the democratic edifice of the government, that is, government by discussion and criticism. His colleagues in the Con-Assembly bestowed on him generous praise and candid approval of his role as the main architect of our Constitution and perhaps, Pattabhi Sitaramayya summed up the sentiments of the Con-Assembly when he said, 'What a steam-roller intellect he brought to bear upon this magnificent task: irresistible, indomitable, unconquerable, levelling down tall palms and short poppies; whatever he felt to be right he stood by, regardless of consequences'.[54]

Notes

1. Dr Babasaheb Ambedkar *Writings and Speeches* (Mumbai, Government of Maharashtra, 1994), Vol. 13, p. 12.
2. Constituent Assembly Debates (CAD), Vol. VII, 30 December 1948, pp. 1136–40.
3. Dr Babasaheb Ambedkar, op. cit. p. 62.
4. CAD, Vol. VII, 9 December 1948, p. 950.
5. Dr Babasaheb Ambedkar, op. cit. p. 1208.
6. Ibid., p. 9.
7. CAD, Vol. VII, 5 November 1948, p. 227.
8. Ibid., p. 244.
9. Ibid., p. 246.
10. Ibid., p. 252.
11. CAD, Vol. vii, 6 November 1948, p. 260.
12. Ibid., p. 275.
13. Ibid., p. 284.
14. Dr Babasaheb Ambedkar, op. cit. p. 50.
15. Ibid., p. 54.
16. Ibid., p. 55.
17. Ibid., p. 56.

18. Ibid., p. 1212.
19. Ibid.
20. Ibid., p. 66.
21. Ibid., p. 390.
22. Ibid., p. 65.
23. Ibid.
24. Ibid., p. 69.
25. CAD, Vol. VII, 6 January 1949, p. 1309.
26. CAD, Vol. VII, 4 January 1949, p. 1239.
27. There were a number of critics who said that there was nothing original in the Draft Constitution. One such critic was M. Ananthasayamam Ayyanger, who said: 'The Draft Constitution is a patch work of some of the old Constitutions of the West – not even some of the modern Constitutions of the West-, with a replica of the Government of India Act, 1935'(CAD, Vol. VII, 9 November 1948, p. 352).
28. Dr Babasaheb Ambedkar, op. cit. p. 59.
29. Ibid.
30. Ibid., p. 60.
31. Some of the critics are mentioned here. Lokanath Misra said: 'The Draft Constitution has given something which is absolutely un-Indian. It is absolutely a slavish imitation of – nay, much more, a slavish surrender to the West' (CAD, Vol. VII, 5 November 1948, p. 242).

    R.K. Sidhwa remarked: 'It has negatived the very idea of democracy by ignoring the local authorities and villages' (CAD, Vol. VII, 6 November 1948, p. 262).

    Pandit Thakur Das Bhargava stated:

    'It has not given a true picture. The real soil of India (village) is not represented by this Constitution' (CAD, Vol. VII, 6 November 1948, p. 284).

    According to N. Madhava Rau:

    'While borrowing some of its provisions from alien sources, including the Government of India Act 1935, it has not woven into its fabric any of the elements of ancient Indian polity' (CAD, Vol. VII, 9 November 1948, p. 388).
32. Dr Babasaheb Ambedkar, op. cit. p. 62.

33. Ibid., p. 60.
34. Ibid.
35. Ibid., p. 61.
36. CAD, Official report, Vol. X, 17 November 1949, p. 610.
37. Ibid.
38. Ibid., 18 November 1949, p. 682.
39. Ibid., 21 November 1949, pp. 736–37.
40. Ibid., p. 742.
41. Ibid., p. 758.
42. Ibid., 22 November 1949, p. 787.
43. Ibid., 23 November 1949, p. 826.
44. Ibid., p. 834.
45. Ibid., 24 November 1949, p. 890.
46. Dr Babasaheb Ambedkar, op. cit. pp. 1207–08.
47. Ibid., p. 1216.
48. Ibid.
49. Ibid., p. 1217.
50. Ibid.
51. Ibid., p. 1214.
52. Ibid., p. 1218.
53. Ibid., p. 70.
54. Ibid., p. xi.

5

The Hindu Code Bill

The Hindu Code Bill, meant to codify the Hindu Law was a progressive measure, introduced by B.R. Ambedkar, on 17 November 1947, in the Constituent Assembly. In fact, the Bill had its origin in a legislation which took effect in the 1937. Ever since that year, the provisions of this Bill had been bandied from one side to the other, from committee to committee. The original Hindu Code Bill was introduced in the Legislative Assembly on 11 April 1947, by J.N. Mandal, Law Member of the Interim Government, after the Law Committee's investigation was complete. A motion was moved in the Constituent Assembly (Legislative) by B.R. Ambedkar on 17 November 1947 to continue the Bill. The Bill sponsored by Ambedkar was a revised one incorporating substantial improvements upon the original Bill, both in the scheme as well as in the content. The debate over the Bill continued for more than four years and remained inconclusive. The Bill was ultimately, 'killed and died unwept and unsung', in the words of Ambedkar.[1]

Ambedkar felt that there was a need for Hindu Code Bill. The need was based on the fact that at the time the Hindu Law was uncodified in a large measure. It remained scattered to innumerable decisions of the Indian High Courts and also of the Privy Council, which formed bewildering motley to the common man and gave rise to constant litigation. Ambedkar thought that it was necessary to give a definite shape and form to the Hindu Law by consolidation and codification.

The principles of codification covered: (i) right to property, ii) order of succession to the property, (iii) maintenance, marriage, divorce, adoption, minority and guardianship. The existing Hindu Law, especially dealing with succession and inheritance led to discrimination against the female heirs. Ambedkar wished to abolish this discrimination in the Hindu Code Bill. The points raised in the Bill for consideration of the House, were these: First, the abolition of birth-right and to take property by survivorship; Second, the giving of half-share to the daughter; Third, the conversion of the women's limited estate into an absolute estate; Fourth, the abolition of caste in the matter of marriage and adoption; Fifth, the principle of monogamy; and sixth, the principle of divorce. Justifying the departures made in the Bill, Ambedkar said:

> The Hindu society is an inert society. It has always believed that law-making is the function either of God or the *Smritis* and that Hindu society has no right to change the law. That being so, the law in Hindu society has remained what it was for generations to come. Society has never accepted its own power and its own responsibility in moulding its social, economic and legal life. It is for the first time that we are persuading Hindu society to take this big step ....[2]

The Hindu Code Bill, after being introduced by Ambedkar in the Constituent Assembly, was moved for referring to the Select Committee on 9 April 1948. The debate in the Select Committee continued for more than four years and still remained inconclusive. Ambedkar felt that the Government and the party in power (the Congress) were not eager to clear the Hindu Code.

The Bill came up, for clause by clause discussion, on the floor of the Provisional Parliament from 5 February to 25 September 1951. On account of the lukewarm support to the Bill by the government, Ambedkar felt dismayed and, therefore, submitted his resignation (Law Minister) to the Prime Minister Pandit Jawaharlal Nehru on 27 September 1951, but continued to participate in the parliamentary debates till 10 October 1951, on the request of the Prime Minister. In his letter of resignation, he expressed that he attached greatest importance to the Hindu Code Bill and would be prepared to undergo any strain on his health to get the Bill through. He wanted the Bill to be taken up on top priority basis on 16 August and be finished by the 1st of September 1951. However, it did not take place. The opponents of the Bill continued obstructive tactics and the Bill could not see the light of the day. Dejected, Ambedkar, ultimately submitted his statement of resignation on 10 October 1951, and left the House in anguish.

Significance of the Bill

The Hindu Code Bill was an interesting and progressive piece of legislation. It aimed 'at changing the basic framework of Hindu Society on more liberal patterns suited to modern times'.[3] Ambedkar believed that the unprogressive character of Hindu society was due to the notion that law cannot be changed.[4] The Bill was the most formidable legislative measure of modern India. It sought among other reforms, to put an end to a variety of marriage systems prevailing in India and legalize only monogamous marriages. It sought to confer on women the right of property and adoption which had been denied to them from ancient times. It put men and women on an equal level in all legal matters.

The significance of the Hindu Code Bill was best given by Ambedkar in his statement of resignation from the Cabinet on 10 October 1951. He was not allowed to present his statement in the Provisional Parliament by the Speaker. He, therefore, quit the House and distributed the copies of statement to the members of Parliament and the Press. In that statement of 10 October, Ambedkar, clearly stated what the significance of the Bill was:

> No law passed by the Indian Legislature in the past or likely to be passed in the future can be compared to it (Hindu Code) in point of its significance. To leave inequality between class and class, between sex and sex, which is the soul of Hindu society, untouched and to go on passing legislation relating to economic problems is to make a farce of our Constitution and to build a palace on a dung heap. This is the significance I attached to the Hindu Code.[5]

Defenders of the Bill

The efforts of Ambedkar to unify the Hindu Code were greatly lauded by a substantial number of members of the Provisional Parliament. Pattabhi Sitaramayya characterized it as an 'interesting piece of legislation for which the country has been waiting for long'.[6] Hansa Mehta called it a 'revolutionary Bill' and 'a great landmark in the social history of the Hindus'.[7] B.V. Keskar said that it was a radical Bill, meant 'to change the very foundations of Hindu society, a society which has remained fossilized for the last thousand years'.[8] K.M. Munshi described the Bill as 'a very big measure'[9] and Deshbandhu Gupta said that it was a very important measure 'as it sought to abolish the artificial barriers that stood in the way of Hindu solidarity'.[10] Begum Aizaz Rasul called it radical and far-reaching and its efforts to codify the Hindu Law would 'certainly be looked upon as one of the most momentous pieces of legislation that has ever been brought forward in this House'.[11] G. Durgabai styled it as 'a great landmark in the social history of India'.[12] The other main defenders of the Bill were H. Siddaveerappa, N.V. Gadgil, Mahavir Tyagi, Upendranath Barman, Col. Ranbir Singh, Pandit Hirday Nath Kunzru, K. Santhanam, Alladi Krishnaswami Ayyar, Acharya J.B. Kripalani, Shrimati Renuka Ray, H.V. Kamath, etc. Among them H.V. Kamath was the most passionate defender of the Hindu Code, and he said that the Bill should be named as *Bhim Smriti*. Speaking in support of this measure, he said:

> As regards the Smritis which are interlinked or interlocked with Dharma, my honorable friend, Dr Ambedkar said the other day that there are perhaps 137 Smritis. I believe he has counted them. Of the Smritis known to Dr Ambedkar there are 137. And now we have got the 138th Smriti because this is also a measure which, although not revolutionary, has introduced changes in our Hindu social relations. So I can apply the same term as has been applied to the other Hindu Social Codes and social texts that have been already written for us. This we call the 138th Smriti. I may call it the *Bhim Smriti*. I hope Dr Ambedkar will pardon me if I refer to this as the *Bhim Smriti*.[13]

The Bill was a forward measure, believed H.V. Kamath, which was meant to lead to the greater glory of Hindu society. It was a step forward towards the codification of Hindu Law.

Praising the role played by Ambedkar, in formulating the Hindu Code Bill, Justice P.B. Gajendragadkar, in a lecture which he delivered in 1951 at Dharwar while the Bill was still before the Provisional Parliament, said:

> It is well-known that Dr Ambedkar can legitimately and justly feel proud for the substantial work done by him in drafting of our Constitution. If with the active cooperation and support of the Prime Minister, who fortunately shares his Law Minister's enthusiasm for the code, Dr Ambedkar is able to pilot the Code through all the stages and give it the pride of place in our Statue Book, I for one would hail it as a time's sweet revenge on the Hindu society as a whole. If Dr Ambedkar gives us Hindu's our code, his achievement would go down in history as a very eloquent piece of poetic justice indeed.[14]

Opponents of the Bill

On the whole, the Hindu Code Bill met with stiff opposition inside the Provisional Parliament. The House was practically divided into two warring groups. The climax reached in the third week of September 1951, when the Bill came up for clause by clause discussion in the Parliament. In a very tense atmosphere, the debate began on 17 September 1951. There were many critics of the Hindu Code. The prominent critics were Shyama Prasad Mookerjee, Pandit Madan Mohan Malaviya, Pandit Thakur Das Bhargava, Pandit Laksmi Kanta Maitra, Mukut Bihari Lal Bhargava, Sardar Hukum Singh, Sardar B.S. Man, O.V. Alagesan, Bakshi Tek Chand, Seth Govind Das, Babu Ramnarayan Singh, etc.

Shyama Prasad Mookerjee, while opposing the Bill said:

> The Hindu Code Bill would shatter the magnificent structure of Hindu culture and stultify a dynamic and Catholic way of life that had wonderfully adapted itself to changes for centuries.[15]

Pandit Madan Mohan Malaviya said that the Bill was against the spirit of the Hindu *Shastras* and the long established customary law and that the Provisional Parliament had no business to interfere with the personal laws of the Hindus.

He warned the government 'not to destroy the fabric of respect for law'.[16]

Pandit Thakur Das Bhargava described the Bill as 'a small measure'. There were some good provisions in the Bill, he said, but at the same time, 'I have not understood fully all the provisions, all the clauses and all the implications of this Bill'.[17] He, therefore, pleaded that Bill should go back to the Select Committee.

Pandit Lakshmi Kanta Maitra felt that there was no need for codification. He was not in favour of 'drastic changes' contained in the Bill. He characterized the Bill as the outcome of Ambedkar's 'megalomania'. He said:

> The country at large is bewildered by the way in which we are dealing with a piece of legislation of this far-reaching importance .... I oppose this Bill, because I feel it is a wholly unwarranted measure and that there has been no demand in the country for a legislation of this kind.[18]

Mukut Bihari Lal Bhargava, while opposing the Bill tooth and nail, said that the only course for it was to throw out this piece of legislation. Few individuals wished this legislation to be thrust upon the country, it could not be accepted. He said:

> The Hindu Law has come into existence as a result of centuries of development, and the Bill is intended to tamper with its time-honoured institutions, customs and usages.[19]

Sardar Hukam Singh and Sardar B.S. Man both opposed the Bill and said that it should not apply to the Sikhs. Sardar Hukam Singh said that in the Preamble it was stated that the Bill was intended to amend and codify the Hindu Law, but he did not find that in this Code. There was nothing of Hindu Law that was being codified here. Divorce was taken from the Christian countries and the law of inheritance from the Muslim Law. The Bill was, therefore, rather a misnomer to call it a codification of Hindu Law.

O.V. Alagesan pleaded that the Bill should not be rushed through, because it contained many weaknesses. The Bill was the result of Ambedkar's 'over-ambitions'. He stated:

> Dr Ambedkar's name is sure to go down in history as the able midwife that assisted at the birth of the Constitution of free India. He wants to add a further feather to his cap and he is justified. His ambition is to supersede the ancient Rishis, Manu, Yajnavalkya and a host of other ancient law givers.[20]

Bakshi Tek Chand emphatically said that the Bill was 'a most truncated and half-hearted measure,' and 'it will do the maximum of mischief to Hindu society and the minimum of good to the members of the female-sex'.[21]

Seth Govind Das said that the idea of introducing a Hindu Code Bill in a country wedded to the secular ideal was 'quite inappropriate'. The Bill should have been made applicable to all citizens of this country.[22]

Babu Ramnarayan Singh said that through the Hindu Code Bill, a conspiracy was being hatched to disrupt the Hindu society; and, in fact, 'it is something like a preparation to invade the Hindu society'.[23]

Ambedkar's Reply

The points raised by the critics of the Bill centred around the facts that, (i) there was really no necessity of such a Bill; (ii) the Hindu society had survived for many centuries, while the ancient society of Rome, Greece and Egypt had disappeared and therefore its laws and social structure must be good; (iii) that the Hindu society had been a very progressive society and that it has been changing; that the Bill is a kind of imitation of the western nations; and that the Hindu marriages are based on sacramental ideal of marriage.

Responding to the critics, Ambedkar demolished each of the above arguments.

He said that one point which had been raised by various speakers generally against the whole Bill, was that there was really no necessity for it. They declared that while the ancient societies of Rome, Greece and Egypt had disappeared, the ancient Hindu society had survived and therefore, its laws and social structure must be good. Ambedkar refuted this argument. He said that the point was: 'Is survival enough, or is it necessary for us to consider whether the plane on which we survive is more important than the mere survival itself?'[24] He continued: 'When I examine the history of India, I find that we have survived as a people who have been from time to time subjugated; vanquished and enslaved'.[25] There were many countries and many communities which had lost in battle and which had been enslaved but some day at some time the vanquished people in other parts of the world had tried to achieve their independence. Ambedkar said that he had not seen any such thing in India. Hence, the argument that merely because we had survived when other communities had passed into history was an argument that did not convince him of the goodness or soundness of the social structure under which the Hindus had been living.

Another argument that Ambedkar did not like was that Hindu society had been a very progressive society. He appreciated one of the great qualities of the Hindu society that it absorbed some things from those who opposed it. But his point was: 'Did the Hindu society change its structure as a result of the absorption of the doctrines of their opponents?'[26] Citing the example of Lord Buddha, Ambedkar said that the Brahminic society accepted his most innocuous dogma of 'ahimsa' but they never accepted his belief in equality. That was the reason that the Hindu society remained stale and stagnant. It did not give up its social structure – the enslavement of the '*Shudra*' and the enslavement of women.[27] It were for this reason, said Ambedkar, that the Hindu Code was essential.

Another argument that had been advanced was that the promoters of the Bill were proceeding in a kind of imitation of the Western nations. Ambedkar made it clear that his ideals were not derived from the Americans or Chinese or from the ancient *Shastras* or the Ramayana or the Mahabharata; they were derived from the Constitution that we had laid down. The very Preamble of our Constitution speaks of liberty, equality and fraternity. The principles laid down in the Constitution form the bedrock of the Hindu Code.[28]

Further, Ambedkar said that the institution of sacramental marriage was not fair and honest. It did not satisfy the ideal of liberty or of equality. He regarded sacramental marriage as polygamy for the man and perpetual slavery for the woman because under no circumstances could the woman get her liberty from her husband, however, undesirable he might have been.[29] As such, Ambedkar pleaded that the Bill was intended to break the slavery of woman and provide her the ability and the capacity to break the contract, when the necessity for breaking the contract was felt.

Reply to Sardar Hukam Singh and Sardar Man

There was a lot of controversy regarding the scope of the Hindu Code. Whether its provisions should apply to the Sikhs, Buddhists and Jains or not? This led to an acrimonious debate.

Sardar Hukam Singh had moved an amendment that it should not apply to the Sikhs. With regard to the question whether this Bill should apply to persons or communities other than Hindus in the strict sense of the word, Ambedkar argued, that it would not be difficult to understand why Sikhs are brought under the Hindu religion, why Buddhists are brought under the Hindu religion, and why Jains are brought under the Hindu religion.

The Buddhists are being brought under the Hindu religion, because, argued Ambedkar:

> When the Buddha differed from the Vedic Brahmins, his difference was limited to matters of creed. Buddha did not propound a separate legal system for his own followers; he left the legal system as it was. It may be that the legal system that then prevailed was a good system; that it had no blemishes and no faults. So, he did not direct his attention to making any changes in the legal system in consequence of the changes that he introduced in certain religious notions.[30]

The similar was the case of the Jains. In a categorical statement, Ambedkar said:

> When Mahavir founded his own religion he did not create a new legal system for the Jains. He allowed the legal system to continue and I think Sardar Hukum Singh will correct me if I am wrong when I say that none of the ten Gurus ever created a law book as such for the Sikhs.[31]

What Ambedkar emphasized was that in the country although religions have changed, the law had remained one. That is why the Sikh follows the law. He asserted that the Jains, Sikhs and the Buddhist have been following a single law system and 'it is too late now for anyone to say that he shall reject this legal system wholesale and will have nothing to do with it. That cannot be done'.[32]

Ambedkar regarded the application of the Hindu Law and the Hindu Code to Buddhists, Jains and Sikhs as a historical development. So far as the Sikhs were concerned, he cited the judgments of the Privy Council when this question was debated much earlier than even 1830, when the decision was taken that the Sikhs were Hindus so far as law is concerned. He reminded Sardar Hukum Singh: 'Just count from 1830 to 1950 – for how many years you have been regarded as Hindus for legal purposes'.[33] He further stated that in law, there is a principle called *stare decisis*, which means a decision taken a long time ago and on which people have gone should better be stayed although it may be wrong.

So, Ambedkar made it very clear in the Constituent Assembly that he would never agree to exempt any province from the operation of the Hindu Code. Quite frankly, he said:

> 'Let there be no doubt about it at all that the Hindu Code shall be a uniform code throughout India. Either I will have that Bill in that form or not have it at all'.[34]

Sardar B.S. Man, a Sikh, did not agree to the views of Ambedkar. He stated that an attempt was being made to codify, but codification 'makes the law rigid whereas custom is not rigid' He pointed out the dangers inherent in codification. He argued that Ambedkar was fashioning out clothes, legal clothes – a sort of *Amritdhara* which would suit every disease from south to the north – and, the clothes that he was trying to fashion out and tailor would be either too loose for southerners or be too tight for the northerners. He reminded Ambedkar to look at the size of the society and its needs – and fashion and tailor the clothes accordingly and not supply ready-made clothes, ready-made medicines, a sort of *Amritdhara* for every disease. He concluded that:

> No attempt should be made upon me as a Sikh to foist any law which is alien and repugnant to my spirit. I for one will not accept it ....[35]

Disagreeing with Sardar Hukum Singh and Sardar B.S. Man, Ambedkar in a bold tone, said:

> Why should you all the time keep on saying, 'I am different. I am not governed by this and I am not governed by that. Therefore, do not make your law binding upon me'. That is the point of my protest.[36]

Ambedkar continued saying that Sardar Man's charge was this that the Sikhs have not been consulted in this matter. His answer to this point was two-fold. Firstly, he said, 'If the Sikhs have not been consulted as Sikhs my contention is that there was no necessity to consult them, because all along the law has assumed that the Sikhs for the purpose of law are Hindus'. And, secondly, he stated that the charge that the Sikhs were not consulted was not founded on facts. Citing the evidence of Rau Committee when it toured and went to Lahore, Ambedkar quoted the names of Sikhs who appeared and made statements before the Committee. They were Justice Teja Singh and Sardar Varyam Singh; the latter came as a representative of the Akali Darbar. Both of them did not oppose the Hindu Code Bill.

Reply to Madan Mohan Malaviya

Pandit Madan Mohan Malaviya was very critical of the Hindu Code Bill. He regarded the Bill very much against the spirit of the Hindu *Shastras.* The Bill might have been prepared innocently but, 'it has within it the potentialities for untold and immeasurable mischief'.[37] He asserted that the Bill should apply after referendum has taken place. He stated that in Hindu society from time immemorial laws had prevailed without the authority of the State, without the authority of the Police, without the authority of any legislature as such. It would be imprudent on the part of the government to make a thoughtless and hasty mistake in demolishing that fabric upon which the respect for and the adherence to the law had prevailed. He asserted that the Provisional Parliament should not interfere into the long established customary law of the Hindus.

Replying to Pandit Malaviya, Ambedkar said:

> I want to assert in this House that I shall hear no argument from any community to say that this Parliament has no right to interfere in their personal law or any other laws. This Parliament is absolutely supreme and we deal with any community so far as their personal law is concerned apart from their religion. Let no community be in a state of mind that they are immune from the sovereign authority of this Parliament.[38]

Ambedkar's Resignation

The debates in the Parliaments had provoked sharp reactions. Ultimately, it was decided that the Parliament should consider the marriage and divorce part of it only. There had been sufficient debate on it. The attitude of Pandit Jawaharlal Nehru, the Prime Minister, was also half-hearted on the Bill. The House did not take any decision on the Hindu Code and it proceeded into other legislative business. This greatly annoyed Ambedkar and he tendered his resignation on the 27 September 1951 to the Prime Minister, the latter requested him to continue for a few days, to which Ambedkar agreed.

Why did Ambedkar submit his resignation? This was made clear by him in his statement that was released on 10 October 1951. The most important cause of his resignation was the treatment which was accorded to the Hindu Code. Ambedkar stated that at one time when discussion was going on the Prime Minister put forth a new proposal, namely, that the Bill as a whole might not be got through within the time available and that it was desirable to get a part of it enacted into law rather than allow the whole of it to go to waste. It was a great wrench to Ambedkar. But he agreed, for, it was better to save a part when the whole was likely to be lost. The Prime Minister suggested that the Parliament should consider the marriage and divorce part. So, the Bill in its truncated form went on. After 2 or 3 days of discussion of the Bill the Prime Minister came up with another proposal. This time his proposal was to drop the whole Bill, even the marriage and divorce portion. This came to Ambedkar as a great shock – a bolt from the blue. He was stunned and could not say anything. He was not prepared to accept that the dropping of the truncated Bill was due to want of time. He was sure that the truncated Bill was dropped because other and more powerful members of the Cabinet wanted precedence for their Bills. He got the impression that the Prime Minister, although sincere, had not the earnestness and determination required to get the Hindu Code Bill through.

In regard to this Bill, Ambedkar had undergone the greatest mental torture. The aid of Party Machinery was denied to him. The Prime Minister gave freedom of vote. The conduct of the Chief Whip of the party was not favourable. He was the deadliest opponent of the Code and was never present to aid Ambedkar by moving a closure motion. For days and hours filibustering had gone on a single clause but the Chief Whip had been systematically absent when the Hindu Code had been under consideration in the House. Ambedkar, in his resignation letter, wrote:

> I have never seen a case of a Chief Whip so disloyal to the Prime Minister and a Prime Minister so loyal to a disloyal Whip. Notwithstanding this unconstitutional behavior, the Chief Whip is really a darling of the Prime Minister .... It is impossible to carry on in such circumstances.[39]

Ambedkar refuted the charge that the Bill was dropped because the opposition was strong. He argued that the Bill had been discussed several times in the Party and was carried to division by the opponents. Every time the opponents were routed. The last time when the Bill was taken up in the Party Meeting, out of 120 only 20 were found to be against it. When the Bill was taken in the Party for discussion, 44 clauses were passed in about in three and a half hours time. This showed how much opposition there was to the Bill within the Party. In the House itself, there had been divisions on three clauses of the Bill – 2, 3 and 4. Every time there had been an overwhelming majority in favour, even on clause 4 which was the soul of the Hindu Code.

Ambedkar, therefore, was quite unable to accept the Prime Minister's decision to abandon the Bill on the ground of time.

He gave this elaborate explanation in his resignation letter because some persons had suggested that he was quitting because of his illness. While repudiating any such suggestion, Ambedkar asserted that he was the last man to abandon his duty because of illness.

Ambedkar was staying on in the Cabinet for the sake of the Hindu Code, because he considered it as the greatest social reform measure ever undertaken by the Legislature in India. He considered that no law passed by the Indian Legislature in the past or likely to be passed in the future could be compared to it on point of its significance. The sole purpose of the Hindu Code was to remove inequality that exists in the Hindu society. To him, legislation relating to economic problems was of less importance in comparison to legislation on social matters, because the soul of Hindu society was inequality. Unless and until, this inequality was not removed by law, the Constitution of India would be no more than a farce, and that would amount to building a palace on a dung heap. This was the significance that Ambedkar attached to the Hindu Code. It was for its sake that he stayed on in the Cabinet notwithstanding his differences.

Ambedkar was staying on in the Cabinet in the hope of doing some good. In this connection, he referred only to three of the statements made by the Prime Minister on the floor of the House.

The first statement made by the Prime Minister was on 21 November 1949, when he gave the following assurance: 'What is more, the government is committed to this thing (Hindu Code). It is going through with it'.[40]

The second statement was made on 19 December 1949, when the Prime Minister said: 'I do not wish the House to think in the slightest degree that we consider that this Hindu Code Bill is not of importance, because we do attach the greatest importance to it, as I said, not because of any particular clause or anything, but because of the basic approach to this vast problem in problems, economic and social'.[41]

And lastly, on 26 September 1951, the Prime Minister said: 'It is not necessary for me to assure the House of the desire of

Government to proceed with this measure in so far as we can proceed with it within possibilities, and so far as we are concerned we consider this matter as adjourned till such time as the next opportunity – I hope it will be in this Parliament – offers itself'.[42]

The last statement of the Prime Minister dated the 26 September 1951, amounted to the dropping of the Bill. Ambedkar could realize the gap between the promises and performance of the Prime Minister. He was aware that his exit from the Cabinet might not be a matter of much concern to anybody in this country. But he wanted to be true to himself and that could be only by going out.

Ambedkar was 'sore at the Prime Minister's mishandling of the Hindu Code Bill, and that was the main factor for his resignation from Nehru's Cabinet'.[43]

Hindu Code: A Precursor of Later Acts

Though the Hindu Code Bill was not adopted by the Provisional Parliament in 1951, Ambedkar's efforts did not go in vain. He believed 'in the efficacy of law and legislation, and he struggled to evolve a codification of Hindu Law in order to fashion India of his dreams, where equality, liberty and fraternity would have an unhindered play'.[44]

Recognizing the need for social repairs, Ambedkar, while introducing the Hindu Code Bill had said:

> That those who want to conserve must be ready to repair and all I am asking of this House is this: that if you want to maintain the Hindu system, the Hindu culture, the Hindu society, do not hesitate to repair where repair is necessary. This Bill asks for nothing more than repairing those parts of the Hindu system which have almost become dilapidated.[45]

The tenets of this Bill were in harmony with the constitutional philosophy of equality of men and women. Ambedkar had 'rebelled against the inhuman elements that were eating into the vitals of Indian society'.[46] The Bill was really a part of 'social engineering'[47] aiming to remove the outdated Customary Hindu Law.

Ambedkar's attempt for repairing the Hindu society through the Hindu Code was not altogether fruitless. The Hindu Code Bill proved to be a precursor of four enactments, adopted later on, by the first Parliament of India. Very soon the Hindu Code Bill was split into four Bills and same were put on the Statue Book of the Parliament. The Hindu Marriage Act, 1955, the Hindu Succession Act, 1956; the Hindu Minority and Guardianship Act, 1956; and the Hindu Adoption and Maintenance Act, 1956, were the four enactments which incorporated the ideas and principles of the Hindu Code Bill formulated earlier by Ambedkar. They give independent status to women and endowed them with the right of adoption, succession and property. Therefore, 'it is truism to say that it is due to Dr Ambedkar that a large part of the Hindu social law is now on par with the legal system prevailing in advanced democracies'.[48] The discussions on the Hindu Code Bill and Ambedkar's role played through the debates thereon are very useful for the students to know more about his sociological and political ideas, and his zeal to repair the damaged parts of the Hindu social order.

The speeches delivered by Ambedkar in the Con-Assembly and the Provisional Parliament, while initiating and defending the Hindu Code Bill reveal, to a great extent, his political ideas. The key features of his ideology were liberty, equality, dignity and social justice – and this he tried to translate into practice. There was practically no gap between his preaching and the practice. His ideology was free from fancies and imagination; it was mainly based on practical utilities and ending of all types of discrimination. The aim of his ideology was social transformation and this he tried to implement through Hindu Code Bill, which was an important piece of legislation, meant to cleanse the rotten structure of the Hindu society and to reinvigorate it.

Notes

1. S.N. Mandal (ed): *Dr. B.R. Ambedkar: His Thoughts and Observations* (New Delhi, National Publishing House, 2004), p. 55.

2. Dr Babasaheb Ambedkar *Writings and Speeches* (Mumbai, Government of Maharashtra, 1995), Vol. 14, Part one, p. 41.
3. V.P. Gupta and Mohini Gupta (eds): *Makers of Modern India, Series II, Dr. B.R. Ambedkar* (Delhi, Ambe Books, 1998), p. 63.
4. D.R. Jatava: *B.R. Ambedkar: A Vision of Man and Morals* (Jaipur, ABD Publisher, 1999), p. 64.
5. Dr Babasaheb Ambedkar *Writings and Speeches*, Vol. 14, Part Two, pp. 1325–26.
6. Ibid., Vol. 14, Part one, p. 12.
7. Constituent Assembly of India (Legislative) Debates (Hereinafter called C.A. (Leg) D), Vol. IV, 9 April 1948, p. 3646.
8. Ibid., p. 3647.
9. Dr Babasaheb Ambedkar, Vol. 14, Part one p. 234.
10. Ibid., p. 235.
11. C.A. (Leg.) D, Vol. IV, 9 April 1948, p. 3648.
12. Dr Babasaheb Ambedkar, Vol. 14, part one, p. 398.
13. C.A. (Leg) D, Vol. II, Part II, 25 February 1949.
14. D.C. Ahir: *The Legacy of Dr. Ambedkar* (Delhi: B.R. Publishing Corporation, 1990), pp. 131–32.
15. Ibid., p. 132.
16. Ibid.
17. Dr Babasaheb Ambedkar, Vol. 14, Part one, p. 323.
18. Ibid., pp. 409, 432–33.
19. Ibid., p. 583.
20. Ibid., p. 750.
21. Ibid., p. 716.
22. Ibid., p. 299.
23. Ibid., p. 388.
24. Dr Babasaheb Ambedkar, Vol. 14, Part Two p. 1159.
25. Ibid.
26. Ibid., p. 1159.
27. Ibid., p. 1160.
28. Ibid., p. 1161.
29. Ibid.
30. Ibid., p. 889.

31. Ibid., p. 888.
32. Ibid.
33. Ibid.
34. Ibid., p. 889.
35. Ibid., p. 1102.
36. Ibid., p. 1172.
37. Ibid., p. 1116.
38. Ibid., p. 1168.
39. Ibid., pp. 1324–25.
40. Ibid., p. 1326.
41. Ibid.
42. Ibid.
43. D.R. Jatava: *Ambedkar: The Prime Mover* (Jaipur, ABD Publishers, 2004), p. 182.
44. M.L. Ranga (ed): *B.R. Ambedkar: Life, Work and Relevance* (New Delhi, Manohar Publisher, 2000), p. 55.
45. Dr Babasaheb Ambedkar *Writings and Speeches*, Vol. 14, Part one, p. 283.
46. Kusum Sharma: *Ambedkar and Indian Constitution* (New Delhi, Ashish Publishing House, 1992), p. 236.
47. D.R. Jatava: *Sociological Thoughts of B.R. Ambedkar* (Jaipur, ABD Publishers, 2001), p. 174.
48. D.C. Ahir: *The Legacy of Dr Ambedkar*, p. 135.

6

Man and Society

Ambedkar's views about man and society form an important aspect of his political ideology. Here, he did not adhere to the traditional notions; instead he formulated his own views better known as revolutionary humanism. To understand properly Ambedkar's concept of revolutionary humanism or social humanism, one must first examine the traditional concept of man and society and thereafter enunciate to what extent Ambedkar departed from them and what type of man and society he visualized.

There were certain concepts of man and society prevalent in India before the advent of Ambedkar on the scene. Let us first examine these concepts in order to have a better understanding of Ambedkar's vision of man and society.

Vedic Concept

The oldest concept of man and society that was prevalent in India was the *vedic* concept. It upheld that man was created by *Prajapati* out of his will in accordance with individual's *Karmas* done in his previous life. 'Man had to pass through a cycle of births and deaths. He could be assigned any form of a being as per his *Karmas.* In each life, man is born to play a certain role and enjoy certain fruits. He will go on transmigrating in the cycle of births and deaths till liberation is achieved through rituals and sacrifices but with the consent and grace of God.

Every time an individual dies, his body disintegrates and his soul, said to be immortal, transmigrates from one place to another'.[1] The Vedic concept, therefore, lays emphasis on *Karma*, God and the transmigration of the soul.

In addition, the Vedic concept also advocated that the society was divinely ordained into four *Varnas* (castes), that is, *Brahmins, Kshatriyas, Vaishyas* and *Shudras*. The duties of each *Varna* have been defined in the Hindu scriptures. This conception of *Varna* has been elaborately defined in *Manusmriti* which has become the classic of Hindu social organization. In short, the Hindu scriptures advocated the theistic concept of man and society. It was closely related to man's *Karma* and fate which were wholly in the hands of divine power. As such, divine social determinism, fatalism and retributory Karma theory were its main ingredients.

Ambedkar rejected outright the Vedic concept of man and society. He believed that it was based on inequality, social oppression and economic exploitation. He held that it promoted caste system, untouchability, slavery and defiled the dignity of human personality. It reduced man into 'dust and dung'. That is why Ambedkar said:

> How can a philosophy which dissects society into fragments, which dissociates work from interest, which disconnects intelligence from labour, which expropriates the rights of man to interests vital to life and which prevents society from mobilizing resources for common action in the hour of danger, be said to satisfy the test of social utility?[2]

The main objections of Ambedkar against the Vedic concept of man and society were that it neither satisfied the test of social utility nor did it satisfy the test of individual justice. He thus rejected the Vedic concept of man and society in toto.

Charvaka, Jain and Buddhist Concepts

The Vedic concept of man and society was theistic, whereas Charvaka, Jain and Buddhist philosophies upheld non-theistic or humanistic concept of man and society. Their concept took man as the centre of study without any supernatural relationship except Jainism, which regarded soul to be supernatural, transmigrating from one birth to another according to its materially generated desires and *Karmas*. However, man was not created by God in these philosophies. So man occupied a prominent place in the universe while living in a particular social situation.

But there were differences among these philosophies over man. According to Charvaka, man is a mixture of matter and consciousness. He regarded man as a living being between birth and death. He asked men to live as freely as they could, enjoy life to the maximum capacity of pleasures and avoid pain as far as possible. He regarded the main aim of human life: 'Eat, drink and be merry'. This is called the hedonistic view of life.

Ambedkar rejected the hedonism as propounded by Charvaka. He did not believe in materialistic mode of life. His outlook was 'humanistic, his novel belief and standards were directly related to the human welfare in this empirical world'. Instead of total materialism, Ambedkar stood for contentment, both mental and spiritual. He said that 'man must grow materially as well as spiritually' and should not follow the hedonistic philosophy 'of being fatten pigs'. Hedonism of Charvaka, according to Ambedkar, was 'pig philosophy' of life. He, therefore, obviously rejected Charvaka's concept of man and society as it was founded on gross hedonism.

Charvaka had said that man is a mixture of matter and consciousness. This was not acceptable to Jainism. According to Jainism, man is composed of matter and soul. Although man is not the creation of God, yet his body contains an eternal soul. The concepts of *Karma, Mukti* (liberation), *Ahimsa* (non-violence), and *Triratna*, that is, right philosophy, right knowledge and right conduct, occupy a central place in Jainism. The Jainism emphasized a life of non-violence and non-possession.

Ambedkar did not accept the Jain view of man and society, because of its emphasis on extremes like total non-violence and asceticism. Ambedkar believed in avoiding the extremes. He laid emphasis on a way of life that is based on moderation.

In contrast to Charvaka and Jainism, the Buddhist concept of man and society was based on moderation. Its core principle was humanism. It was based on love and friendship. It emphasized righteous conduct based on moral precepts. It advocated liberty, equality and fraternity.

Ambedkar was attracted towards the Buddhism as it was based on moderation. Gross hedonism of Charvaka and the total non-violence and asceticism of Jainism, did not find place in Buddhism. What impressed Ambedkar most was the middle-path of Buddhism. He saw in Buddhism 'a new hope for man, new democratic element and new social order in accordance with the spirit of India's constitutional philosophy'.[3]

Christianity and Islam

Both the Christianity and Islam advocate theistic concept of man and society. They have given man a very insignificant place in the divine scheme of things. They discard the theory of man's *Karmas*. They believe that man was created by divine power, yet he had no direct link with God or Allah. 'In Christianity, Jesus Christ is the intermediary between God and man, whereas in Islam, Mohammad, as the last messenger of Allah, is there to be remembered after the name of Alṃighty'.

The Christian doctrine of man and society consists of belief in God, stress on the necessity of faith in God and belief in the original sin of man and the possibility of salvation through faith in Christ and the grace of God. In other words, God is the father who looks after man's needs if he obeys Him.

The Islamic concept of man and society is also based on the will and grace of Allah. The five pillars of the Islamic way of life are – belief in Allah, prayer, fasting, Zakat and pilgrimage to Mecca. Man and his natural laws are the creations of Allah. Allah is the owner of everything. Nothing belongs to man. The Islamic concept of society is a 'close corporation' of all those who believe in Allah and Mohammad as the last messenger.

Ambedkar did not believe in the theistic concept of man and society as advocated by the Christianity and Islam. He saw man in a different context 'of social situation wherein the oppressed man had to face and fight against the fundamentalists belonging to the theistic religions. He found man all alone, neither soul nor God helped him, and thus, his concept of man had a humanistic connotation, quite different from the concept of Hinduism, Jainism, Islam, Christianity, etc.'[4]

Medieval Concept

A host of saints, religious reformers and sects in medieval India had spoken about man and society. Through their ideas and preachings they had attacked the inequalities, caste discriminations, untouchability and other social evils. Though the saints and sects had discarded the exploiting tendencies that were widespread in medieval India, their efforts did not yield the desired results. Despite their honest efforts, 'the human relations in the empirical world did not come up to their expectation'. Since they could not eliminate the social evils, they brought God in their preachings and emphasized the spiritual equality of all beings before Him. God remained the governing principle of society. Even this idea of giving central place to God did not prove fruitful, because the Vedic principle of *Varnas* was deeply rooted. In short, the medieval concept of man and society was coated in God.

Ambedkar discarded the medieval concept of man and society. He did not believe in any kind of theistic concept. He did not want to leave man at the mercy of God. What he wanted was that the downtrodden should rise and stand himself for his own emancipation by his own efforts. He wanted that the man should free himself from the bondage of theism. In the words of D.R. Jatava:

> Ambedkar rejected all those concepts of man and society, which had brought the oppressed and the distressed in relation with the false idea of God, eternal soul, transmigration, re-incarnation, retributive theory of Karmas, etc. He was not satisfied with the medieval mode of social life, though he appreciated the social role of saints like Kabir and Nanak.[5]

Gandhian Concept

Mahatma Gandhi was the contemporary of Ambedkar. In his concept of man and society, Mahatma Gandhi had carried on the spirit of *Varnas.* He considered man to be a spiritual being, yet placed him under the 'divine social mechanism'. Though Gandhi condemned untouchability, he was an advocate of *Varnashrama Dharma.* He had a faith in the Vedic version of *Varnas.* He regarded it better than what was contained in the *Manusmriti.* In his view, 'the Vedic theory of Varnashrama Dharma could be applied to the whole world in order to establish the ideal of Ramarajya'. Mahatma Gandhi conceived and worked out a concept of Sarvodaya society. It was based on truth, non-violence and the creation of an egalitarian social order. In short, Gandhi also gave to God and soul a prominent place in his ideology.

The Gandhian concept of man and society did not attract the attention of Ambedkar. He regarded it as 'a replica of Varna and caste mechanism'. Ambedkar also pointed out certain contradictions in the Gandhian concept of man and society. On the one hand, Gandhi upheld divine social governance and on the other, he advocated the Sarvodaya society as a man-made society. According to Ambedkar, it was difficult to reconcile these two contrasting concepts of man and society. While rejecting the Gandhian concept, Ambedkar asked the downtrodden 'to be beware of Gandhism as it was based on a series of self-contradictions'.

The importance of Ambedkar lay in the fact that he advocated a new concept of man. According to him, 'it is man alone who could study himself in a particular situation and with the help and guidance of his fellow beings he could find out some solution for the problems he is confronted with. No body can help him except his own mind and effort, though it needs similar understanding of his fellow beings'.[6]

Ambedkar's political ideology is not a speculation regarding utopian ideal, but it is an attempt to provide empirical solutions to the complex problems of the society. Ambedkar in his writings and speeches has expressed his views on many political issues. They comprised the theoretical as well as practical aspects. From the functions of the state to the intricacies of every small detail of the Constitution, he has adumbrated his political ideology.

Social Humanism

The basic ideas of Ambedkar regarding man and society are reflected in his concept of social humanism or revolutionary humanism. The two cardinal components of social humanism are *Samata Samaj* and *Samatagrahi*. The former is his concept of society and the latter the concept of man. He believed that by experimenting and linking these two components, the depressed classes can achieve the goal of Samata Samaj (egalitarian society) and thus they can become changed men, that is, the true Samatagrahis.

Ambedkar pursued a humanist approach in Indian politics, because of his unflinching faith in the emancipation of the weak and the distressed people of society. His humanism was nurtured on social equality, the brotherhood of all human beings, meaning that man has to be interpreted in the perspective of '*bahujan hitaya, bahujan sukhaya*'. His humanism, therefore, had roots not only in the humanistic spiritual enlightenment but also in the materialistic well-being of man. To this end, the entire politics should be directed; otherwise the socio-economic emancipation of the weak and distressed would not be possible. Ambedkar said that since politics was associated with power and authority, it could be utilized for the well-being of the weaker sections of society. It must be made an instrument for liberating them from social tyrannies and deadening slaveries perpetrated in the names of order, culture and religion. As a defiant humanist, Ambedkar did not accept the metaphysical ideas like soul, God, heaven, *moksha,* transmigration, re-incarnation, etc. He had an ardent faith in man, the human-beings that live in society. Man for him, was the centre of study, and philosophy, as he thought of it, was nothing but 'a standard to measure the conduct of man' in the light of liberty, equality and fraternity. Ambedkar recognized the revolutionary nature of Buddhist philosophy and culture, for it was Buddha who heralded the spirit of revolt against social inequality, economic suppression, political tyranny and religious discrimination. The Buddhist movement asked the people to evolve right relations between man and man in all fields of life so that the principle of '*bahujan hitaya, bahujana sukhaya*' could be materialized. It prepared the foundation of a humanistic culture, a prosperous and glorious civilization, from which Ambedkar picked up his political and social ideas to fight against the forces of social determinism, political tyranny and economic oppression.

Ambedkar was an advocate of the theory of individual and political freedom, including the sanctity of human rights to all people. He believed not only in man's right to life, liberty and property, but also in moral rights of the individual to lead a respectable life in society. He wanted to strike a balance between liberty and equality. In it lies his attempt to harmonize political democracy and social democracy. For him political democracy could not last unless there lay at the base of it social democracy which recognized liberty, equality and fraternity as the principles of a good life. Without equality, liberty would produce the supremacy of the few over the many. Equality, without liberty, would kill individual initiative. Without fraternity, liberty and equality could not become a natural course of things. Thus, the principles of liberty, equality and fraternity formed an inseparable trinity in Ambedkar's theory of individual and political freedom.[7]

The political ideology of Ambedkar tilted in favour of the weaker sections of society, in order to develop a sturdy and robust sense of self-help, self-respect and self-emancipation. Only in this sense they could make themselves able to enjoy political freedom and individual rights. So he championed the cause of intellectual and social emancipation and stressed the need of removing glaring economic inequalities, otherwise the people suffering from those could blow up the democratic structure of our political system. Being a champion of freedom and human rights, Ambedkar was a great humanist who believed in cooperation, tolerance, fellowship, peace and progress, in social and political life and he wanted that the traditional shackles of caste and untouchability that had so long imprisoned the mind of Indian society should be removed forthwith. Ambedkar taught the significance of individual creativity and social obligation in his humanist approach to politics. A sincere concern for the lowly, the forlorn, the humiliated and the distressed was the positive feature of Ambedkar's political thought. As a humanist, he refused to be blind to the sufferings of the vast sections of humanity.

Social Precedes Political

The core of political thinking of Ambedkar is contained in two of his statements – the rights are protected not by law but by social and moral conscience of society, and a democratic form of government presupposes a democratic form of society. He considered democracy essentially as a form of society of a more associated living and a social conscience, the only safeguard of all rights. The roots of democracy are to be searched in social relationships, in terms of associated life among the people who form a society. For him, social relationships are the key to democracy. Ambedkar is a social democrat in spirit and practice. His special contribution to political thought lies in his linking up liberty, equality and fraternity to the concept of social democracy, which in turn, he relates to democracy as a form of government. He further reminds the limitations of social democracy in everyday functioning. As he categorically stated while addressing the Constituent Assembly (25 November 1949), 'Political democracy can not last unless there lies at the base of it social democracy' which means, 'a way of life which recognize liberty, equality and fraternity as the principles of life'. In this sense, he defined democracy as a form and method of government whereby revolutionary changes in the economic and social life of people are brought about without bloodshed.

In most of the speeches and writings of Ambedkar, the central theme is social reformism. He often debated and confronted on the issue of precedence of social over political issues. Politics have to be necessarily connected to the social issues. The very foundations of democracy lie in associated living in society. On the issue of giving primacy to social over political, he differed with Congress and socialists. This is well reflected in all his writings in general and especially in *Annihilation of Caste* and *What Congress and Gandhi Have Done to Untouchables.*

Political Ideology of Ambedkar

Ambedkar was influenced by all the major political traditions of his times. His political thought has emerged from the three grand traditions of political thought, i.e. liberal, conservative and radical. The unique feature about him is that he has transcended all these traditions. He was influenced by the ideas of John Dewey, the pragmatic American and his teacher. The Fabian Edwin R.A. Seligman had considerable impact on his thought. He often quoted Edmund Burke, the conservative British thinker, though we can't brand Ambedkar as conservative. Ambedkar's notion of liberty comes close to T.H. Green and H.J. Laski.

Ambedkar's philosophy is primarily ethical and religious. He thoroughly explored the Indian traditions and its philosophical systems in a unique way. He developed political concepts like democracy, justice, state and rights from his understanding of Indian society and the functioning of its institutions on the moral grounds. He was very critical of the institution of caste, which influences all the spheres of individual's life and the Indian society as a whole. He further discussed how individual is related to society and how individual's freedom is limited by other social forces. He was critical of authoritarian Hindu social order and argued in favour of democratic society. He probed into the moral and social foundations of India and gave new meaning to the lives of disadvantaged people. Reason and rationality played a role in his actions, writings and speeches. The methodology he used was very scientific rather than speculative. He was influenced by the assumptions of modernity. He was well informed in many areas of Indian history, polity, culture, anthropology and philosophy. He quoted many thinkers in his writings, including those who influenced him.

His political theory is rooted in moral premises. It is as an ideal to be realized. He was very much critical about the Hindu social order. He argued that Hinduism is not qualified to be a community. Buddhism was projected as the ideal having the value of community grounding on morality. He considered that Buddhism attempted to found society on the basis of 'reason' and 'morality'.

His conception of community was very novel. He did not confirm to either Hindu ideal community or Marxist conception of community based on participation in production process. His conception of community was moral and ethical. It was not automatically available for participation in common affairs. His idea of community had to be created through hard and torturous process of moral transformation.

Faith in Man

Man is the most important component of society and focal point of Ambedkar's political ideology. In Ambedkar's view, man was not created by any supernatural power. Man himself is the creator of his own social being including the resultant virtues and evils. The entire social order is the creation of all human beings, irrespective of whether it is good or bad. According to Ambedkar,

> Man is the creator, reformer and also rebellious by nature. He exists, because he creates, reforms and rebels against what he wishes to uproot. Man does so with all sense of justice and utility.[8]

Ambedkar was fully convinced of the uniqueness of man, his ability, courage and respective capacity. To him, man is not a means to an end but an end in himself. The ultimate purpose of all activity is the good of man, and as Aristotle put it, the good life. It is a man who gives meaning to society. Man, to him, is something more than God. He did not believe in God or any supernatural being who can help man and remove his miseries. Man himself can mitigate his own woes, slavery and poverty. He said,

> You must abolish your slavery yourself. Do not depend for its abolition upon God or superman. Your salvation lies in political powers and not in making pilgrimage and observance of fasts. Devotion to scriptures would not free you from your bondage, wants and poverty; your forefathers have been doing it for generations, but there has been neither respite nor even a slight difference in your miserable life in any way ... your religious fasts, austerities and penances have not saved you from starvation.[9]

This strong faith in human dignity, prestige and power led Ambedkar to discard the belief in fatalism or pre-determinism, held by the people, because it is responsible for social stagnation. Ambedkar was one of the great humanists. Being a great jurist, he rejected belief in the existence of God on rational and empirical grounds. He said:

> No body has seen God. People only speak of God. God is unknown and unseen. Nobody proves that God has created the world. The world has evolved and is not created. What advantage can there be in believing in God? It is unprofitable. It only ends in creating superstition.[10]

Ambedkar remarked,

> The appearance of Tulsi (a Hindu family plant) leaves around your neck will not relieve you from the clutches of the money-lenders; because you sing song of Rama, you will not get a concession in rent from the landlord ....[11]

To Ambedkar the belief in God or supernatural being is a belief in falsehood. He did not want man to depend upon any supernatural factor, because it leads man to loss of self-reliance, courage and confidence. A man forgets his creative ability and also the social responsibility that he is expected to exhibit with the help of his own intelligence and power. Ambedkar opposed supernaturalism and believed in man; he looked upon him as the centre of his thought and action.

Equality

A society, which does not preach equality between man and man, woman and man, is opposed to the principle of social justice. It is not worth surviving. Ambedkar had a deep faith in practical discipline and wisdom, as well as the principle of equality between man and man and the demand made upon the people to exercise some moral function. The principle of equality, though not practicable in an absolute manner is the foundation of justice – economic, social and political. It is also the basis of all democratic institutions. It is necessary factor in human relations. Without adopting it, society cannot have the best men.

Ambedkar believed men are born unequal. Some are robust, others are weaklings. Some have more intelligence, others have less or none. Some have more capacity, others have less. Some are well to do, others are poor. But all have to enter into what Darwin called 'the struggle for existence and survival of the fittest' only fittest tend to survive. Why is it so? This is because of rule of inequality. Ambedkar argued,

> In the struggle for existence, if inequality be recognized as the rule of the game, the weakest will always go to the wall. Should this rule of inequality be allowed to be the rule of life?[12]

Even more, to Nietzsche, only the superman must survive and rule over the masses in accordance with his own commands. In Nietzsche's philosophy, the role of equality has no value.

Ambedkar here differed from Darwin and Nietzsche. To him, the question however was: 'Is the fittest the best from the point of view of society'. But there is no positive answer. Ambedkar wrote,

> It is because of this doubt that religion preaches equality, for equality may help the best to survive even though the best may not be the fittest. What society wants is the best and not the fittest.[13]

Obviously, if society is to save the best from ruin, then the principle of equality between man and man must be adopted as the rule of life. Ambedkar further argued,

> Can you respect or believe in a religion which recommends action that brings happiness to oneself by causing sorrow to

> others, or happiness to others by causing sorrow to oneself or sorrow to both oneself and others?[14]

Ambedkar argued that a society based on *Varna* or caste is a society which is based on a wrong relationship. In fact, a pattern of social relationship based on hereditary or hierarchical order cannot, in any way, disburse justice to the members of the society as a whole.

Hero-Worship

Ambedkar was totally against hero-worship in the political life of the country, because it prevents a spirit of inquiry, a sense of creativity and an independent attitude of mind. Hero-worship is, in fact, against the spirit of democracy.

This caution is far more necessary in the case of India, than in the case of any other country. Because in India *Bhakti* plays a part in politics unequalled in magnitude than the part it plays apart in politics of any other country in the world. *Bhakti* may be a road to the salvation of the soul; but in politics, *Bhakti* or hero-worship is a sure road to degradation and eventual dictatorship.[15]

Ambedkar criticized Indian journalism for worshipping heroes blindly. 'Journalism was once profession, and it has now become a trade. It has no more moral function than the manufacture of soap; it does not regard itself as the responsible adviser of the public ... to accept a hero and worship him has become its principal duty'.[16] Such a trend in Indian journalism still persists. It gives undue publicity to those things, which need not deserve so much. Ambedkar observed:

> Never has the interest of the country has been sacrificed so senselessly for the propagation of hero-worship. Never has hero-worship become as blind as we see it in India today.[17]

According to Ambedkar,

> Hero-worship in the sense of expressing our unbounded admiration is one thing. To obey the hero without thinking is a totally different kind of hero-worship. There is nothing wrong in the former while the latter is no doubt a most pernicious

> thing'.[18] 'The former is only man's respect for anything noble and true; while the latter is the villain's fealty to his lord and is a sign of debasement. The former does not take away one's intelligence to think and independence to act. The latter makes one a perfect fool. The former involves no disaster to the state. The latter is the source of positive danger to it.[19]

In this way, Ambedkar warned the people against the spirit of irrational and blind hero-worship which today, prevails in the country. The condemnation of hero-worship will lead us to the new values of social and political life.

Thoughts on Society

Ambedkar's views of society are different from those of others. As observed by Aristotle, 'man is by nature and necessity a social animal. Hence he lives in society. Thus society is quite natural, essential, eternal and universal. It is instrumental in evolving such an atmosphere which would be conducive not only for the satisfaction of his primary wants, but for the development of his personality'.[20]

To Ambedkar, society was not an organism as some people hold; it was based essentially on human attitudes. The organization has certain essentials, which go to make up a real view of society. Ambedkar said:

> Men do not become a society by living in physical proximity any more than a man ceases to be a member of his society by living so many miles away from other men. Secondly, mere similarity in certain habits and customs is not enough to constitute a society. Parallel activity, even if similar, is not sufficient to bind men into a society.

He cited the living example of Hindu festivals. The different castes observe similar festivals, yet these parallel performances of similar festivals among the different castes and groups, have not been able to bind them into one 'integral whole'. The different castes do not possess things in common sense of spiritual unity and brotherhood, the soul of a society.

For constituting society, what is necessary for a man, is to share and participate in a common activity so that the same emotions are aroused in him that animates the others. Making the individual a sharer or partner in the associated activity so that he feels its success as his success, its failure as his failure, is the real thing that binds men and makes a society of them.[21]

Thus society is another name for more or less cordial inter-relationship between the human beings living in a geographical area.

Ideal Society

Ambedkar, however, visualized an ideal society based on 'liberty, equality and fraternity'.[22]

> An ideal society, in his view, should be mobile, should be full of channels for conveying a change taking place in one part to other parts. In an ideal society there should be many interests consciously communicated and shared. In other words there must be social endosmosis.[23]

He was, of course, quite aware of the fact that 'no where is human society one single whole. It is always plural'.[24] The questions to be asked in determining what an ideal society constitutes, are; How numerous and varied are the interests which are consciously shared by the groups? How full and free is the interplay with other forms of associations? Are the forces that separate groups and classes more numerous than the forces that unite? What social significance is attached to this group life.[25] Thus, he contemplates a society which is plural in character, but not static, rigid, traditional and orthodox in behaviour. It would give fair and equal chance to each and everybody for their progress and bind all the people into one common cultural bond. 'Ethnically' he stated, 'all people are heterogeneous. It is the unity of culture that is the basis of homogeneity'.[26] The unity of culture obviously could be developed only when the society is based on liberty, equality and fraternity.

Here, it is necessary to explain in brief the underlying principles of society: Liberty, equality and fraternity. According to Ambedkar, liberty includes civil liberty and political liberty. Equality means 'moral equality'. It is essentially an ethical value which recognizes equality of opportunity for each and every one without making any unjust distinctions between man and man, such as caste, class, creed or sex. However, equality also denies the undue right of strong to exploit the weak. Fraternity means, 'fellow feeling'. It is 'a sentiment which leads an individual to identify himself with the good of others'.[27] Fraternity is, he observed, 'the name for the disposition of an individual to treat the object of reverence and love and the desire to be in unity with his fellow beings'.[28] He defined justice as 'simply another name for liberty, equality and fraternity'[29] However, he gave much more importance to equality. 'Fraternity and liberty,' he stated, 'are really derivative notions. The basic and fundamental conceptions are equality and respect for human personality. Fraternity and liberty take their roots in these two fundamental conceptions. Equality is the original notion and respect for human personality is a reflexion of it. So that where equality is denied, everything else may be taken to be denied'.[30]

Means of Realizing the Ideal Society

It is, however not impossible to bring into reality the ideal society depicted by Ambedkar. This could be realized by the following ways.

First, it is necessary to do away with the caste-ridden social order. 'Reason and morality,' he states, 'are the two most powerful weapons in armoury of a reformer'.[31] 'They should be put to use. It is necessary "to destroy the belief in the sanctity of the Shastras", and to make every man and woman free from the thraldom of the Shastras'.[32] Then they would be willingly ready to inter-dine and inter-marry.

Second, Ambedkar suggested to accept the scheme of state-socialism; in which agricultural land and key industries would be nationalized. Neither there would be forced labour nor dependency. State-socialism ensures one-man, one-value; as such every individual would lead his life with dignity.

Third, he advocated that the political structure should be such that every one would be able to get equal share in the power. All the people would enjoy their fundamental rights and fulfill their obligations. Untouchability would be abolished and its practice would be an offence punishable by law. There should be non-parliamentary government so that the problem of minorities would be solved and they would be able to associate with the national stream.

Fourth, restructuring of the society, socially, economically and politically could be done not by bloody revolution but by constitutional means. He had no faith in any unconstitutional or extra constitutional methods like civil disobedience, strikes, fasts, etc. He contemplated to solve all the problems within the framework of the constitution.[33]

In sum, Ambedkar visualized an integrated society in which there is love for all and malice towards none.

Society and Individual

There are two contrasting views of the relation between society and individual. First, thinkers like Fitche and Hegal maintain that society is superior to individual. It has power and prestige over the individual interests. Society in itself is an independent body whose commands and rules are binding on all men and women. On the other hand, thinkers like Locke, maintain that society is nothing more significant than a name for a group of individuals, who alone are of significance and whose interests are alone based on the social order. To Locke, individuals are by nature 'all free, equal and independent'. Society is simply 'the people who make up its membership'.

Ambedkar, as a humanist, did not believe either in the superiority of social order or in the superiority of individual. Society exists in the individual and the individual cannot live without society. He believed in an integrated view of man and society. Man apart from man is impossible. In other words, the individual is not superior to society as capitalism holds: society is not superior to the individual, as communism believes, but society and the individual, to Ambedkar are inter-dependent. Ambedkar regarded man, in his political philosophy, as an element of society, not in isolation, as a rational being essentially endowed with reason; apart from society man has no meaning and value. It is the man who forms society and it is also the society that recognizes man and his relations with other human beings. Ambedkar's view of society and the individual may be summed up in the dictum – Man is the cause of social relations.

Man is not for social relations, but social relations are for man and therefore, the social relations should be based on the common rules of morality, in order to serve all men, in all circumstances and at all times.

In Ambedkar's view, man was not created by any supernatural power. Man himself is the creator of his own social being including the resultant virtues and evils. Man is the creator, reformer and also rebellion by nature. He exists, because he creates, reforms and rebels against what he wishes to uproot. Man does so with all sense of justice and utility.

Ambedkar asked: 'Who will remove the evils of poverty, ignorance, caste and untouchability?' The answer he gave was: 'Only man, no one else'. To sum up, one can quote the words of D.R. Jatava:

> The revealing aspect of Ambedkar's thoughts is that the matters, directly related to God and its creation, soul and its transmigration, reincarnation and its redeeming dose, citadel of heavenly abode, *Karma* and its effects on the next life, *moksha* (salvation) and its union with Brahma, miracles of the divine spirits, predetermined fate of human beings, etc. do not find place in Ambedkar's philosophy and approach to the problems of man and society. For these ideas and beliefs in no way improved the lot and quality of the life of the weak, the lowly and oppressed. Man is himself responsible for what he is, and it is only man, who can solve the problems and remove the hardships by his own efforts. Thus, the ideas and concepts that Ambedkar nourished defend an independent existence of man and ask human beings to be responsible, honest and liberal to maintain the order of social equality and rights of the individual. All this signifies the dignity of mankind.[34]

Thus, Ambedkar broke with the past and inaugurated a new and intensely interesting concept of man and society. He was inspired by his humanistic, rationalistic and pragmatic ideology. He rejected the theistic concept of man and society that man was a depraved animal, marked with graded inequality at birth and having no chance of progress. He abandoned the concept of ascetic morality and hedonism. He was less fearful of the Devil and the God. For him, everything was changing and man must stand on his own feet to meet the challenges of life and to end the social inequalities that had been rampant in Indian society. He thus introduced a new concept of man with emphasis on rationalism and empiricism. Man alone can do away with the age of bastards and profligate theologists who had created a society as if to illustrate Aristotle's saying that 'man, when separated from law and justice, is the worst of all animals'.

Notes

1. D.R. Jatava: *B.R. Ambedkar: Study in Society and Politics* (New Delhi, National Publishing House, 1998), pp. 28–29.
2. Dr Babasaheb Ambedkar *Writings and Speeches*, Vol. 3, 1987, p. 71.
3. D.R. Jatava, p. 33.
4. Ibid., p. 34.
5. Ibid., p. 35.
6. Ibid., p. 36.
7. Ibid., p. 8.
8. Ibid., p. 36.
9. Dhananjay Keer: *Dr. Ambedkar Life and Mission* (Bombay, Popular Prakashan Pvt. Ltd., 1990), p. 235.
10. Dr Babasaheb Ambedkar *Writings and Speeches*, Buddha and His Dhamma, Vol. 11 (Mumbai, Government of Maharashtra, 1992), p. 251.
11. Dhananjay Keer, op. cit. p. 218.
12. Dr. Babasaheb Ambedkar *Writings and Speeches*, Vol. 11, p. 308.
13. Ibid.
14. Ibid., p. 309.
15. Keer, op. cit. pp. 411–412.

16. B.R. Ambedkar: *Ranade, Gandhi and Jinnah* (Bombay, Thacker and Co. Ltd., 1943), pp. 48–49.
17. Ibid.
18. Ibid., p. 59.
19. Ibid., p. 60.
20. Op. cit. Sukhbir Singh: History of Political Thought, Vol. I (Meerut, Rastogi Publications, 2006), p. 144.
21. Dr Babasaheb Ambedkar *Writings and Speeches*, Vol. 1 (Bombay, Government of Maharashtra, 1979), p. 51.
22. Ibid., *Writings and Speeches* Vol. I, p. 57.
23. Ibid.
24. Ibid., p. 64.
25. Ibid.
26. Ibid., p. 6.
27. Dr Babasaheb Ambedkar *Writings and Speeches*, Vol. 3 (Bombay, Government of Maharashtra, 1987), p. 44.
28. Ibid., p. 97.
29. Ibid., p. 25.
30. Ibid., p. 66.
31. Dr Babasaheb Ambedkar *Writings and Speeches*, Vol. 1, op. cit. p. 74.
32. Ibid., p. 68.
33. R.K. Kshirsagar: *Political Thought of Dr. Babasaheb Ambedkar* (New Delhi, Intellectual Publishing House, 1992), p. 34.
34. D.R. Jatava: *B.R. Ambedkar: Study in Society and Politics* (New Delhi, National Publishing House, 1998), pp. 213–214.

7

State and Government

Ambedkar attached more importance to society than to the State. The State, to him, has 'to provide against internal disorder and external aggression'.[1] He did not consider State to be an absolute one. He did not agree with the idealist view of the State as a separate, mystic personality, 'a march of God on earth' upon which the individual depended for his existence. To him, it was the people who made the State and without them there could be no State. He laid stress on 'fellow-feeling' or 'social union' as one of the essential elements of the State. A mere assemblage of people in a definite territory could not be able to maintain its political sovereignty without attaining social integrity.

Ambedkar did not agree with Hobbes, Hegal, Bosanquet-the supporters of the absolute theory of the State. For him, the State is not machinery of exploitation or of violence, but a machinery to bring about desired welfare of the people. He proposed that the State is a means to achieve an end of well-being of the people. Of all the organizations, the State is a supreme organization, legally empowered to control and co-ordinate various aspects of social life, and capable to protect the people whenever it is necessary. To him, stability of the State rested on deference and sympathy. He was therefore, against the doctrine of civil disobedience. He remarked,

> 'To believe in civil disobedience is to believe in anarchy'.[2]

He conceived the State as an organization, the aim of which is (i) to maintain the right of every subject to life, liberty and pursuit of happiness and to free speech and free exercise of religion; (ii) to remove social, political and economic inequality by providing better opportunities to the submerged classes; and (iii) to make it possible for every subject to enjoy freedom from want and freedom from fear.[3] The State had to serve the interests of man and society as a servant and not as a master. To him, the true freedom of man was not merely political. It was also social, economic, intellectual and spiritual. According to Ambedkar, a good state was that which guaranteed protection against persecution of one community by another and also against internal disturbances, violence and disorder in any part of its territory.[4] It meant that the State is not an absolute one. It has to abide by the wishes of the people. There should be harmony between different organizations existing in the State.

State and Law

According to Ambedkar, law is an important factor in maintaining social peace and justice among different groups of people. It is a guardian of liberty and equality.

> All citizens are equal before the law and possess equal civic rights. Any enactment, regulation, order, custom or interpretation of law by which any penalty, disadvantage or disability is imposed upon or any discrimination is made against any citizen shall cease to have any effect.'[5]

To him, law was not only a legal function. It also regulates the life of the whole society and nation as well. It keeps within limits all men irrespective of caste, colour and creed. His faith in individual liberty and dignity led him to the rule of law. All persons have intrinsically equal value. It is the duty of a government to see that the people are not deprived of equality before law. Ambedkar said:

> No State shall make or enforce any law or custom which shall abridge privileges or immunities of citizens; nor shall any State deprive any person of life, liberty and property without due process of law; nor deny to any person within its jurisdiction equal protection of law.[6]

To see that there is no misrule of law is the most important function of a morally formed government of the people.

Ambedkar supported the principle of law behind the law. He was very much impressed by the American Constitution in which the concept of law behind the law is found. This concept follows the federal view of society and State. Society is an integrated way of living based on various voluntary associations. The State is one of them. There is to be a higher authority, the function of which is to define the relationships of each part to the whole. That is done by a State through law, though law is not essentially the product of the State.

The concept of law behind the law has been severely criticized, because it opens the door to rebellion and anarchy. However, according to Ambedkar, the possibility of revolt is everywhere if the masses are miserable and poor. Moreover, as he rightly opined, men do not rebel upon little affairs; light and transient causes and if the circumstances are such that give rise to rebellion, then the things must be changed and be set right. People count much in relation to formation of law.

According to Ambedkar, law is an obligation, which depends upon the social and moral conscience of the people. Ambedkar said:

> As experience proves, rights are protected not by law but by social and moral conscience of society. If social conscience is such that it is prepared to recognize the rights which law chooses to enact, right will be safe and secure. But if the fundamental rights are opposed by the community, no law, no parliamentary, no Judiciary can guarantee them in the real sense of the world.[7]

Ambedkar sought a harmony between the people and the legal power of the State.

State and Religion

Ambedkar's approach towards religion was rational, utilitarian and social. Religion strengthens social organization and promotes the spirit of devotion to the common good. Ambedkar has rightly observed that,

Religion as social force cannot be ignored.[8]

Following Burke, he stated that, true religion is the foundation of society, on the basis of which a civil government rests and seeks its sanction.[9]

However, Ambedkar's approach towards religion was not traditional one. Traditional and popular point of view of religion is, in his words, 'belief in God, belief in soul, worship of God, curing of the erring soul, propitiating God by prayers, ceremonies, and sacrifices'.[10] He did not believe in this traditional connotation of religion. His approach towards religion was rational, social and utilitarian. Religion strengthens social organization and promotes the spirit of devotion to the common good. The State therefore, should neither be indifferent nor coercive towards religion.

According to Ambedkar, the State should guarantee to its citizens,

> The liberty of conscience and the free exercise of his religion including the right to profess, to preach and to convert within limits compatible with public order and morality.[11]

He stood for the religious freedom. He knew that the religious freedom is the soul of Indian culture and civilization. He said:

> Parents and guardians should be entitled to determine the religious education of children up to the age of sixteen years.[12]

Ambedkar wanted his people to steer clear of all religious fanaticism; coercion which has been the bane of human society for long came in for scathing attack at his hand. It is pity that most of the people are prepared to die for the sake of their religion rather than live according to it. To him 'the centre to religion is man, the base is morality, the aim is secular welfare of mankind and means is the righteous conduct embedded in social responsibility that all human beings owe towards their fellow-beings living in human society and the relevance of a religion, consists in the trinity ideal of Liberty, Equality and Fraternity to bring about the necessary change in its social norms and human relations'.

He did not favour any religious coercion either by some community or by the State. State coercion, especially in religious matters was least desirable in Ambedkar's scheme of social and political life. He had a strong faith in the principle of Secularism. To law, all religions are respectable. Ambedkar said, 'The State shall not recognize any religion as state religion'.[13] Secularism is a blend of tolerance, liberty and equality leading towards a synthesis between nationalism and internationalism, though even in this rational attitude, some people may discover an element of isolationism. But he did not tolerate wrong ideals and practices. The practice of caste and untouchability, economic exploitation and social tyranny, can no longer be tolerated. His secularism was of a radical type and rebelled against any religious ill treatment, hatred and discrimination.

Linguistic States

In a memorandum submitted in 1948, to the Linguistic Provinces Commission, Ambedkar had expressed his views on the reorganization of states on linguistic basis. While acknowledging the danger to the unity of India inherent in the creation of linguistic provinces with their pride in race, language and literature developing into mentalities of being separate nations, Ambedkar saw certain definite political advantages in the reconstitution of provinces on linguistic basis. On receipt of the report of the States Reorganization Commission, he found it necessary to modify his views to some extent, and penned his final views on the formation of linguistic states in the book titled *Thoughts on Linguistic States* which was published in 1955. He gave his valuable opinion on the problem, the country was facing, of States reorganization. Obviously, after having witnessed from very close angle, the developments taking place in respect of linguistic reorganization of the states from 1947 to 1955, he was actually impelled to suggest his solution on the very acute problem of states reorganization.

Ambedkar observed that, in general, 'One State, One Language' is a universal feature of almost every State – Germany, France, Italy, England and the United States of America, etc. in the western hemisphere, it is a general 'rule' and not a dogma. Wherever there has been departure from this rule, there has been danger to the State. The danger of disintegration and degeneration is inherent in multilingual states. Ambedkar said 'India cannot escape this fate, if it continues to be a congery of mixed States'.[14] A multilingual State is, thus, unstable and a unilingual State is stable.

To Ambedkar, the unity and integrity of India was most important. While accepting the principle of linguistic provinces, he stated,

> 'It must provide against the break up of India's unity'.[15]

He very rightly observed:

> A State is built on fellow-feeling. The existence of this fellow-feeling is the foundation of a stable and democratic State.[16]

However, he observed that the fellow-feeling is a 'double-edged feeling' as it creates 'fellowship for one's own kith and kin and anti-fellowship for those who are not one's own kith and kin'.[17] While creating fellow-feeling it is imperative to avoid the possibility of anti-fellow-feeling. Thus, the solution must fulfill two tests. One, it should be such that it should create fellow-feeling and two, it should avoid the possibility of anti-fellow-feeling.

He was, however, aware of the fact that homogeneity does not require linguistic unity. He said very categorically that, 'the facility to speak a common language does not ensure homogeneity which is the result of many other factors'.[18] In India, there is close relation between the caste, language and region. In Maharashtra, the majority caste is Maratha. In Andhra, the Reddis, Kammas and Kapu Communities are in dominating position. If the States are organized on linguistic basis, it would mean 'handing over of Swaraj to a communal majority'[19] and they may 'go to war against other States'.[20] Therefore, he thought that,

> There must be definite checks and balances to see that communal majority does not abuse its power under the garb of a linguistic state.

He provides linguistic basis of the State, at the same time he attempts to maintain India's unity.[21]

He favoured linguistic principle as the basis of States reorganization, but objected to making the language of the State its official language. He thought that there should be one official language through-out the country. He thought for the purpose of maintaining cultural unity of the province, it is not necessary to have the language of the province as its official language. At the beginning making State language as its official language may not be harmful, but in the long run it may prove to be fatal to the national unity. This would result in having several small nationalities often antagonistic to each other, in a country. In that case unity and integrity of the country would be in grave jeopardy.[22]

Ambedkar thought that the States should be reorganized on the basis of 'one state, one language.'[23] In India numerous languages are spoken. Therefore, he thought that 'One State, One Language' was the practical and efficacious formula of States reorganization.

The official language of India should be Hindi and until India becomes fit for this purpose, English'.[24] A linguistic State with its regional language as its official language may easily develop into an independent nationality. The road between an independent nationality and an independent State is very narrow. If this happens, India will cease to be modern India we have and will become the medieval India consisting of variety of States indulging in rivalry and warfare. Even in federal units also Hindi should be the official language and until a particular State becomes fit to have Hindi as its official language, English should be continued. He was however, not ready to accept the regional language as the official language of the State, the regional language should be one of the criteria on which the State should be organized, but it should not be the official language of the State.

By linguistic States he meant one of two things. It can mean that all people speaking one language must be brought under the jurisdiction of one State. It can also mean that people speaking one language may be grouped under many States provided each State has under its jurisdiction people who are speaking one language.[25] The Commission took the view that the creation of one single State for all people speaking one and the same language was the only rule to be observed.

Thus, Ambedkar contemplated to instill cultural unity in the respective States by creating them on linguistic basis and in the nation but accepting Hindi or English as a national official language. This may prove to be good to prevent the possibility of linguistic hatred, narrow parochialism and petty communalism and to instill the sense of fellow-feeling in the people throughout the nation. Ambedkar said,

> It would be better if India follows the road of linguistic States. Though there are some difficulties. Yet there is no other way than to make the way to democracy easy, to remove racial and cultural difference.[26]

In most emphatic terms, he declared,

> Any Indian, who does not accept this proposal as a part and parcel of a linguistic State, has no right to be an Indian .... He cannot be an Indian in the real sense of the word except in a geographical sense .... With regional language as official languages, the ideal to make Indian one united country and to make Indians, Indians first and Indians last will vanish.[27]

However, his thoughts were not properly appreciated in those days. The organization of the States in India is not based on any definite principle as such. Therefore, the problem of discord and disharmony between Centre and States as well as the State and State is in vogue today. The problem of north versus south, linguistic majority versus linguistic minority and communal majority versus communal minority are still in existence today. Consequently, the secessionist or separatist forces have become more active, assertive and militant. In order to achieve communal harmony, national integration and economic development, India needs to adhere to his thoughts as expeditiously as possible.[28]

Government

What is government? According to Garner, the government is, 'the agency or machinery through which common policies are determined and by which common affairs are regulated and common interests promoted. Without a government the population would be an incoherent, unorganized anarchic mass with no means of collective action'. According to Robert Dahl, the government is an organization 'that successfully upholds a claim to the exclusive regulation of the legitimate use of physical force in enforcing its rule within a given territorial area'. Thus, the government is one of the essential elements of the State. It is like a managing committee which manages the affairs of any company or organization, manages the affairs of the State. The government is a machinery which enacts the laws, which implements the laws and which interprets the laws. It consists of three organs – legislature, executive and judiciary.

Ambedkar however opined that,

> Government is based on the obedience to authority.[29]

He stated that, 'Willingness to obey the authority of government is a factor equally necessary for the success of any scheme of self government'.[30] Willingness to render obedience to the authority of the government is as essential for the stability of government as the unity of political parties on the fundamentals of the state. It is impossible for any sane person to question the importance of obedience in the maintenance of the state. He enumerated the factors on which political obligation is based. They are indolence, deference, sympathy, fear and reason. He observed:

> To believe in civil disobedience, is to believe in anarchy.[31]

He firmly believed that, 'law and order is the medicine of the body politic, and when the body politic goes sick this medicine must be administered'.[32] It is the one and only means which can save the country from anarchy. Thus Ambedkar prescribed civil disobedience as a last resort.

He however wanted to have responsible and good government, he said,

> We must have a government, in which the men in power will give their undivided allegiance to the best interest of the country. We must have a government in which men in power, knowing where obedience will end and resistance will begin, will not be afraid to amend the social and economic code of life which the dictates of justice and expediency so urgently call for.[33]

Forms of Government

There are several forms of government, such as monarchy, oligarchy, democracy and dictatorship etc. Ambedkar favoured democracy and condemns anarchy and dictatorship. He realized that dictatorship and anarchy, both are incompatible with individual's liberty. This is why, he felt the need of a sufficient strong and responsible government under which liberties are well protected, although, certain functional and constitutional checks should be brought to bear upon the government so that the liberty to the common man is not jeopardized.

Like Rousseau, Ambedkar was also conscious of the fact that the majority rule may not necessarily be, as it is not always, in the interest of the whole community. He was aware of the fact that the majority rule may result in oppression of the individual or minorities. Ambedkar's main concern, therefore, was to safeguard the individual as against the tyranny of the majority. And this he aimed to achieve not by taking away all power from the government and reducing it to a nullity, but by formulating a scheme of 'checks and balances' on the lines of American Constitution.[34] But the nature and form of checks and balances must be determined by two considerations. Ambedkar said:

> The first necessity is of establishing a correlation between the political Constitution and social institutions of the country, if democracy is to make real. As the social institutions of countries differ in their form, the checks and balances in its political Constitutions must also differ. The second is the necessity of providing a firm flooring to the servile classes

> against the possibility of their being pressed down by the governing classes, by reason of their superior power.[35]

From the above view point, Ambedkar maintained that the will of the majority is essential for good as well as responsible government, but for him it should necessarily provide concessions and considerations to the will of the minorities. Hence, as a staunch advocate of parliamentary system of government, and in fact, as a practical political scientist, he introduced this system in the Constitution of free India, which was welcomed by all political thinkers of the East and the West. Referring to the preamble to the Constitution of India, Barker said, 'I am more moved to quote it because I am proud that the people of India should begin their independent life by subscribing to the principles of a political tradition which we in the west call western, but which is now something more than western'.[36] This Constitution provides equality of opportunity to all with equal human rights and maintains the parliamentary system and upholds individual liberty.

Parliamentary Government

The Constitution of India provides for a parliamentary system of government on the British model, in preference to the presidential form of the American model. A section of the House led by K.T. Shah, that was opposed to this system, pleaded for the adoption of the presidential system of the American type. To them, parliamentary system stood for instability and can work only in a political society with a high degree of political maturity and constitutional discipline. They wondered whether such pre-requisites were available in the political life of India. The parliamentary system, in view of its removable character of the executive, might lead to political chaos and constitutional crisis. But the Draft Constitution envisaged a removable parliamentary system of executive. Ambedkar gave the following explanation, justifying it:

> A democratic executive must satisfy two conditions – (i) it must be a stable executive and (ii) it must be responsible executive. Unfortunately it has not been possible so far to

> devise a system which can ensure both in equal degree. You can have a system which can give you more stability but less responsibility, or you can have a system which gives you more responsibility but less stability. Looking at it from the point of view of responsibility, a non-Parliamentary Executive being independent of Parliament tends to be less responsible to the legislature, while a Parliamentary Executive being more dependent upon a majority in Parliament becomes more responsible. The Parliamentary system differs from a non-Parliamentary system in as much as the former is more responsible than the latter but they also differ as to the time and agency for assessment of their responsibility. The Draft Constitution in recommending the Parliamentary system of executive has preferred more responsibility to more stability.

To some of those who were familiar with Ambedkar's views on the subject, this came as a great surprise and a visible transformation in his views. Not long before he had expressed in most categorical terms his preference for an irremovable non-parliamentary system in the Memorandum he submitted to the Constituent Assembly on behalf of the All-India Scheduled Castes Federation. It was published in 1947, under the title *States and Minorities*. He had provided in this model Constitution that the Union and State Executive shall be non-parliamentary (not removable before the term of the legislature). He, obviously, had in his mind not only the American but the Swiss model too, when he provided that 'Members of the Executive could be non-legislators in which case they shall not have the right to sit in the legislature, speak, vote and answer questions'.[37] He had also stated that the special features and requirements of the parliamentary executive, being what they are, make the system absolutely unsuitable for India. Further, 'if adopted, it would result in permanently vesting executive power in a communal majority … (which) will be free to run the administration according to its own ideas of what is good for the minorities. Such a state of affairs could not be called democracy; it will have to be called imperialism'. The introduction of such a system of government 'will be full of menace to the life, liberty and pursuit of happiness of the minorities in general and of the untouchables in particular'.[38] He was also of the opinion that the parliamentary system of the British type would not be successful in India and its chances were 'very slender'. He was convinced that 'in view of the clashes of castes and creeds there is bound to be a plethora of parties and groups in the Legislature in India', which may result in the instability of the executive.

Ambedkar had thought, an irremovable executive, modelled largely on American type would serve the following purpose:

1. To prevent the majority from forming a government without giving any opportunity to the minorities to have a say in the matter.
2. To prevent the majority from having exclusive control over administration and thereby make the tyranny of the minority by the majority impossible.
3. To prevent the inclusion by the majority, in the executive, representatives of the minorities who have no confidence on the minorities.
4. To provide a stable executive necessary for good and efficient administration.

One fails to understand as to why there was such a complete swing to the opposite in Ambedkar's views and stand on this problem as the Chairman of the Drafting Committee. As indicated in his speech in the Assembly, he defended the parliamentary system with a removable executive. He argued that such a system with a removable executive provided a greater degree of responsibility, which was the need of the country.

This sudden transformation in his views can possibly be explained in the light of the following points.

In the first place, it should be remembered that his proposals as contained in *States and Minorities* were intended mainly to be the demands of a minority group. He had, therefore, to plead in it for and on behalf of the scheduled castes and lay emphasis on such things as would protect their interests at any rate. His plea for an irremovable executive was one such. But as the principal architect of the Constitution, he could not afford to think only on a sectional basis and give expression to his personal views and preferences. Secondly, Indians had developed familiarity with parliamentary institutions – at least from a distance, during the long period of British rule. Finally, a more important factor than anything else was, that Prime Minister Nehru had already expressed his preference for the parliamentary system in his speech earlier in the Assembly. Pandit Nehru was the Chairman of the Union Constitution Committee, on the basis of whose report, the Drafting Committee had to proceed. The support for adopting this system came from an important section of the Assembly consisting of K.M. Munshi, Sir Alladi Krishnaswami Iyer and others.

Ambedkar had, therefore, no alternative but to give legal shape to the parliamentary system with a removable executive by writing it into the Constitution and justify its adoption by the Assembly.

Nation and Nationalism

Closely related to the State and government is Ambedkar's concept of nation and nationalism. The concepts of nationalism and national integration assume prime importance especially in Indian society which is more heterogeneous than homogeneous. They are obviously the indicator of the nation's strength, tranquillity and over all progress. Ambedkar defined nationalism as,

> A social feeling, it is feelings of a corporate sentiment of oneness which makes those who are charged with it to feel that they are kith and kin. It is a feeling of 'consciousness of kind' which on the one hand binds together those who have it and on the other severs them from those who are not of their kind. It is a longing not to belong to any other group; but their own.[39]

National feeling is a feeling of consciousness of kind. It is in a sense belonging together and leaving aside the rest. This national feeling is double edged feeling. It is at once feeling fellowship of one's own kith and kin and anti-fellowship feeling for those who are not one's own kith and kin.

Though to Ambedkar, national feeling has both a fellowship and an anti-fellowship element, there is no room for race-hatred, caste-feeling and social prejudices in his concept of nationalism.

He would definitely agree with Vivekananda who preached 'I am thoroughly convinced that no individual or nation can live by holding itself apart from the community of others, whenever such an attempt has been made under false ideas of greatness, policy or holiness – the result has always been disastrous to the secluding one'.

Thus, national integration is a process in which people though divided on many counts, feel emotionally one. It is a common sentiment of being one community, irrespective of the factors, if any, which foster plurality. It is a fact that there are several divisive forces which pose potential danger to our national integration; such as casteism, regionalism, linguism, communalism, capitalism, feudalism and many others. It is very difficult, though not impossible, to achieve national integration in such a traditional society.

Ambedkar thought that the pre-condition of achieving national integration was the realization of the fact that India was not a nation. He categorically said that, 'I am of the opinion that in believing that we are a nation, we are cherishing a great delusion. How people divided into several thousands of castes be a nation? The sooner we realize that we are not as yet a nation in the social and psychological sense of the word the better for us'.[40] He took a very realistic view of the Indian society that, in this country one finds really two nations – a ruling nation and a nation which is a subject nation[41] 'touchables and untouchables'. Thus, when once the people in India realize that they are divided between several nationalities, they would, naturally try to find out rationally the cause of such divisions and strive to root out the fissiparous tendencies from the society. This shows his pragmatic approach towards the ills of the society which enabled him to make a correct diagnosis of it and suggest appropriate, effective and corrective measures for the same.

Indian society is, however, infected with following elements which directly or indirectly hamper the growth of national integration in our country.

1. Undoubtedly, casteism has played an unparalleled havoc in Indian society. It is the outcome of caste system which has got religious sanction under the *Vedas* and the *Shastras*. Therefore, it is deeply rooted in the Hindu society and people could not dare to oppose it due to fear of divine wrath. The caste system has 'completely disorganized and demoralized the Hindu'.[42]

   He exhorted that the real remedy on the evil of caste system is to have inter-caste marriage. Fusion of blood is necessary for removing the barriers of caste. However, he was aware of the difficulty in inter-caste marriages. According to him caste is a notion either of superiority or inferiority vis-à-vis other castes. Unless and until the 'notion' as such changes there cannot be fusion of blood. That 'notion' requires to be changed first. In order to change that 'notion', it is necessary 'to destroy the belief in the sanctity of the *Shastras*,'[43] 'to dynamite the *Shastras*'. In order to reform the puritan Hindu society, he had suggested certain measures, which were – (i) there should be one standard book of religion (ii) priesthood must at least cease to be hereditary and (iii) there should not be discrimination against any one on the ground of caste or untouchability.

2. Ambedkar did not ignore the importance of economic factor in the formation of an integrated society. He thought that in free India there should not be economic inequality and exploitation either by landlords or money lenders and feudals in the society. He categorically said that, the freedom which was being demanded and the Britishers were to concede, was the freedom to few money lenders and feudals. 'Freedom to money lenders and feudal only does not mean freedom to the country. When the peasants and labourers would be free, then only the country would be free in the real sense'.

   He introduced a Bill to amend the Bombay Hereditary Office Act, 1874 in Bombay Legislative Assembly in March 1928, in order to rescue the Watandar Mahars from the bondage of hereditary work as Mahars. He formed Independent Labour Party in 1936, especially to vent the grievance of the landless, poor tenants, agriculturists and workers. There was stated in the manifesto of the party that they would undertake to make laws for the welfare of the peasants and workers. It was the policy of the party to nationalize by industries in the larger interests. He wrote in his book 'State and Minorities' the objectives of the government would be, *inter alias*, 'to make it possible for every subject to enjoy freedom from want and freedom from fear'.[44] Further, he provided the scheme for state socialism for economic equality.

But, he thought that the social order should precede economic order, otherwise all the efforts to bring a new economic order would be futile. Therefore, he thought to reform the social order at the first so as to facilitate the arrival of new economic order which was set to take place under state socialism. Thus he did not foresee an integrated society without eradicating exploitation and economic inequality.[45]

3. It is but, a fact that the Indian society is divided on the basis of narrow parochialism and petty linguism. In order to overcome the barriers of regionalism and linguism, he prescribed some remedies:

   First, the state should be organized on the basis of 'One State, One Language' formula and not on 'One language, One State'. As far as possible, they should be small and uniform in size and equal in resources.

   Second, the official language of all states should be Hindi instead of respective regional languages.

   Third, in addition to one central capital there should be a second capital preferably at Hyderabad in the south for bridging the gulf of mistrust between north and south.

   Fourth, adequate provisions should be made for protection of the minorities (in the state organized according to the new scheme).

   This abundantly speaks for his realistic sense and gesture of bridging the gap between several region and linguistic minorities. His idea of small and viable states and a strong

Central Government was beneficial to both the union as well as the states, and this could have been useful in minimizing the emergence of caste politics in the states. Small states would have been useful in avoiding regional imbalance also.[46]

4. Communalism is a big threat to national integration. There are several communities in our country, such as Hindu, Muslims, Scheduled Castes, Tribes, Sikhs, Jains, Buddhists and Christians.

   In the pre-Independent era, the communal problem was obviously the problem of Hindus, Muslims and the Scheduled Castes. Their separate religious status and socio-economic situation were, of course, the root causes of the communal problem. However, this problem was becoming more and more conspicuous with the growth of the aspiration of respective communities to share power in and take benefits of the growing democratic institutions in our country.

   Ambedkar, the spokesman of the depressed classes, said, 'The depressed classes form a group by themselves; which is distinct and separate from the Muhammadens and although they are included among the Hindus, they in no sense form an integral part of that community'.[47] Their unique socio-religious and economic position constrained him to state that,

   'The scheduled castes are more than a minority and any protection given to the citizens and to minorities will not be adequate for the scheduled castes.[48]

   He said emphatically to the majority Hindus that,

   'In the name of democracy there must be no tyranny of the majority over the minority'.[49]

   In order to solve the problem of scheduled castes, he proposed some solutions as:

   (a) There should be separate electorate for the scheduled castes to adequate reservations in the legislature.
   (b) They should have reservation in the services in proportion to their population.

(c) Provisions should be made for facilitating higher education of scheduled castes; and

(d) They should be given waste and uncultivated land for the purpose of agriculture and a separate Settlement Commission should be appointed for that purpose.

Ambedkar was very optimistic regarding national integration. He said that, 'I am quite convinced that given time and circumstances nothing in the world will prevent this country from becoming one'.[50] But he further said, that the most vital need of the day is to create among the mass of the people the sense of a common nationality, the feeling not that, they are Indians first and Hindus, Muhammadens or Sindhis and Kanarese afterwards, but that they are Indians first and Indians last. If that be the ideal then it follows that nothing should be done which will harden local patriotism and group consciousness'.[51]

Although Ambedkar was a staunch nationalist and visualized an integrated society in the real sense, he was misunderstood by some obscurantist and communalists. He was called an anti-national, communalist and 'stooge' in the hands of Britishers. However he was so sincere in his cause, firm in his determination, uncompromising in his conviction, unparallel in his intellectual honesty and confident of his ability that he remained unperturbed irrespective of all the criticisms against him.

Ambedkar's perspective of national integration was very comprehensive, rational and real. He visualized an integrated society, based on liberty, equality, fraternity and social justice. He was of the firm opinion that unless the society is based on these principles, it cannot achieve integration at all. Mere religious or ideological appeal without substantial change in the structure, philosophy and attitude will not be helpful in achieving a cohesive society.

Nationalism and Patriotism

Nationalism and patriotism are two different, but relative terms. Both are such vital ideas related to human society without having any relation to human needs and social conditions, that their true meaning cannot be determined. But in this country, as Ambedkar observed:

> Nationalists and patriots are a peculiar people. A patriot and a nationalist in India is one who sees with open eyes his fellowman treated as being less than man. But his humanity does not rise in protest. He knows that men and women for no cause are denied their human rights. But it does not prick his civic sense to helpful action. He finds whole classes of people shut out from public employment. But it does not rouse his sense of justice and fair play. He perceives hundreds of evil practices that injure man and society. But they do not sicken him with disgust.[52]

To Ambedkar, patriotism demanded action in right direction and reaction against all wrongs. Mere attachment to the land is half-hearted patriotic spirit. He wished a patriot and a nationalist to have in them a full-blooded faith in doing justice and good to the needy, the lowly and the weak.

Ambedkar, crusader of the downtrodden masses, did not strive for power in the name of patriotism. As he observed, 'the patriot's one cry is power and more power for him and for his class'.[53] He did not belong to such a class of patriots in Indian society – 'I am glad I do not belong to that class of patriots – I belong to that class which takes its stand on democracy and which seeks to destroy monopoly in every shape and form. Our aim is to realize in practice our ideal of one man and one value in all walks of life, political, economic and social'.[54]

To Ambedkar, patriotism and nationalism meant democracy, liberty and equality. His view of patriotism and nationalism obviously created a spirit of social brotherhood and a determination to improve the lot of the people who live in the same country but are not otherwise treated as full men. Patriotism should attach more importance to bettering the life of the degraded masses, uneducated people and sick citizens. And it is because of the awakening of such a spirit in patriots and nationalist that they demand the ending of imperialism, bureaucracy, social tyranny, forced labour, casteism, communalism, poverty, illiteracy, unemployment, ill treatment and insecurity.

Secularism and Nationalism

Ambedkar always believed in only one nationalism, i.e. the Indian nationalism. He did not hold any religious view of nationalism such as Hindu nationalism or Muslim nationalism. Some people have associated it with the rule of the majority and its monopoly of power, which Dr Ambedkar vehemently opposed. Ambedkar said:

> Unfortunately for the minorities in India, Indian nationalism has developed a new doctrine which may be called the Divine Right of the Majority to rule the minorities according to the wishes of the majority. Any claim for the sharing of power by the minority is called communalism while the monopolizing of the whole power by the majority is called Nationalism.[55]

Ambedkar never allowed his nationalistic spirit to submit to such a type of irrationalism.

However, secularism did not mean that the state shall not take into any consideration 'the religious sentiments of the people'. It meant that there should be no imposition of any religion upon the people. They can accept different religions in accordance with their conscience. But he did not want irrational nationalism in the name of religion. Religious difference, though natural in Indian society, should not in any way hamper the development of a strong current of national unity. What he wanted was that 'religion should be the binding force which deepens the solidarity of human society'. It is the social solidarity, which can lead the people to happiness, national unity, military strength and political stability.

Thus Ambedkar, as the champion of secularism, advocated for religious tolerance and condemned all kinds of hypocrisy and oppression in the name of religion and nationalism. Otherwise, national relations will be a violation of the basic principles of democracy and contrary to the best interest of government and religion. Nationalism and secularism should try to build up a fellowship of believers by bringing them together for emotional integration and social unity.

A Rational Attitude towards Nationalism

'Nationalism, to Ambedkar, was not the spirit of the whole revivalism of India's past. No doubt, he looked back to the past with respect and reverence, but he believed in making a distinction between a good or a bad, a right or a wrong, a workable or an unworkable scheme of social and national life'.[56] His attitude towards nationalism was rational. He wanted the people to discard what is not good and true in the past and invited them to study the present. In Buddhist traditions, he found many things useful for the man today.

Ambedkar did not like extreme nationalism, which creates a spirit of intolerance. Extreme nationalism easily develops into irrationalism and is hardly conducive to human welfare. Ambedkar knew well that humanity progresses only when there is a spirit of co-operation, i.e. social brotherhood, and not when there is too much of inequality and injustice. Nationalism, to him, should not be prejudiced and inhuman, aggressive and intolerable.

Nationalism, in Ambedkar's political philosophy, demands not only the liberation of every slave country, but also the freedom for all subjects and subjugated masses even in free countries. So nationalism to him appeared as something more than mere political freedom. The real object of nationalism is the people. Without raising the whole level of the common masses, nationalism cannot survive. It has to broaden the minds of men in the line of liberal humanitarian nationalism, preserving at the same time, certain ideals and objectives, the material and spiritual growth of man and unity of all human beings. Nationalism is always based on cultural and spiritual factors. It is closely related with man's life, pride and activity. Ambedkar said:

> Nationalism is a fact which can neither be eluded nor denied. Whether one calls it an irrational instinct or positive hallucination, the fact remains that it is potent force which has a dynamic power to disrupt empires. Whether nationalism is the cause or the threat to nationalism is the cause, is a difference of emphasis only.[57]

He regarded nationalism as a real force in human life. In fact nationalism sometimes is so blind that it causes enmity and anger even among those who have lived together for centuries. Muslim nationalism was so irrationally intense that it disrupted the long and aged unity of Indian people.

Ambedkar recognized the efficacy of nationalism as the most dynamic forces of modern history. National unity was the fundamental aim of his political thought. The spirit of his nationalism started with humanistic cause of the poorest of poor in the world. He wanted equality and civil rights for those who were deprived of them for centuries past. His nationalism was not merely an empty state of mind, but it was based on a full-blooded humanistic faith in the greatness of his country and the dignity of its citizens.

Ambedkar wanted the spiritual unity of the people. He said, 'What is wanted is not merely political unity but a true union of heart and soul, in other words social unity. Political unity is worth nothing, if it is not the expression of real union. It is as precarious as the unity between persons, who without being friends become allies of each other ... personally; I do not think that permanent union can be made to depend upon the satisfaction of mere material interests'. It is clear that the unity of the country not only political and social, but also spiritual, was the supreme concern of his freedom movement.

The real thing is the recognition of nationalism as strong enough to produce war in spite of the people's resistance. It has devastatingly enough, proved itself to be no outward creed but a vital force to be reckoned with. Obviously Ambedkar regarded nationalism as a real force in human life. It has now become an affair of life and death to most of the people in the world. He defined nationalism as an individual instinct related to human mind. This is a very strong force that can disrupt the empires, and this instinct is always undestroyable. Nationalism, according to him is the absence of caste system. The social brethren irrespective of class, creed or caste and the brotherly interaction in the society meant nationalism. The people inter-related and tied with each other with the strong instinct of brotherhood and oneness meant nationalism. Dr Ambedkar always strongly opposed the terrorist activities in the name of national love, the conservative activities of slavery and hero-worship.

Ambedkar's views about nation and nationalism formed an important aspect of his political ideology. His concept of democracy clearly indicated that democracy means co-existence, the roots of democracy are always found in social interaction. Ambedkar's political thought must satisfy two conditions. Nationalism in relation to a nation should be based fundamentally on a strong feeling of social unity. Without it, nationalism cannot exist. And nationalism, in relation to internationalism, should be founded on human brotherhood. Otherwise, it may create conflicts and cause wars among the different countries of the world. In other words, nationalism should not be a tyranny and menace to any other community and country.

Notes

1. B.R. Ambedkar: *State and Minorities* (Bombay, Thacker and Co. Ltd., 1947), p. 3.
2. B.R. Ambedkar: *Pakistan or Partition of India* (Bombay, Thacker and Co. Ltd, 1946), p. 294.
3. B.R. Ambedkar: *State and Minorities*, p. 3.
4. Ibid., pp. 108–111.
5. Ibid., p. 9.
6. Ibid.
7. B.R. Ambedkar, *Buddha and His Dhamma* (Bombay, Siddhartha College Publication, 1957), pp. 34–35.
8. Dr Babasaheb Ambedkar *Writings and Speeches*, Vol. 3 (Bombay, Government of Maharashtra, 1987), p. 23.
9. Dr Babasaheb Ambedkar *Writings and Speeches*, Vol. 1, p. 23.
10. B.R. Ambedkar: *Buddha and His Dhamma*, p. 226.
11. B.R. Ambedkar: *State and Minorities*, p. 11.
12. Ibid.

13. Ibid.
14. B.R. Ambedkar: *Thoughts on Linguistic States* (Jalandhar, Bheem Patrika, 1977), p. 11.
15. Dr Babasaheb Ambedkar *Writings and Speeches*, Vol. 1 (Bombay, Government of Maharashtra, 1979), p. 104.
16. Ibid., pp. 143–144.
17. Ibid.
18. Ibid., p. 106.
19. Ibid., p. 137.
20. Ibid., p. 135.
21. R.K. Kshirsagar: *Political Thought of Dr. Babasaheb Ambedkar* (Delhi, Intellectual Publishing House, 1992), p. 175.
22. Ibid., p. 175.
23. Dr Babasaheb Ambedkar *Writings and Speeches*, Vol. 1, p. 143.
24. Ibid., p. 145.
25. Ibid., p. 146.
26. D.R. Jatava, *Social Philosophy of B.R. Ambedkar* (Agra, Phoenix Publishing House, 1965), p. 138.
27. B.R. Ambedkar: *Thoughts on Linguistic State*, p. 12.
28. R.K. Kshirsagar: *Political Thought of Dr. Babasaheb Ambedkar*, p. 179.
29. Dr Babasaheb Ambedkar *Writings and Speeches*, Vol. 8 (Bombay, Government of Maharashtra, 1990), p. 299.
30. Ibid., Vol. 8, p. 300.
31. Ibid.
32. Dr Babasaheb Ambedkar *Writings and Speeches*, Vol. 1, p. 359.
33. Dr Babasaheb Ambedkar *Writings and Speeches*, Vol. 2 (Bombay, Government of Maharashtra, 1982), p. 505.
34. B.R. Ambedkar: *What Congress and Gandhi have Done to the Untouchable* (Bombay, Thacker and Co. Ltd., 1946), p. 242.
35. Ibid.
36. D.R. Jatava, *Political Philosophy of Ambedkar* (Agra, Phoenix Public Agency, 1965), p. 182.
37. B.R. Ambedkar: *State and Minorities* – What are their Rights and How to Secure Them in the Constitution of Free India? 1947, p. 35.
38. Ibid., p. 36.

39. B.R. Ambedkar: *Thoughts on Pakistan* (Bombay, Government of Maharashtra, 1990), p. 31.
40. Bhagwan Das (ed): *Thus Spoke Ambedkar* (Jalandhar, Bheem Patrika Prakashan, 1969), p. 188.
41. Ibid., p. 75.
42. Dr Babasaheb Ambedkar *Writings and Speeches*, Vol. I (Bombay, Government of Maharashtra, 1979, p. 51.
43. Ibid., p. 68.
44. B.R. Ambedkar: *State and Minorities* (Lucknow, Buddha Vihar, Risaldar Park, 1978), p. 9.
45. R.K. Kshirsagar: *Political Thought of Dr. Babasaheb Ambedkar*, p. 192.
46. Ibid., pp. 192–193.
47. Bhagwan Das (ed.): *Thus Spoke Ambedkar*, Vol. I, p. 19.
48. B.R. Ambedkar: *States and Minorities*, p. 5.
49. Bhagwan Das, Vol. I, p. 70.
50. Ibid., p. 133.
51. Dhananjay Keer: *Dr. Ambedkar Life and Mission* (Bombay, Popular Prakashan, 1992), p. 122.
52. Bhagwan Das: *Thus Spoke Ambedkar*, Vol. I, p. 19.
53. D.R. Jatava: *Political Philosophy of Ambedkar*, p. 75.
54. Ibid., p. 75.
55. B.R. Ambedkar: *State and Minorities*, Thacker and Co. Ltd., Bombay, 1947, p. 52.
56. B.R. Ambedkar: *Annihilation of Caste* (2nd ed), B.R. Kadrakar, 1936, pp. 77–78.
57. B.R. Ambedkar: *Pakistan or the Partition of India*, p. 207.

8

Democracy and State Socialism

Ambedkar is widely known as a staunch protagonist of democracy in its true spirit. He had discussed certain aspect of democracy in his famous speech delivered before the members of the Poona District Law Library, on 22 December 1952. His thoughts on democracy are found in his many other books also. He defined, democracy, in a speech at Poona as, 'a form and a method of government whereby revolutionary changes in the economic and social life of the people are brought without bloodshed'. In democracy, the persons who are duly authorized by the people to rule over them try to introduce changes in social and economic life of the people, so that the welfare of the people could be possible. The people also accept and respond positively to those changes without resorting to bloodshed. If there are certain differences with the government they settle those differences amicably and within the framework of the Constitution. There cannot be opposition from any corner for the sake of opposition.

Ambedkar took a rationalistic and comprehensive view of democracy. He wrote: 'Democracy is not merely a form of government. It is primarily a mode of associated living of conjoint communicated experience. It is essentially an attitude of respect and reverence towards fellowmen'. He was fully aware of the fact that political democracy will not succeed without social and economic democracy. According to him, social and economic democracy is the tissue and fibre of political democracy. His vision of a democratic society was one in which there will be neither an oppressed class nor a suppressed class; equality before law and administration and functioning of moral order in society. He felt that society based on liberty, equality and fraternity should be the only alternative to a caste society.

While addressing the Constituent Assembly on the 26 January 1950, Ambedkar said:

> We are going to enter into a life of contradictions. In politics we will have equality and in social and economic life we will have inequality. In politics we will be recognizing the principle of 'one man, one vote and one man, one value'. In our social and economic life we shall, by reason of our social and economic structure, continue to deny the principle of 'one man, one value'. How long shall we continue to deny equality in our social and economic life? If we continue to deny it for long, we will do so only by putting our political democracy in peril. We must remove this contradiction at the earliest possible moment or else those who suffer from inequality will blow up the structure of political democracy which this Assembly has so laboriously built up.

So he attached highest importance for establishing the principle of 'one man, one vote', 'one man, one value, which alone can make democracy complete and real. This is the soul of democracy. In other words, political power, economic strength and social position should be shared equally by all sections of society in a democracy.

Love and faith in the dignity of the weak, the poor and the lowly, both in their individuality and sociality, developed in Ambedkar an ardent faith in the democratic way of life. He aspired for having a government of the people, for the people and by the people. According to Ambedkar, democracy means no slavery, no caste and no coercion. He wanted free thought, and expression that is choice and capacity to live and let live, which according to his conscience, would be the right path to democracy. The aim of democracy, to Ambedkar is essentially the practical interest of society as a whole, and not of any class, group or community. All individuals have to be welcomed into the common social living on the ground that they possessed common humanity. Men have different capacities, different choices and functions, yet every one of them should find an honourable and equal place in the social organization. To him,

> Real democracy is opposed to suppression of minorities. The suppression and exploitation of minorities in any form is the negation of democracy and humanism. If suppression is not stopped, then democracy degenerates into tyranny.[1]

Political Democracy

According to Ambedkar, political democracy rests on four[2] premises. They are:

1. The individual is an end in himself.
2. The individual has certain inalienable rights which must be guaranteed to him by the Constitution.
3. The individual shall not be required to relinquish any of his constitutional rights as a price of any privilege.
4. The State shall not delegate power to private persons to govern others.

Obviously, the dignity of the individual, political liberty, social progress and human rights with necessary constitutional safeguard form Ambedkar's basic decent democratic ideals in the political democracy.

The democratic principle of life, liberty and pursuit of happiness are considered to be the essentials of human life in Ambedkar's concept of democracy. He attached more importance to human well-being and human rights. His view of democracy, hence opposed authoritarianism, dictatorship, fascism and anarchism which have no sympathy for individual rights of free thought and movement.

The essence of democracy, to Ambedkar, is that as many members of a society as possible should share the exercise of human rights. It means that there should be equal opportunity for all citizens and harmony among the claims of each person. The majority, which controls the government in democracy, must defend, minority rights, because by denying them, the majority denies the essence of democratic life to them. Only when there is proper adjustment between the rights of man and his institutions, good democracy and humanism is best secured. Discrimination in human rights is the very negation of social and political democracy.

He, however stated that political democracy cannot be successful unless there is social and economic democracy. The society must be free from conflicting social groups and economic groups. There should be casteless and classless society for the success of democracy. Therefore, he thought to base his ideal society on liberty, equality and fraternity. For achieving economic equality he proposed 'State Socialism'.

It is, however a fact that the majority in our country is not political. In the election, people give prior preference to the candidates of their respective community. Therefore, Ambedkar, by and large concluded that we have communal majority in our country.

So he had deliberately proposed to have non-parliamentary government in our country. Though he was strong proponent of parliamentary democracy, he moulded his opinion in view of social milieu and electoral attitude in India. He stated in his famous book *States and Minorities* (1947), that, 'non-parliamentary in the sense that it shall not be removable before the term of the legislature'.[3] In other words, the term of the union executive would be co-existing with the term of the legislature. The Parliament would not be empowered to oust the government by passing no-confidence motion on the strength of its communal majority.

The Prime Minister shall be elected by the whole house by single transferable vote. He would not be elected by the bare communal majority in the garb of a political party, whatsoever. The Prime Minister would be leader of the whole House and not of a single majority party.

The representatives of the minorities in the Cabinet would be elected by members of each minority community in the legislature by single transferable vote. They would not be nominated by the Prime Minister himself and they would not be removed by him.[4]

However, the representatives of the majority community in the executive shall be elected by the whole House by single transferable vote. This would bring cohesion between all the members of all the communities in the legislature.

A member of the Cabinet need not be the member of the legislatures, they would have the right to sit in the legislature, speak, vote and answer questions.

A member of the Cabinet may resign his post on a censure motion or otherwise but shall not be liable to be removed except on impeachment by the House only on the ground of corruption or treason. He thought to keep him above the petty political or communal consideration.[5]

However, when the Constituent Assembly was formed and it elected Ambedkar as Chairman of its Drafting Committee, he had to change his thoughts in view of the majority decision. He could not insist on the scheme of non-parliamentary government. He thought that people may exercise the right of adult franchise very conscientiously without any favour or fear of any caste.

Conditions for the Success of Democracy

Ambedkar had very explicitly stated the conditions which are necessary for the successful working of democracy. They can be stated in brief as under:

1. *Equality* – For the success of democracy, the first and foremost necessary element is equality. He had stated that there must be no glaring inequalities in the society. There should not be an 'oppressed class' and there should not be a 'suppressed class'. The divided society has within itself the 'germs' of a bloody revolution. His ideal society is based on liberty, equality and fraternity, which he had derived from his preceptor, the Buddha. However, he gives primary importance to equality in this trinity. Fraternity and liberty are really derivative notions. Equality is the original notion and respect for human personality is a reflexion of it. So that where equality is denied, everything else may be taken to be denied.

Ambedkar means by equality, social and economic equality. His ideal society is casteless and classless society. He said very categorically that political democracy can not be successful unless there lies at the base of it social democracy. He gave a grave warning that 'how long shall we continue to deny equality in our social and economic life? If we continue to deny it for long, we will do so only by putting our political democracy in peril'.

2. *No Perpetual Authority to Rule* – Today, it has been provided in the democratic Constitution of India that after every five years those who are in power must go to the people and seek a fresh mandate from the people. According to Ambedkar, in democracy, nobody has any perpetual authority to rule and perpetual subjection to other but that rule is subject to sanction by the people and can be challenged in the House itself.[6] He said categorically that, 'As a king has no Divine Right to Rule, as also a majority has no Divine Right to Rule'. Majority rule is tolerated only because it is for a limited time and subject to right to have it changed, and secondly, because it is rule of political majority which has submitted itself to the suffrage of a minority and not a communal majority. He had rightly observed that in India, 'the majority is not a political majority. In India the majority is born. It is not made'. That is the difference between a communal majority and a political majority. A political majority is not a fixed or a permanent majority. It is a majority which is always made, unmade and remade. A communal majority is a permanent majority.

   It means that there should be no hereditary class to rule. There is always a possible tendency among those who are in authority to remain in power. They do not want to leave their places. This spoils the very basis of democratic tradition and strikes at the root of democratic practice, freedom and opportunity.

3. *Two Party System* – The condition for the successful working of democracy is the strong opposition to the ruling majority; unless there are two parties, one is to rule and other is to oppose, there can not be democracy. In his words,

> Two parties are necessary to keep government from being despotism'.[7]

He thought that there must be an effective veto power against the authority of those who are ruling the country. There can not be veto against the king, but in democracy it must be exercised against the party in power.

The dogmatic, totalitarian viewpoint holds that there is only one truth and from that position to the one-party state there is a direct line. The democratic viewpoint holds that different men perceive different aspects of truth, mainly in the light of their lives and experiences and there will be at least two sides to any major question. Ambedkar likes the democratic viewpoint, because it also gives respect to opposition party. In communist political organization, there is no need for an opposition party, rather it kills an opposition, which to him, is an act of inhumanity and barbarity. This mentality should no longer have a place in civilized countries.

4. *Equality in Law and Administration* – There must be equality not only before law, but there must be equality of treatment in administration. The personnel in administration need to be most sincere and efficient. The members of the ruling party should not interfere if any action is taken against any offender. In other words, the personnel in administration should be permanent, uncorrupt and efficient so that everybody would be able to get justice. The administration must be well responsive, responsible and impartial. It should command obedience to authority.

   There ought to be distinction between what is called 'Political Offices' and 'Civil Offices'. The British Government maintained distinction between political offices and civil offices. In USA, the 'spoil system' is no more in existence. Ambedkar thought in India also the administration should be above politics and should not allow at any rate any interference in the administration.

   He however observed that,

   > The administration is completely in the hands of Hindus. It is their monopoly. From top to the bottom it is

> controlled by them .... Their one aim is to discriminate against the untouchables and to deny and deprive them not only of the benefits of law, but also of the protection of the law against tyranny and oppression. The result is that the untouchables are placed between the Hindu population and the Hindu ridden administration, the one committing wrongs against them and the other protecting the wrong-doer, instead of helping the victims.[8]

It is because of this reason that he demanded reservation for the depressed classes in the services in order to change the composition of the administration and fill in with their own brethren to help them and to boost up their morale.

5. *Constitutional Morality* – Ambedkar had rightly observed that 'a Constitution which contains legal provisions is only a skeleton. The flesh of the skeleton is to be found in what we call constitutional morality'. The observance of constitutional morality for the successful working of democracy is another condition. Constitutional morality means some conventions – some moral obligation, that the people must observe. However, in England it is called the usages and conventions of the Constitution. Political actors in England are invariably bound to those conventions.

Constitution needs to be observed in its letter and spirit. The Constitution provides a mere skeleton or some basic principles. However, each and every rule of public life can not be provided in the Constitution. The detail in the legal skeleton could be filled in by healthy principles or conventions which are always based on justice and which evolve in the course of history.

Ambedkar referred to the convention laid down by King Windsor Edward III who had to abnegate the throne as he married an ordinary woman against the wishes of the Parliament. He referred with admiration, the convention laid down by President Washington who of his own refused to contest for Presidentship of the USA. for the third consecutive tenure on the ground of constitutional morality. Ambedkar resigned his Ministership (Law ministry), when there arose a discord between him and

Pandit Nehru on the issue of Hindu Code Bill, as he thought there should be perfect unity and harmony among the members of the Cabinet.

According to Ambedkar, to save democracy and strengthen its roots, the people must establish some conventions and follow some constitutional morality. No doubt Ambedkar thought so, but this cannot be done without mass education and integrity of the people.

6. *No Tyranny of Majority* – In democracy, there are always two rival parties striving to compete against each other for getting political power. The party proving its majority forms the government and the party in the minority forms the opposition. However, it is not expected from the majority to impose its tyranny over the minority. He states:

   'The minority must always feel safe that although the majority is carrying on the government the minority is not being hurt, or the minority is not being hurt below the belt'.[9]

   However, to Ambedkar, there should not be constant agitation, continuous adjournment motions and violent speeches or outbursts. Such a spirit in democratic set up is harmful to democracy. The opposition party is expected to co-operate with ruling party by constructive criticism and fruitful suggestions in the matter of governance of the State. He advocated that there should be free and fair discussion in the parliament. Every member of a minority party should be treated with due respect and dignity and should be heard; irrespective of his view. It is however necessary to have political majority or minority and not communal majority or minority. The majority party should try to see such an atmosphere on the floor of parliament and even outside the parliament, in which a revolutionary spirit or unconstitutional spirit would not develop. [10]

7. *Moral Order* – According to Ambedkar, democracy requires the existence of a moral order in the society. He contemplated that politics can not be devoid of ethics. The government may pass the laws and implement them but unless there is morality in the society; law can not achieve any success. According to Laski: 'It is my activity which gives legality to the law. Law, therefore, has to make its

way to acceptance through those channels of the mind'. Unless the people observe some moral principles to hold themselves together for common purposes, the State cannot function in any way. Politics without ethics is empty and a constant peril to the prospect of democracy.

According to Ambedkar, the majority of the people are left to be governed not so much by law as by morality. Law plays a small part in human society, only when there is dispute and disorder. In this regard, he praised Laski who referred this aspect of democracy much in his writings. 'The only person who, I think, has referred to this aspect of democracy is Laski. In one of his books, he has very categorically stated that the moral order is always taken for granted in democracy. If there is no moral order, democracy will go to pieces as it is going now probably in our own country'.[11]

Ambedkar had no faith in value-free politics. He said:

> Politics has become a kind of sewage system intolerably unsavory and unsanitary. To become a politician is like going to work in the drain.[12]

Once he reportedly said that, 'Politics has become a game of scoundrel, but for me it is a mission'. He, however, put before the people an ideal as to how politics could be a mission.

8. *Public Conscience* – The last but not the least is the condition of public conscience which is essential for the successful working of the democratic Constitution. According to Ambedkar, public conscience means,

> Conscience which becomes agitated at every wrong, no matter who is the sufferer; and it means that everybody whether he suffers that particular wrong or not, is prepared to join him in order to get him relieved.[13]

Larger number of young boys and girls, belonging to the white race, joined the struggle of the Indians in South Africa. There are many white people who have, physically and mentally, supported the Negroes in their fighting against social injustice in the USA. This is all due to what Ambedkar called a faith in public conscience.

But Ambedkar, with a sense of surprise, found an utter lack of public conscience in the people of urban areas, even among the so-called modernist in India. He stated very categorically that there is South Africa everywhere in India, however, he felt strange as to why there could not be any non-scheduled caste who could take up the cause of the oppressed people in India. He rightly observed that it was because of lack of 'public conscience'. He thought that the non-Dalits should come forward to liberate the Dalits. If they failed to do so, the oppressed people would develop revolutionary mentality which could prove to be grievously dangerous to democracy.

Ambedkar's thoughts on the conditions precedent for the successful working of democracy in India are really most significant and relevant to the Indian society.

State Socialism

There are several types of socialism such as Utopian Socialism, Scientific Socialism, Fabian Socialism, Syndicalism Socialism, Guild Socialism, Democratic Socialism, Gandhian Socialism and State Socialism. However, there is one common thread behind all types of socialism. It is that socialism aims at the control of the means of production by the State that is of essential and basic industries for the equitable distribution of wealth produced.

According to Leo Huberman, 'Socialism is a system in which, in contrast to capitalism, there is common ownership of the means of production instead of private, planned production for use instead of anarchic production for profit'. Thus socialism is a doctrine which envisages a classless society having common ownership of the means of production and equitable distribution of production among all the members so as to achieve socio-economic justice.

Now it is proposed to know the ideas of Ambedkar on State Socialism and to know that how far his State Socialism is different from or similar to the Scientific Socialism of Karl Marx.

Ambedkar had developed the theory of State Socialism in his book *States and Minorities* originally prepared to be submitted to the Constituent Assembly in the year 1947. Accordingly, State Socialism envisages,

> Putting an obligation on the state to plan the economic life of the people on lines which would lead to the highest point of productivity without closing every avenue to private enterprise and also provide for the equitable distribution of wealth.[14]

Ambedkar's idea of socialism is an attack on poverty. He did not agree with those men who develop sort of stoic endurance and resignation towards poverty. He agreed with Buddha, who does not comfort the poor by praising their poverty, nor did he sublimate poverty as a happy state for man to live in. To Ambedkar, poverty and socialism cannot exist together. One should remember that State Socialism aims at reducing those social and economic conditions of inequality in which some people live without working and some people work without decent living. Therefore, his concept is based on the principles of justice and right. It wanted the removal of everything, which is evil, but by the peaceful and legislative means.

Ambedkar advocated State Socialism in the field of industry and also ownership in agriculture with a collectivized method of cultivation. Ambedkar was one of the few Indians who demanded nationalization of insurance. He was of the firm opinion that the plight of 60 million untouchables who were landless labourers cannot be ameliorated through consolidation of land or by tenancy legislation, only collective farms can solve the problems of the landless labourers.

Ambedkar keenly observed the State Socialism. His plan had two special features.

> One is that it proposes State Socialism in important fields of economic life. The second special feature of the plan is that it does not leave the establishment of State Socialism to the will of the Legislature. It establishes State Socialism by the Law of the Constitution and thus makes it unalterable by any act of the Legislature and Executive.[15]

Ambedkar did not wish to leave the establishment of State Socialism to the will of the legislature. He wanted that constitutional law should prescribe the economic structure of society. It had some vital purpose. 'The purpose', he said, 'is to protect the liberty of the individual from the invasion by the other individuals. The connection between individual liberty and the shape and form of economic structure of society may not be apparent to everyone. Nevertheless the connection between the two is real'.[16] Many persons have to relinquish their constitutional rights in order to gain their livelihood. State Socialism and political democracy are not incompatible; therefore Ambedkar wanted to establish State Socialism not through dictatorship but through political democracy. He wrote:

> The problem, therefore, is to have State Socialism without dictatorship, to have State Socialism with Parliamentary Democracy, the way out seems to retain parliamentary democracy and to prescribe State Socialism by the law of the constitution so that it will be beyond the reach of the parliamentary majority to suspend, amend or abrogate it. It is only by this that one can achieve the triple object, namely, to establish socialism, to retain parliamentary democracy and avoid dictatorship. [17]

Ambedkar desired to include the programme of socialism in the fundamental rights. But Sardar Vallabhai Patel and J.B. Kriplani refused it to do so.

His views regarding State Socialism would be interpreted and elaborated as under:

1. Ambedkar thought that the State should be under obligation to plan the economic life of the people. This implies that he had staunch belief in the State. The social order which he visualizes is based on the basic postulates of liberty, equality and fraternity.[18] In this social order every one is at liberty to acquire property, tools and materials as being necessary for earning a living to keep the body in due state of health. The supporters of caste system apparently deny the 'liberty' to choose one's own profession. Ambedkar stated that men are different from each other in respect of heredity, social atmosphere and his

own efforts, but they should be given equal opportunity for their development.

He said that 'the connection between individual liberty and the shape and form of the economic structure of society may not be apparent to everyone. Nevertheless, the connection between the two is real.[19] Undoubtedly, 'the individual is an end himself' and 'the individual has certain inalienable rights which must be guaranteed to him by the constitution'.[20] However, in the economic system based on private enterprise the individuals rights are, undermined, if not violated. He stated that unemployment and fear of starvation may compel him to lose his rights given under the Constitution.

Therefore, he was of the opinion that it is not enough to enumerate fundamental rights in the Constitution, but to create necessary economic situation in which the people would be able to enjoy those rights. Therefore, there is need of state intervention in the economic life of the society. He did not agree with the proposition that where the state refrains from intervention, what remains is liberty. When the state refrains from intervening in the economic life of the people, there will be liberty, but that liberty would be to the capitalists to enslave the poor and nothing more. Therefore, he proposed 'to limit not only the power of government to impose arbitrary restraints but also of the more powerful individuals or to be more precise to eliminate the possibility of the more powerful having the powers to impose arbitrary restraints on the less powerful by withdrawing from the control he has over the economic life of the people'.[21] He therefore, stated that the state should fulfill its obligation towards the society in maintaining the triple object of liberty, equality and fraternity.

2. In order to avoid exploitation of one class by another, there should be equitable distribution of wealth. Therefore, he stated:
   (a) The key industries or which may be declared to be key industries shall be owned and run by the State.
   (b) The industries which are not key industries but which are basic industries shall be owned by the State and

shall be run by the State or by corporation established by the State.

(c) Insurance industry shall be in public sector and insurance will be compulsory for every citizen.

(d) Agriculture shall be State industry.

3. Private sector and entrepreneurs shall have a role in the economy but it shall not be dominating. He proposed nationalization of key and basic industries including land, but leaves other industries for the private enterprise. It implied that there is no bar on private property in his State Socialism. Private property may exist in the form of small scale and cottage industries, personal savings, domestic animals and other means of production for individual's maintenance. In his State Socialism, no person shall be disqualified to hold any public office or exercise any trade or calling by reason of his or her religion, caste, creed, sex or social status.

4. The State shall acquire the subsisting rights in such industries, insurance and agriculture land held by private individuals whether as owners, tenants or mortgages and pay them compensation in the form of debenture equal to the value of such property. The State shall determine how and when the debenture holder shall be entitled to claim cash payment.

   The debenture shall be transferable and inheritable property but neither the debenture holder, nor the transfer from the original holder, not his heir shall be entitled to claim the return of the land or interest in any industrial concern acquired by the State or to be entitled to deal with it in any way.

   The debenture holder shall be entitled to interest on his debenture at such rate as may be defined by law to be paid by State in cash or in kind as the State may deem fit.

5. The agriculture industry shall be organized on the following basis:

   (i) The State shall divide the land into farms of standard size and let out the farm for cultivation to the residents of the village as tenants made up of groups of families to cultivate the land collectively in accordance with rules and directions issued by government.

(ii) The tenants shall share among themselves in the manner prescribed, the produce of the farm left after the payment of charges properly leviable on the farm.

(iii) The land shall be let out to villagers without distinction of caste or creed and in such manner that there shall be no landlord, no tenant and no landless labourers.

(iv) It shall be obligatory on the part of the State to finance cultivation of the collective farms by supply of water, animals, manures, implements, seeds, etc.

(v) The State shall be entitled to levy the following charges on the produce of the farm –

  (a) a portion for land revenue;

  (b) a portion to pay the debenture holders; and

  (c) a portion to pay for the use of capital goods supplied.

(vi) The State shall prescribe penalty against those tenants who willfully break the condition or neglect to make best use of the means of cultivation or otherwise act prejudicially to the scheme of collective farming.

(vii) The State shall finance for industry and see that there will be rapid industrialization and maximum production.[22]

(viii) The whole scheme of State Socialism would be an inseparable part of the Constitution. There should be three reasons for this provision. (1) There should be continuity for the success of planned economy, especially for the long term plans. If they are discontinued abruptly on any unreasonable ground, it may be futile. (2) It can not be expected under Parliamentary system that the plans would be continued by the new government. One party may agree to it, but it is not certain that others would agree to it. (3) In our country, he stated, 'the majority is a communal majority'. It may try to protect the caste interests rather than class interests. Probably they may not tolerate that the poor and weaker sections of the society would take the benefit of the plans.

Then whether to accept dictatorial form of government in place of Parliamentary Democracy in order to secure continuity for the successful implementation of the economic plans? He did not want to exchange Parliamentary Democracy for dictatorship for the success of State Socialism. 'The way out', he stated, 'seems to be to retain Parliamentary Democracy and to prescribe State Socialism by the law of the Constitution so that it will be beyond the reach of a parliamentary majority to suspend, amend or abrogate it. As only by this one can achieve the triple object, namely, to establish socialism, retain Parliamentary Democracy and avoid Dictatorship'.[23]

6. State Socialism presupposes abundant production. It is natural that if there is no abundant production, there cannot be adequate and equitable distribution. Therefore, he stated that the State should formulate such a plan which would lead 'to highest point of productivity'. It is true that unless the nation increases its production, it cannot meet the needs of people.
7. According to Ambedkar any kind of discrimination is a menace to socialism, because it snatches from the individuals their fundamental right and it is derogatory to man's dignity. A true socialist to him would not tolerate ill-treatment and oppression, because this is opposed to socialism. The problem of socialism, in India, is more social than economic. There are traditional beliefs, which induce the people to look upon one another as low and high thereby acquiring social status and prestige, though these people may not be able to achieve these things by their ability alone. Man is a member of society. So it is the bounden duty of society to remove hindrance from the way of socialism by minimizing occasions for ill-treatment, oppression, conflict and frustration. The true test of socialism, in India, is not how far it helps men to solve their present problems, but how far it breaks down the traditional barriers that separate man from man.

To Ambedkar, the then present social system economically, socially, politically and morally was not suited to create a socialist spirit among the people. It required radical changes in all spheres.

8. To Ambedkar, 'culture is essential for man. That being so, the aim of human society must be enabling every person to lead a life of culture, which means the cultivation of mind as distinguished from the satisfaction of mere physical wants'. The life of culture is not possible unless there is sufficient leisure. It is only when there is sufficient leisure that a man can devote himself to a life of culture. According to Ambedkar 'leisure means the lessening of the toil and effort necessary for satisfying the physical wants of life'. The most urgent need that socialism has to face here in this country is how to provide leisure to every individual. To Ambedkar it is possible only when machine takes the place of Man. There is no other means of producing leisure. Machinery and modern civilization are thus, indispensable for emancipating man from leading the life of a brute, and for providing him with leisure and for making a life of culture possible.[24] To him, a democratic and socialist society must assure 'a life of leisure and culture to each one of its citizen'.

Attitude towards Marxism

What are similarities and differences between State Socialism propounded by Ambedkar and Scientific Socialism propounded by Karl Marx? Both Karl Marx (1818–1883) and Ambedkar (1891–1956) were very much concerned with the problem of the exploited humanity. Karl Marx was obviously aware of the severity of problem of the Proletariat Class in European countries. He himself had to undergo difficulties due to unemployment and poverty. Ambedkar was aware of the gravity of the problem of the downtrodden communities including the poor labourer classes in India. He himself had bitter experience of untouchability and poverty. Therefore, their hearts melted to see the agony of the exploited classes. However their perception of the society, their experience with the society, their ideology of emancipation of the suffering masses and ways and means to attain the objective so dear to their hearts were different.

1. Ambedkar accepted Marx's interpretation of history partially, yet he differed from him on many points. To Marx, history was the result of 'economic forces'. To Ambedkar, 'the impersonal forces are a determining factor which cannot be denied, but that effect of impersonal forces depended on man must also be admitted'.[25] It is man who controls some of the impersonal forces and makes possibilities for instrument and machines, which are the basis of modern culture and civilization. All economic activities are not undertaken and accomplished by implements and instruments, but by living men and women. Economic force, thus, dependant on the minds and wills of human being. Ambedkar here criticized Marxism, which denies man a proper place in human society.

   Ambedkar in his thought lays complete faith in man and his ability to control economic forces in harmony with social problems. From this point of view, he differed from Marxism, which regarded 'economic relation as the be-all and end-all of human life'.

   It is not the material existence of man which decides his fate, but he himself can change his adverse situation. According to Ambedkar, 'Man, therefore, is a factor in the making of history and those environmental forces whether impersonal or social, if they are the first and not the last things'.

2. Karl Marx observed that, 'the history of all hitherto existing society is the history of class struggle'. There has been constant conflict of interests between 'haves' and 'haves not'. In the modern age these classes are known as Bourgeoisie and Proletariat.

   The statement of Karl Marx referred above might be true in respect of other countries, but it can not be so in respect of India. Indian society is basically a caste society. Caste system was a permanent arrangement of suppression and exploitation. On the contrary, class cannot be permanent, though practically it is difficult to enter in but not impossible to do so. At least few industrious, enterprising and intelligent people could hope to achieve higher status in a class society but not in a caste society.

Indian history obviously reflects caste and communal problems rather than economic problems.

3. In the opinion of Ambedkar, the problem of the scheduled caste was obviously social rather than economic, where as the problem of Proletariat, in the opinion of Karl Marx, was economic. The caste system generates the sense of superiority or inferiority in relation to others not because one caste is economically rich and other is poor, but because one feels superior or inferior as a principle of caste system providing in the *Shastras*. Ambedkar said that, 'Self respect is more important than the material gains. Our struggle is for honour, for self-respect, not for the economic progress'.[26]

   While suggesting remedy on the economic ills of Proletariat, Karl Marx said that the Proletariat must first of all acquire political supremacy. Ambedkar also suggested the same remedy on the ills of scheduled castes. He said that, 'we can have one power and that is the political power. This power we must win. Armed with this power, we can protect the interests of our people'.[27] Thus, so far as remedy on the problem of the Proletariat as well as the scheduled castes is concerned, the views of both the thinkers were identical.

4. The ways and means, which Marxists wish to adopt in order to bring about communism, were not dear to Ambedkar. Karl Marx stated that, 'the ends can be attained only by the forcible overthrow of all existing social conditions. Let the ruling classes tremble at a communist revolution. However, Ambedkar believed in a constitutional means as a way of attaining power. To Ambedkar, violence, force and killing of the opposed, as the means of social and political change, appeared as erroneous and inhuman. He appealed to the mighty millions, 'do not be allured by the communists success, I am quite confident that if we all become one tenth as enlightened as the Buddha was, we can bring about the same results by the methods of love, justice and goodwill'.

5. Karl Marx condemned religion and religious activity as 'the opium of the people and the vale of woe'. Ambedkar did not agree with Marxism when it says 'Religion is an evil,

because it is sheer speculation and imagination; rather it is cry in the wilderness, wholly groundless and unscientific'. Whereas to Ambedkar, religion is essentially man's valuable heritage, after studying the various religions of the world, Ambedkar came to the conclusion that in question regarding the betterment of human life and social organization, religion plays a decisive role. Although he discarded Hinduism and embraced Buddhism which is basically rational and which believes in liberty, equality and fraternity, it is not mere change from one religion to another, it implies a protest against the religious myths, God, soul, heaven, superstitions and all humbug and acceptance of a way of life based on rationalism. As a Buddhist, he believed in atheism. Marx also believed in atheism.

6. Karl Marx advocated for imposing dictatorship of Proletariat. On the contrary, Ambedkar had indomitable faith in democracy. He believed that dictatorship is dictatorship, whether it is by Proletariat or capitalist. He had staunch faith in the trinity of liberty, equality and fraternity. His ideas seemed to be very much relevant to the modern age. The idea of dictatorship of Proletariat seems to be redundant.
7. In Karl Marx's opinion, State is the instrument of exploitation of the Proletarian; hence it needs to be destroyed. This cannot be accepted. The nature of state, however, depends on the nature of the persons who form the government. Ambedkar believed in State as an instrument of social change and social welfare.

It could be summarized in the words of Dongre that 'Dr Ambedkar seeks to establish a balance between State ownership and private enterprise, but communism wants complete State monopoly. Ambedkar wants to retain Parliamentary Democracy in which the communist have no faith. Ambedkar is opposed to dictatorship for which communist stands'.[28]

In sum, Ambedkar thought to make the plans of State Socialism an inseparable part of the Constitution. It would come through the Constitution and not through the bloody revolution. Subsequently, it would come in operation through the apparatus of democratic government duly composed of all the sections of the society. Every individual would be able to enjoy the fundamental rights, including the rights to legal remedies. The age-long exploited and oppressed scheduled castes would get certain special safeguards and it would be highly difficult to parliamentary majority to repeal or abridge those safeguards, thus, in his State Socialism, everybody would get justice. His State Socialism envisaged a classless and casteless society in which every human being was entitled to liberty, equality and fraternity. Individual's welfare was the end and State Socialism was the means to achieve that end. Reason, morality and justice were its basic postulates.[29] Obviously his State Socialism was very much pragmatic and relevant to the Indian structure.

Thus, in Ambedkar's political thought, the most precious things were the individual freedom and common good. His ideas and ideals revolved around the welfare of man. He had a deep faith in fundamental human rights, gender equality, dignity of the individual, social and economic justice, secularism, non-violence, constitutional morality, promotion of social progress and better standards of living in all spheres of human life. His political ideology was of utmost significance for social transformation in our country.

Notes

1. Bhagwan Das: *Thus Spoke Ambedkar*, Vol. I (Buddhist Publishing House, Jalandhar, 1963), pp. 41–44.
2. Bhagwan Das: *Thus spoke Ambedkar*, Vol. III (Bangalore, Ambedkar Sahitya Prakashan, 1979), p. 172.
3. B.R. Ambedkar: *State and Minorities* (Thacker and Co. Ltd., Bombay, 1947), pp. 43–46.
4. R.K. Kshirsagar: *Political Thought of Dr. Babasaheb Ambedkar* (Intellectual Publishing House, Delhi, 1992), p. 56.
5. Ibid.
6. D.R. Jatava: *Political Philosophy of Ambedkar* (Phoenix Publishing Agency, Agra), 1965 p. 101.

7. B.R. Ambedkar: *Ranade, Gandhi and Jinnah* (Thacker and Co. Ltd, Bombay), 1943 p. 237.
8. B.R. Ambedkar: *States and Minorities* (Lucknow, Buddha Vihar, 1978), p. 50.
9. Bhagwan Das: *Thus Spoke Ambedkar*, Vol. III (Bangalore, Ambedkar Sahitya Prakashan, 1979), p. 46.
10. Ibid., p. 47.
11. Ibid., p. 48.
12. B.R. Ambedkar: *Ranade, Gandhi and Jinnah*, (Thacker and Co. Ltd, Bombay), 1943, p. 227.
13. Bhagwan Das: *Thus Spoke Ambedkar*, Vol. III (Bangalore, Ambedkar Sahitya Prakashan, 1979), p. 49.
14. B.R. Ambedkar: *States and Minorities*, p. 42.
15. B.R. Ambedkar: *State Socialism* (Bheem Patrika Publication, Jalandhar), p. 13.
16. B.R. Ambedkar: *States and Minorities*, pp. 31–32.
17. B.R. Ambedkar: *State Socialism*, p. 13.
18. B.R. Ambedkar: *Annihilation of Caste* (1936), Dr. Babasaheb Ambedkar *Writings and Speeches*, Vol. 1, Education Dept., Government of Maharashtra, 1979, p. 57.
19. B.R. Ambedkar: *State and Minorities*, p. 43.
20. Ibid., p. 43.
21. Ibid., p. 45.
22. Ibid., pp. 22–24.
23. B.R. Ambedkar: *State and Minorities*, p. 47.
24. B.R. Ambedkar: *What Congress and Gandhi have Done to the Untouchables* (Bombay, Thacker and Co. Ltd., 1946), p. 249.
25. B.R. Ambedkar: *Ranade, Gandhi and Jinnah* (Bombay, Thacker and Co. Ltd., 1943), p. 5.
26. Bhagwan Das: *Thus Spoke Ambedkar*, Vol. II (Buddhist Publishing House, Jalandhar, 1968), p. 145.
27. Ibid., p. 35.
28. M.K. Dongre: *Economic Thoughts of Dr. B.R. Ambedkar* (Ambedkar Sanjay Publication Nagpur, 1974), p. 47.
29. R.K. Kshirsagar: *Political Thoughts of Dr. Babasaheb Ambedkar*, p. 133.

9

Social Justice

The concept of 'Social Justice' is broader in scope than 'Justice'. The concept of justice is a hoary one. The Greek philosopher, Plato regarded justice as the true principle of social life. 'The Republic', therefore is called 'a treatise concerning justice'. It constitutes the most important part of his political philosophy. According to Ernest Barker, 'Justice is the hinge of his thought, and the text of his discourse'.[1] In his contemporary world, Plato saw, 'stasis' everywhere – cities so divided that their citizens stood 'in the posture of gladiators' against one another. He saw 'unrighteousness rampant and injustice enthroned'.[2] He saw ignorance supreme and parading up and down in the guise of knowledge. Plato found in justice the remedy for curing these evils.

It should be noted that before Plato many theories of justice were prevalent. Plato reviewed a number of traditional theories of justice – propounded by Cephalus, Polemarchus, Thrasymachus and Glaucon – and rejected them. According to Cephalus, 'Justice consists in speaking the truth and paying one's debt'; Polemarchus spoke, 'Justice seems to consist, in giving what is proper to him'. Thrasymachus, defined justice as 'the interest of the stronger', in other words, 'might is right'. Glaucon regarded justice as 'the interest of the weaker'. Plato rejected these definitions because they treated justice as something external and artificial. For Plato, justice is the primary moral value and is intrinsically linked with other essential moral qualities.[3] It is the right condition of the human soul; it is internal as it resides in the human soul. Justice exists both in the individual and the State. But it exists on a larger scale and in a more visible form in the State. Individually, justice is a 'human virtue' that makes a man self-consistent and good; socially, justice is a political consciousness that makes a State internally harmonious and good. It meant that a class should do its work in that social cadre or political plan to which it was called by its peculiar propensities. Plato's three classes were – the rulers, soldiers and artisans based on the principles of wisdom, courage and desire, respectively. To Plato, 'Justice is a product of class division and specialization of functions'; it is 'giving to every man his due'.[4] And his due is to be assigned the particular task which he is best qualified by aptitude and training to perform. His definition is unusual in that it has no legal or juristic connotation. It is not concerned with the rights of an individual against the State. Even his threefold categorization of man's instincts and capacities is naive. His arbitrary assignment of men to one or another of the three classes, depending upon their individual aptitudes, also destroys freedom. His conception of justice is moral and not legal. It is in no sense a juristic definition. It is a system of duties, not of rights. In contrast to Plato's meaning of justice, the modern concept of social justice is wider in scope. The concept of social justice is legal, juristic, and proclaims a system of rights and freedom for an individual.

Another Greek philosopher, Aristotle, propounded the concept of 'distributive justice'. For him, the end of the State is the promotion of good life. The realization of this end depends on the realization of a life of common action. The life of common action may become a possibility, provided the citizens of a State act in conformity to the laws of the State, that is, they should develop in themselves that great quality which is known as the law-abidingness. And since law-abidingness is a complete virtue, in that sense, justice is also a complete virtue. Justice, therefore, to Aristotle is the name of that great moral virtue and excellence of character which is so essential for dealing with social and public relation. According to him, to provide a system of rights in relation to the society is the business of the distributive justice. To protect these rights against the infringement by others, is the work of the corrective justice.

Aristotle's distributive justice is the name of that principle of distribution by which goods, services, honour and offices are distributed among the citizens of the State. But the principle of distribution is based upon the worth or virtue of an individual. It recognizes and preserves distinction between the worthy and non-worthy. It counters equality of the unequal and ensures that a man's rights, duties and rewards should correspond to his merit and social contribution. Aristotelian distributive justice is, thus, the other name of proportionate equality.

Both Plato and Aristotle were the great thinkers who developed the concept of justice. They differ in many fundamental respects from each other.[5] First, Aristotelian justice lays emphasis on a system of rights, while Platonic justice attaches more importance to duties. Second, Aristotle's justice is legal in character, whereas Platonic justice is essentially moral and philosophical. Third, Aristotelian justice establishes equality between different members of the State, while the Platonic justice establishes a hierarchy of classes. But inspite of these differences, the aim of both the philosophers is to find out a principle of capability through which unity, harmony, virtue and happiness can be established in society.

It may be mentioned here that both Aristotelian and modern social justice lay emphasis on the rights and duties of citizens. But the difference between the two is that social justice attempts a classification of rights – social, political, economic, legal and fundamental, and attaches a corresponding duty only in relation to that right. Further, both Aristotle's and modern social justice are founded on equality. But the concept of equality – social, economic, political and legal – which the social justice contemplates, is very much beyond the purview of Aristotle. Aristotle's proportionate equality is very much limited in comparison to equality as advocated by modern thinkers of social justice. In Aristotle's proportionate equality, a citizen is rewarded according to his capacity or ability, but the social justice endeavours to pay its citizens not only according to their capacity or ability, but also according to their needs. Social justice even goes further to protect the interests of the downtrodden through a variety of constitutional or legal devices. It is here that social justice rises to the higher and truer conception of justice.

The above elaboration relating to the concept of justice as propounded by Plato and Aristotle would help us in understanding the meaning of social justice in its true perspective. Social justice is composed of two words: 'Social' and 'Justice'. Each has specific meaning, and when conjoined with each other they convey a correct sense.

Social Justice Explained

The word 'social' is connected with society and the way it is organized. Its scope is very wide, including social issues, problems and reforms, thereby calling for social and economic change. It also refers to the position of depressed or disadvantaged classes in society and the measures to be taken for their advancement. It is social engineering, that is, an attempt to change society and to deal with social problems according to particular political beliefs. Such a socio-economic change can be brought through law. It aims towards the creation of political, economic and social democracy, combining the principles of socialism, with the greater personal freedom of democracy and the ending of class or caste distinctions. So the word 'social' has a wide connotation, connected with society and how it should be organized, and what should be its social values and structure.

The word 'Justice' means the fair treatment of people: which means law based on the principles of justice and rationality, that is, equal rights and justice for all, irrespective of class, sex, race or caste distinctions. It means that the state should deal with the people correctly and completely; it should be morally fair and reasonable; and it should frame just laws and enact them justly.

Social justice therefore is a combination of the meanings of 'Social' and 'Justice'. Its dimensions are very broad. However, an attempt made by Usha Kapoor in her 'Observation Remarks' on 'Dr Ambedkar and Social Justice', is fair enough to convey the meaning of social justice. She says:

> Social justice is a tridimensional concept – it is a prime democratic value, a prime social ethic and an instrument of social transformation. As a democratic value, it connotes political equality and freedom, the acceptance of the principle of 'one man, one vote'. As a social ethic, it is a matter of the rejection of caste and class barriers by clearing the social conscience of the traditional notion of inequality between man and man. As an instrument of social transformation, it provides leverage to the state to check social disparities and imbalances through legislative action.[6]

It is this concept of social justice which, perhaps, Ambedkar pleaded, being a great crusader for the rights of the downtrodden and weaker sections of Indian society.

It is very difficult to give an exact definition of social justice. Its general features can be gauged from the following narration of Zafar A. Khan given in his paper, 'Social Justice and the Indian Constitution: Ambedkar's Perspective':

> Social justice is understood as the right of the weak, aged, destitute, poor, women, children and other under-privileged persons, to the protection of the state against the ruthless competition of life ... Social justice is not confined to a fortunate few but takes within its sweep, large masses of disadvantaged and underprivileged segments of society; justice which not only penetrates and destroys the inequalities of race, sex, power, position or wealth but is also heavily weighed in favour of the weaker sections of humanity.[7]

Social justice, therefore, is the equitable distribution of the social, material and political resources of the community. It is socio-economic revolution to transform the society and at the same time maintaining its unity and harmony. It has to ensure to the people that the rule of law becomes meaningful in order to make justice a reality for them. It is, therefore, used in a comprehensive sense, including both economic justice and social justice. It takes within its sweep the objective of removing all inequalities and discriminations, and affording equal opportunities to all citizens in social affairs and economic activities. Social justice, accordingly, is meant 'to wipe every tear from every eye'.

The above concept of social justice was ably expounded by B.R. Ambedkar during the course of the framing of the Indian Constitution.

Vision of a Just Society

Ambedkar held that social justice is a means towards the creation of a just society, or an ideal society. His just society is a casteless society, based on the principles of social justice. His just society is based on the principles of liberty, equality and fraternity.

Ambedkar developed his vision of a just society after exploring the nature of Indian society or social order. He made a comprehensive analysis of the Hindu social order based on four classes or *Varna* system and pointed out its drawbacks and debilities. He rejected the basic principles of the Hindu social order, that is, graded inequality, fixity of occupations and caste-status based on birth. He upheld a basic change in the rigidity of the caste structure and suggested its total annihilation. This was the starting point of his ideal society.

Ambedkar provided a picture of 'just' or 'ideal society' in his well-known work, *Annihilation of Caste*. He said:

> An ideal society should be mobile, should be full of channels for conveying a change taking place in one part to other parts. In an ideal society there should be many interests consciously communicated and shared. There should be varied and free points of contact with other modes of association. In other words there must be social endosmosis.[8]

Ambedkar's ideal society is based upon two fundamental principles. 'The first is that the individual is an end in himself and that the aim and object of society is the growth of the individual and the development of his personality. Society is not above the individual and if the individual has to subordinate himself to society, it is because such subordination is for his betterment and only to the extent necessary. The second essential is that the terms of associated life between members of society must be regarded by consideration founded on liberty, equality and fraternity'.[9]

In this observation of Ambedkar, writes James Massey, the main point needs to be noted is that in the caste-based society, an individual person has no place, where in Ambedkar's proposed society individual is the final end. Also, in the caste-based society a person's relationship with the member of his or her class or with the members of these classes were already fixed, but in Ambedkar's visioned society other relations have to be based on liberty, equality and fraternity.[10]

Besides the two essential principles, one of the most important components is 'justice', or the 'principle of justice', because according to Ambedkar 'the norm or the criterion for judging right and wrong in the modern society is justice', and again justice according to him, 'is simply another name for liberty, equality and fraternity'.[11]

Ambedkar's concept of a just society is based on social justice – the key features of which are individual as an end in himself and his relations to be governed on the principles of liberty, equality and fraternity.

Key Components of Social Justice

The key components of Ambedkar's concept of social justice are liberty, equality and fraternity.

The first component is liberty. Liberty, Ambedkar said, to be real must be accompanied by certain social conditions. In the first place there should be social equality. 'Privilege tilts the balance of social action in favour of its possessors. The more equal are the social rights of citizens, the more able they are to utilize their freedom .... If liberty is to move to its appointed end it is important that there should be equality'.[12]

In the second place, there must be economic security. 'A man may be free to enter any vocation he may choose ... yet if he is deprived of security in employment, he becomes a prey of mental and physical servitude incompatible with the very essence of liberty .... The perpetual fear of the morrow, its haunting sense of impending disaster, its fitful search for happiness and beauty which perpetually eludes, shows that without economic security, liberty is not worth having. Men may well be free and yet remain unable to realize the purposes of freedom'.[13]

In the third place there must be knowledge made available to all. In the complex world man lives at his peril and he must find his way in it without losing his freedom. 'There can, under these conditions, be no freedom that is worthwhile unless the mind is trained to use its freedom. (Given this fact) the right of man to education becomes fundamental to his freedom. Deprive a man of knowledge and you will make him inevitably the slave of those more fortunate than himself ... deprivation of knowledge is a denial of the power to use liberty for great ends. An ignorant man may be free ... but he cannot employ his freedom, so as to give him assurance of happiness'.[14]

Ambedkar held that the above three conditions social equality, economic equality and availability of knowledge – are essential to make liberty real. In antique society or Hinduism liberty is not real because of the absence of three conditions in it. He believed that in a just society, liberty can be real.

The second component of social justice is equality. It means all men are equal, all men are of the same essence and the common essence entitled them to the same fundamental rights and to equal liberty. There is no equality in antique society, because it is based on the principle of gradation and rank. He says:

> The system of rank and gradation is, simply another way of enunciating the principle of inequality so that it may be truly said that Hinduism does not recognize equality.[15]

The antique society or Hinduism is a denial of equality both social as well as religious, leading to a degradation of human personality. He held that in the modern society based on social justice equality would be its main component.

The third component of social justice is fraternity. Fraternity is opposed to individualism. It is another name for fellow feeling. It consists in a sentiment which leads an individual to identify himself with the good of others whereby 'the good of others becomes to him a thing naturally and necessarily to be attended to like any of the physical conditions of our existence'. It is because of this sentiment of fraternity that the individual does not 'bring himself to think of the rest of his fellow creatures as struggling rivals with him for the means of happiness, whom he must desire to see defeated in their object in order that he may succeed in his own'.[16]

Ambedkar believed that individualism would produce anarchy. It is only fraternity which prevents it and helps to sustain the moral order among men. Fraternity is a natural sentiment, and Ambedkar quoted with approval, the following words of J.S. Mill:

> The social state is at once so natural, so necessary, and so habitual to man, that, except in some unusual circumstances or by an effort of voluntary abstraction he never conceives himself otherwise than as a member of a body; and this association is riveted more and more, as mankind are further removed from the state of savage independence. Any condition, therefore, which is essential to a state of society, becomes more and more an inseparable part of every person's conception of the state of things which he is born into, and which is the destiny of a human being. Now, society between human beings, except in relation of master and slave, is manifestly impossible on any other footing than that the interests of all are to be consulted. Society between equals can only exist on the understanding that the interests of all are to be regarded equally. And since in all states of civilization, every person, except an absolute monarch, has equals, every one is obliged to live on these terms with some body; and in every age some advance is made towards a state in which it will be impossible to live permanently on other terms with any body. In this way people grow up unable to conceive as possible to them a state of total disregard of other people's interests.[17]

This is the real sentiment of fellow feeling or fraternity, and in its absence an ideal society is inconceivable. Fraternity, therefore, is a significant component of social justice.

The core components of social justice, according to Ambedkar, are liberty, equality and fraternity. Social justice means a complete change in the fundamental notions of life. It means a complete change in our look and in attitude towards men and things. It means a new life. But a new life, pulsating with the ideals of social justice, cannot enter a body that is dead (antique society). He, therefore, said:

> But a new life cannot enter a body that is dead. New life can enter only in a new body. The old body must die before a new body can come into existence and a new life can enter into it. To put it simply, the old must cease to be operative before the new can begin to enliven and to pulsate. This is what I meant when I said you must discard the authority of the Shastras and destroy the religion of the Shastras.[18]

What Ambedkar pleaded was social change or transformation; and social change and social justice are synonyms.

Bases of Social Justice

The true bases of social justice, according to Ambedkar are to be found in Buddhism, not in Marxism. Having read them and being interested in the ideology of both, Dr Ambedkar made a comparative evaluation of both and realized that there was something in the Buddha's teachings that was of great worth.

Ambedkar appreciated the Marxian version that the purpose of philosophy is to reconstruct the world; and that the workers are exploited by the owners who misappropriate the surplus value and that the exploitation leads to greater and greater impoverishment of the workers. He rejected the key features of Marxism; inevitability of socialism, revolution, class struggle and dictatorship of the proletariat. He was also not prepared to accept the economic interpretation of history as the only explanation of history. Ambedkar said that though Marx pleaded economic equality, he missed the importance of liberty and fraternity. He believed that Marx laid emphasis on only one pillar of social justice, that is, economic equality; whereas the other pillars of social justice, such as, liberty and fraternity were neglected by Marx. As such, according to Ambedkar, much of the Marxian creed has been disapproved by history and much has been demolished by his opponents. As a result of this criticism much of the ideological structure raised by Karl Marx 'has broken to pieces'.

The true bases of social justice, according to Ambedkar, are rooted in the creed of Buddha. Buddha's teachings are very vast and form the corpus of social justice. Buddha said:

> Religion is necessary for a free society; religion must relate the facts of life and not to theories and speculations about God, or Soul, or Heaven or Earth; real religion lives in the heart of man and not in the Shastras; man and morality must be centre of religion; the function of religion is to reconstruct the world; all human beings are equal; worth and not birth is the measure of man; fellowship towards all must never be abandoned; freedom from superstitions and inequalities; war is wrong unless it is for truth and justice; nothing is infallible, everything is subject to change, etc.[19]

This is the creed of fraternity, which Ambedkar derived from Buddha. And fraternity is an important plank in Ambedkar's concept of social justice.

Ambedkar believed that humanity does not only want economic values, it also wants spiritual values to be retained. He pleaded that the Buddha's method was to change the mind of man: to alter his disposition, so that whatever man does, he does it voluntarily without the use of force or compulsion. The main means to alter the disposition of men is Buddha's *Dhamma* and the constant preaching of this *Dhamma*. So, social justice is a very broad concept, meant to alter the disposition of Man, through the ideals of liberty, equality and fraternity. Social justice is both an economic and spiritual creed. In the words of Ambedkar:

> Humanity does not only want economic values, it also wants spiritual values to be retained. Permanent dictatorship has paid no attention to spiritual values and does not seem to intend to. Carlyle called political economy a 'pig philosophy'. Carlyle was of course wrong. For man needs material comforts. But the communist philosophy seems to be equally

> wrong for the aim of their philosophy seems to fatten pigs as though men are no better than pigs. Man must grow materially as well as spiritually. Society has been aiming to lay a new foundation was summarized by the French Revolution in three words: Fraternity, Liberty and Equality. The French Revolution was welcomed because of this slogan. It failed to produce equality. We welcome the Russian Revolution because it aims to produce equality. But it cannot be too much emphasized that in producing equality society cannot afford to sacrifice fraternity or liberty. Equality will be of no value without fraternity or liberty. It seems that the three can co-exist only if one follows the way of the Buddha. Communism can give one but not all.[20]

This gives us a clue to Ambedkar's concept of social justice, that is, fraternity, liberty and equality must co-exist. Since this is the path tread by Buddha, it can be said that the true bases of Ambedkar's social justice are embedded in Buddhism.

Power to be Exercised with Wisdom

Ambedkar held that the way to achieve social justice lies in the fact that the power should be exercised with wisdom. He said that there are three tactics or strategies by which the future could be decided. Either there should be surrender by the one party to the wishes of the other – that is one way. The other way is to call a negotiated peace. The third way is to open war; Ambedkar was appalled at the idea of solving the problems of social justice or social change by the method of war. The religious toleration or communal harmony which is an important principle of social justice must not be secured by the method of war or force. He said:

> I have no hesitation and I do want to place before this House in the clearest terms possible that if war comes in this country and if that war has any relation to the issue with which we are confronted today, it will not be a war on the British. It will be a war on the Muslims. It will be a war on the Muslims or which is probably worse; it will be a war on a combination of the British and the Muslims. I cannot see how this contemplated war be of the sort different from what I fear it will be.[21]

Ambedkar quoted a passage from Edmund Burke's great speech on conciliation with America. He believed this might have some effect upon the temper of the members of the Constituent Assembly. He reminded the House that when the British people were trying to conquer the rebellious colonies of the United States, and living them under their subjection contrary to their wishes, Edmund Burke, while repelling this idea of conquering the colonies, had said:

> First, Sir, permit me to observe, that the use of force alone is but temporary. It may subdue for a moment; but it does not remove the necessity of subduing again; and a nation is not governed which is perpetually to be conquered. My next objection is its uncertainty. Terror is not always the effect of force and an armament is not a victory. If you do not succeed, you are without resource for, conciliation failing, force remains; but, force failing, no further hope of reconciliation is left. Power and authority are sometimes bought by kindness; but they can never be begged as alms by an impoverished and defeated violence .... A further objection to force is, that you impair the object by your very endeavours to preserve it. The thing you fought for is not the thing which you recover; but depreciated, sunk, wasted and consumed in the contest.[22]

Ambedkar believed that it would be perilous to ignore these weighty words. The problem of solving the Hindu-Muslim antagonism by force or war would be a grave mistake. The communal harmony should be maintained by peaceful methods of consent and conciliation. Power should be exercised with wisdom. That is the only way by which 'we can carry with us all sections of the country'. That is the only way to promote social justice.

Interpreting Ambedkar's views it can be said that the efforts to bring social justice or social change through the use of force would be perilous. The maintenance of communal harmony is a principle of social justice. No society can be united in the absence of communal harmony. All in all, what Ambedkar meant was that unless and until power is exercised with wisdom, the issues of social justice would not be successfully solved. Here, Ambedkar's views are more or less akin to Plato, who, in his *The Republic*, wrote:

> Until philosophers are kings, or the kings and princes of this world have the spirit and power of philosophy, and wisdom and political leadership meet in the same man, ... cities will never cease from ill, nor the human race.[23]

Unguided by wisdom or rationality, social justice would be in disarray. Social justice is an internal part of wisdom. In fact, Ambedkar equated power with wisdom, and if power is bereft of wisdom, social justice would be damaged or ruined. Wisdom, knowledge, thought, intellect and reason should be requirements of power; and if it is not be so, the social justice would remain barren of vitality. Political power and wisdom (rationality) should meet together to make social justice effective.

Methods for Promoting Social Justice

Ambedkar believed that social justice should be obtained through constitutional methods or means. The social and economic change should be secured through peaceful ways, instead of the bloody methods of revolution. The methods of civil disobedience, non-cooperation and *satyagraha* should be abandoned.

Social justice should never be obtained through revolution. Rebellion is the worst method to secure social justice, because it threatens the very foundations of civil society. If it is successful, it means the destruction of government and the triumph of anarchy; even if it fails, it can only be put down at the cost of much bloodshed and disorder. Ambedkar's views about rebellion or revolution are almost similar to that of Luther; the latter said:

> Rebellion is not just plain murder; but it is like a great fire which sets a land ablaze and lays it waste; therefore rebellion brings with it a landfull of murder and bloodshed; it creates widows and orphans and destroys everything, like the greatest of all disasters.[24]

Ambedkar upheld that for the attainment of social and economic transformation revolutionary methods are unjustified, because such methods are 'nothing but the Grammar of Anarchy'. According to Ambedkar:

> When there was no way left for constitutional methods for achieving economic and social objectives, there was a great deal of justification for unconstitutional methods. But where constitutional methods are open, there can be no justification for these unconstitutional methods. These methods are nothing but the Grammar of Anarchy and the sooner they are abandoned, the better for us.[25]

Thus, social justice obtained through constitutional means, he held, is more durable and lasting, promoting fraternity and ushering in a new social order.

A Document Vibrant with Social Justice

Ambedkar's ideology of social justice is clearly reflected in the Indian Constitution of which he was the principal architect. The Constitution is a document vibrant with social justice. The preamble, the directive principles of state policy and the fundamental rights form a trinity of social justice, and are 'the core of the commitments to the social revolution'. This trinity is the conscience of the Constitution and a vehicle to bring social change. It promotes egalitarianism, secularism, welfare society and a just social order. It discourages casteism, communalism and a feudalistic nature of society. It provides effective mechanism to translate its goals into reality. It is meant to promote constitutionalism for a better tomorrow.

The Preamble is the mirror of the Constitution. It is a manifesto of the aims and aspirations of social justice. It solemnly resolves to secure all its citizens justice: social, economic and political, liberty of thought, expression and belief; faith and worship; equality of status and of opportunity; and to promote among them all fraternity assuring the dignity of the individual and the unity and integrity of the nation. This is indeed the core of social justice embedded in the Constitution. While concluding the debate on the preamble in the Constituent Assembly, Ambedkar said:

> I say that this preamble embodies what is the desire of every member of the House that this Constitution should have its roots, its authority, its sovereignty from the people, that it has.[26]

Social justice relates to the creation of a new social order. The key features of that new social order is given in the chapter on Fundamental Rights. The people of India have the right to equality, right to freedom, right to life and personal liberty, right against exploitation, right to freedom of religion, cultural and educational rights, and right to constitutional remedies.

In addition to these, the directive principles of state policy also express in categorical terms the ideas of social justice. The Directives lay down to minimize the inequalities, to make available to all the citizens adequate means of livelihood, to distribute ownership and control of material resources so as to subserve the common good, to avoid concentration of wealth, equal pay for equal work, to protect the health of workers; men and women, the tender age of children against abuse, to protect the youth against exploitation and the like. The state is also required to provide free legal aid to the poor, right to work, right to education and public assistance in cases of unemployment, old age, sickness and disablement; to make provision for securing just and humane conditions of work and for maternity relief, etc. The state has to provide free and compulsory education for children below the age of 14 years, to promote the educational and economic interests of the scheduled castes and scheduled tribes and other weaker sections, to raise the level of nutrition and scheduled standard of living and to improve the public health, etc.

Though social justice has not been defined in the Indian Constitution; the preamble, the directive principle of state policy and fundamental rights clearly illustrate the philosophy of social justice. Social justice, it may be said, is 'a relative concept taking in its wings the time and circumstances, the people, their traditions and aspirations, their turmoil and torrents, their backwardness, blood, sweat and tears'.[27]

Reservation of Seats

The preamble, the directive principles of state policy and the fundamental rights convey the ideology of social justice in a general sense. For the downtrodden and the weaker sections of the society, the Constitution provides reservation of seats in legislatures and services. The policy of reservation for the disadvantaged section is an instrument to promote social justice. The Articles from 332 to 340 deal with the reservations. These special provisions regarding reservation of seats for the depressed and the weaker sections are meant to accelerate the pace of social revolution. These are the 'imperatives towards social transformation and reconstruction of the Indian society, which constitute the gist of social justice'.[28]

In short, the constitutional safeguards to the downtrodden groups (SCs, STs, OBCs and women) form the core of social revolution.

No social justice can ever advance a step further if the society is not free from untouchability. To quote Ambedkar:

> Most parts of the world have had their type of populations called the lowly. The Romans had their slaves, the Spartans had their helots, the British their villains, the Americans their Negroes and the Germans their Jews. So the Hindus have their untouchables. But none of these can be said to have been called upon to face a fate which pursues the untouchables. Slavery, serfdom, villainage all have vanished. But untouchability still exists .... The untouchable is worse off than the Jew .... Yet nobody sees to take any notice of the untouchables – some sixty millions of soul, – much less espouse their cause.[29]

Ambedkar's crusade against slavery, serfdom and untouchability and ultimately its abolition in any of its forms by the Constitution of India could justly be styled as one of his greatest achievements towards promoting the cause of social justice.

Ambedkar's theory of social justice was shaped by his personal experience of being an untouchable in his early life and by his western education. His social thought ultimately led him to emerge as the champion of the downtrodden. Because of his early sufferings due to the practice of untouchability, he determined to fight against the social evil which was at last abolished through the Constitution of India in whose drafting he played a key role. Even the abolition of untouchability was not enough; he made provisions in the Constitution regarding their (depressed classes) reservations in legislatures and services in order to improve their socio-economic status and to bring social change.

A New Social Order

To Ambedkar, social justice meant creation of a new social order – one of its key features being the empowerment of women. To liberate the Hindu women from the bonds of lawless social laws, Ambedkar, as the Law Minister of India, introduced the Hindu Code Bill in the Provisional Parliament. The Bill related to the codification of Hindu laws regarding the women's rights to inheritance, succession, marriage, divorce, etc. It was meant to promote the culture of equality among Hindu men and women. Initially, Pandit Nehru, the Prime Minister, supported the Bill, but at the later stage he backed out, and this hurt the feelings of Ambedkar, who submitted his resignation in September 1951. The details of the Bill and the debate held on it have been described in the chapter 'The Hindu Code Bill'.

Finally, time had proved that Ambedkar was right and subsequently the Hindu Code Bill was split into four Bills and were passed separately by the Parliament in 1955–56.

In Ambedkar's concept of social justice the reconstruction of society on the basis of the culture of equality and empowerment of women has been a significant feature. His mission was to liberate the women from outdated social customs, thereby, to reconstruct the society and to usher in a new social order.

Minority Rights

Social justice is not antagonistic to minority rights. In the Constituent Assembly, while advocating the rights of the minorities, Ambedkar proceeded on the assumption that national well-being depended upon the rights enjoyed by the minorities. He considered that constitutional safeguards for the preservation of religious, cultural and linguistic identity of the minorities would bend them to unite as one nation by the bond of fraternity. It would enable the minorities to become equal partners in nation-building.

In the Constituent Assembly when clause 18 regarding cultural and educational rights of minorities was moved by Sardar Patel, three members of the House, namely, Mohanlal Saksena, Mahavir Tyagi and K.M. Munshi, pleaded that the said clause be referred back to the Advisory Committee for reconsideration. They pleaded that the rights of minorities should be relative, that is to say, 'we must wait and see what rights the minorities are given by the Pakistan Assembly before we determine the rights we want to give to the minorities in the Hindustan area'.[30]

At this stage, speaking in the Constituent Assembly on the absoluteness of rights of minorities, Ambedkar said:

> Now, Sir, with all deference, I must deprecate any such idea. Rights of minorities should be absolute rights. They should not be subject to any consideration as to what another party may like to do to minorities within its jurisdiction. If we find that certain minorities in which we are interested and which are within the jurisdiction of another State have not got the same rights which we have given to minorities in our territory, it would be open for the state to take up the matter in a diplomatic manner and see that the wrongs are rectified. But no matter what others do, I think we ought to do what is right in our own judgment and personally I think that the rights which are indicated in clause 18 are rights which every minority, irrespective of any other consideration is entitled to claim. The first right that we have given is the right to use their language, their script and their culture. We have stated that 'there shall be no discrimination on the ground of religion, language, etc. in the matter of admission into state educational institutions. We have said that 'no minority shall be precluded from establishing any educational institution which such minority may wish to establish'. It is also stated there that whenever a State decides to provide aid to schools or other educational institutions maintained by the minority, they shall not discriminate in the matter of giving grant on the basis of religion, community or language. Sir, I cannot understand how there can be any objection to these rights which have been indicated in clause 18.[31]

Keeping in mind the supreme goal of national unity and integrity, Ambedkar upheld the legitimate rights of minorities in a democracy. He regarded that the discrimination of any sort, whether minority or majority, was inconsistent with the goal of social justice.

Social Humanism

Ambedkar's ideology of social justice is synonymous with his social humanism. According to D.R. Jatava, Ambedkar's social humanism were based on the following principles: (i) equality among human beings; (ii) every human being as an end in himself; (iii) right of every human being to social, economic, political and religious freedom; (iv) to make every human being free from want and fear; (v) to maintain liberty, equality, fraternity, and to strive to secure redemption from oppression and exploitation of man by man, of class by class, and of nation by nation; (vi) to stand for a democratic society under a parliamentary system of government; (vii) to believe in non-violence as an instrument of social change and adopt peaceful and persuasive methods to avoid class conflicts and the possibility of civil war; (viii) to avoid any 'ism' or any theory or dogma in its extreme aspect; (ix) need for spiritual discipline; and (x) firm foundation of universal love, equality and human brotherhood that the Buddha taught.[32]

Ambedkar's theory of social justice is, broadly speaking, a replica of his social humanism.

Democracy and Social Justice

Ambedkar believed that 'if we wish to maintain democracy not merely in form, but also in fact,' then social and economic revolution, through constitutional means, is essential. The social and economic objectives as enshrined in the Indian Constitution form the grammar of social justice.

He said that political democracy is not enough. It must be accompanied by economic and social democracy. Inequality in social and economic life is hazardous for the realization of social justice. On the economic plane, there are some in Indian society who have immense wealth as against many who live in abject poverty. On the social plane, 'our society is based on the principle of graded inequality which means elevation for some and degradation for others'.[33] These contradictions must be eliminated through the proper implementation of the principles of social justice.

Ambedkar believed that the structure of democracy cannot last unless there lies at the base of it social democracy. By social democracy, he meant 'a way of life which recognizes liberty, equality and fraternity as the principles of life'.[34] What Ambedkar calls social democracy is, in fact, a part of social justice. As such, unless the principles of social justice are not chewed and digested by both the government and people of India, democracy at the top would be barren of life and a life of contradictions would prevail. Social justice can alone put an end to the life of contradictions in Indian society.

Social Justice: A Unique Blend

Ambedkar's concept of social justice is not a spontaneous creation; it is the outcome of so many factors that influenced his course of life. The four major factors that led to the formulation of the ideology of social justice were: (i) consequences of the operation of caste system; (ii) the ethos of freedom struggle; (iii) the impact of western liberalism and (iv) the impact of Buddhism. The brand that Ambedkar prepared, by blending together the four streams, is called the ideology of social justice. Social justice is, therefore, a pleasant or useful combination of Ambedkar's experience of different thoughts.

The first factor that weighed on Ambedkar's mind was that the consequences of caste system in Hindu society are dangerous for building a cohesive society. Describing the consequences of the operation of *varna* or caste system in India, he said:

> The effect of castes ethics of the Hindu is simply deplorable. Caste has killed public spirit. Caste has destroyed the sense of public charity. Caste has made public opinion impossible. A Hindu's public is his caste. His responsibility is only to his caste. His loyalty is restricted only to his caste. Virtue has become caste-ridden and morality has become caste-bound.

> There is no sympathy to the deserving. There is no appreciation for the meritorious. There is no charity to the needy. suffering, as such, calls for no response. There is charity, but it begins with the caste and ends with the caste. There is sympathy, but not for men of other caste.[35]

Ambedkar was appalled to see the horrors of caste-ridden society. To him, inequalities that existed appeared appallingly bad. Comparing inequalities as prevalent in the western countries and in India, he observed:

> In Europe it is true that the strong has not shrunk from exploitation, nay the spoilation of the weak, but there, the strong have never contrived to make the weak helpless against exploitation so shamelessly as was the case in India among the Hindus. Depriving property and education from the larger sections of the society they have been completely made disabled for direct action against their pitiable conditions. There have been social revolutions in other countries of the world. Why has not there been a social revolution in India? A simple answer is that the caste system is in the interest of the upper strata of the society. It is human nature that once he is well settled he would not allow to get disturbed.[36]

Social justice, in a sense, is a protest against the fossilized caste system of the Hindus which 'deadens, paralyses and cripples the people from helpful activity'. Social justice is a plea for social revolution and resurgence of Indian society on the modern principles of liberalism that started from the age of enlightenment in the west.

The second factor that helped Ambedkar to develop the principles of social justice was the ethos of the Indian freedom struggle. It was in 1917, that the Indian National Congress had passed the following resolution:

> This Congress urges upon the people of India the necessity of justice and righteousness of removing all disabilities imposed by custom upon the depressed class, the disabilities being of a most vexatious oppressive character subjecting those classes to considerable hardship and inconvenience.[37]

This resolution of the Congress was epoch-making in socio-political history of India, nay, in the development of the concept of social justice.

The third factor was the impact of western liberalism upon Ambedkar. His education abroad and vast learning of western political philosophy made him familiar with the ideas of liberalism and democracy. This has already been discussed in the preceding chapters.

The last factor was Ambedkar's thorough study of Buddhism, from where he derived the ideas of social democracy, liberty, equality and fraternity.

All these ideas were assimilated by Ambedkar and he put them together in a harmonious whole and that harmonious whole can be called social justice.

Social justice, therefore, is the philosophy of good life. It is, indeed, 'a prime democratic value, a prime social ethic and an instrument of social transformation'.[38]

Notes

1. E. Barker: *Plato and His Predecessors* (London, 1952), p. 153.
2. C.L. Wayper: *Political Thought* (New Delhi, B.I. Publications, 1974), p. 16.
3. Forsyth and Keens-Soper (eds): *A Guide to the Political Classics* (Oxford, Oxford University Press, 1988), p. 25.
4. M. Judd Harmon: *Political Thought from Plato to the Present*, p. 34.
5. Sukhbir Singh: *History of Political Thought*, Vol. I (Meerut, Rastogi Publications, 2006), p. 161.
6. Mohammad Shabbir (ed): *Ambedkar on Law, Constitution and Social Justice* (Jaipur, Rawat Publications, 2005), p. 292.
7. Ibid., p. 306.
8. Dr Babasaheb Ambedkar *Writings and Speeches*, Vol. 1 (Mumbai, Government of Maharashtra, 1989), p. 57.
9. Ibid., Vol. 3, p. 95.
10. Mohammad Shabbir, p. 159.

11. Dr Babasaheb Ambedkar, *Writings and Speeches*, Vol. 3, 1987, p. 25.
12. Ibid., p. 39.
13. Ibid.
14. Ibid.
15. Ibid., p. 25.
16. Ibid., p. 44.
17. Ibid., pp. 44–45.
18. Ibid., Vol. 1, pp. 77–78.
19. Ibid., Vol. 3, 1987, p. 442.
20. Ibid., p. 462.
21. Ibid., Vol. 13, 1994, p. 13.
22. Ibid., pp. 13–14.
23. Michael Curtis (ed): *The Great Political Theories* (New York, Avon Book Division, 1961), p. 49.
24. David Thomson (ed): *Political Ideas* (Middlesex, Penguin Books, 1970), p. 44.
25. Dr Babasaheb Ambedkar *Writings and Speeches*, Vol. 13, p. 1215.
26. Mohammad Shabbir, op. cit., p. 310.
27. Ibid., p. 310.
28. Ibid., p. 313.
29. B.R. Ambedkar: *Mr. Gandhi and the Emancipation of the Untouchables* (Jalandhar, nd), p. 11.
30. Constituent Assembly Debates, 1 May 1947, pp. 504, 507–508.
31. Dr Babasaheb Ambedkar *Writings and Speeches*, Vol. 13, pp. 20–21.
32. D.R. Jatava: *Social Philosophy of Dr. Ambedkar* (Agra, Phoenix Publishing House, 1965), p. 91.
33. Dr Babasaheb Ambedkar *Writings and Speeches*, Vol. 13, p. 1216.
34. Ibid.
35. Ibid., Vol. 1, 1979, p. 57.
36. Mohammad Shabbir, op. cit. p. 177.
37. Ibid., p. 173.
38. Ibid., p. 292.

10

Relevance

The 19th century is generally styled as the age of renaissance in India. The enlightenment, revival and vitalization of modern India was one of the significant phenomenon of world history. The period of time extending from the 18th century to the middle of the 19th century had presented a spectacle of thorough economic decline, political prostration, social stagnation and cultural decadence. India had become a colony of the British Empire. The failure of the Great Mutiny of 1857 had buttressed British imperialistic hold on the country.

After the failure of the Great Mutiny of 1857, the mind and soul of India had began to awaken. There occurred gradually a rise in the forces of nationalism and with it there arose a demand for social and economic reshaping. A dynamic upsurge of new social activity appeared in the programmes and preachings of social reformers in the 19th century. Simultaneously, India came into contact with modern military technology, communications and the advanced ideas of western rationalistic and thought-currents. With the introduction of western learning in India, a new spirit of intellectual quest was generated, and it applied itself to religious, social, economical and political problems.

The intellectual renaissance of India in the second half of the 19th century was a significant factor in the rise of modern Indian nationalism. The awakening of the Indian spirit manifested its creativism first in the realms of philosophy, religion, culture and political self-consciousness came as an inevitable consequence. Indian renaissance was primarily moral and spiritual. There arose the social reform movements, such as, the *Brahmo Samaj*, the *Arya Samaj*, the *Prarthana Samaj* and the Ramakrishna Movement. The key feature of social reform movements was revivalism. They advocated the shaping of life on the basis of ancient scriptures – the *Vedas*, the *Upanishads*, the *Gita* and the *Puranas*. They put a new humanistic and cosmopolitan interpretation upon the old scriptures. They were reformist in their orientation and advocated ending of untouchability, removal of caste distinctions, widow's remarriage, inter-marriage, inter-dinning and women's education. They had a rocklike faith in the *Vedas* and believed that the problems of life should be solved in accordance with *Vedic* canons. Believing in God, soul, theism (faith) and rebirth, they aimed towards the moral purification of an individual and social reconstruction. They were prophets of perfect Vedism. Their main objective was the resurrection of past glory and greatness of the country on the basis of *Vedic* idealism.

This sentiment of revivalism was generated as a reaction against the great challenge thrown by an alien civilization, which was politically dominant and economically powerful. It is 'out of the clash of the new mechanical civilization of the Occident and the old pietistic and religious cultures of India, we find the emergence of new India'.[1] As a defense mechanism against the impact of an alien political power in the country, the old cultures of the land began to revive and reassert themselves. This, in brief, is the genesis of revivalism of the 19th century in India,

In addition to, there occurred another event of great significance in 1885. This was the founding of the Indian National Congress. The Congress during its first phase from 1885 to 1905 was under the influence of moderate leaders; and from 1905 to 1916, the extremist leaders dominated the Congress. However, the nature of the Congress underwent a great change with the advent of Mahatma Gandhi and his launching of non-cooperation movement in 1920–21.

At this period of time, Ambedkar had started taking interest in the abolition of social evils and untouchability; and gradually by 1930s he became a national figure. The Hindu social reform movements aiming towards the revival of the old scriptures did not attract his attention. He detested the very idea of resurrecting the past glory. He looked upon reformism as a half-hearted attempt towards the abolition of untouchability. He unfolded in a merciless way the contradictions inherent in the ancient scriptures – the *Vedas,* the *Upanishads* and the *Puranas.* He demolished the concept of the infallibility of the *Vedas.* He uprooted its basic tenet of the *Varna* system which was based on graded inequality. He advocated the abolition of caste. He categorically blasted the theories of theology, soul and rebirth. Instead, he held that Man was more important than God. Man occupied a central place in his ideology. He advocated a drastic social change through peaceful methods. His method was the application of critical reason to meet the problems of life. All in all, Ambedkar initiated a new ideology, quite in contrast to the ideals of reformist movements of the 19th century. His ideology in due course proved more relevant to the situation in comparison to the ideology of the revivalist movements. Its relevance was demonstrated in practice at the time of the framing of India's Constitution.

In the preceding chapters, much has been written about the ideology of Ambedkar. In this chapter, the relevance of his ideology is put very succinctly.

Rationality

In the modern Indian social tradition, Ambedkar was first and supreme in the development of socio-political ideology rooted in rationality. He was young in his soul and never lost the boy's insatiable curiosity. To great curiosity, Ambedkar allied great faith in reason. He believed that life and the world were rational and that the laws formulated by the government should be based on rationality.

Ambedkar's faith in reason and rationality was unshakeable. He said that all rational rules should replace the supernatural. Consciousness is created by reason. Reason is the only means of knowing reality. Theology and morality should be based on reason. Rational men ought to be free to pursue their interests and customs that have been erected to block their path should be altered or destroyed so as to permit them greater liberty. Morality should be founded not on scriptures and theology, but on rationality, that is, the changing needs and aspirations of society; and not any unchanging revelation or dogma, should determine the good. The orthodox scriptures, metaphysics, theology and supernatural sanctions should be swept away as they are antagonistic to reason. For Ambedkar, reason was triumphant. He discarded *Vedas*, scriptures and theology, and evolved a new ideology of reason. Like Descartes, he was confident of the power of reason. He exalted rationality and believed that social order should be guided by it.

Ambedkar argued that man should employ reason for the speedy progress and the transformation of society. Perfectability of human race is impossible without reason. The Indian Constitution of which he was the main architect is the living monument of Ambedkar's reason-drafted social and political order. He upheld that consciousness is created by reason and upon conscience and justice all man-made laws should be based. His conviction was that the downtrodden would never be free till the last page of *Manusmriti* is burnt or strangled with the entrails of the last priest (Brahmins). He asserted that the very first step towards social transformation is the destruction of *Manusmriti*'s power in which intolerance and graded inequalities have its roots. *Manusmriti* and *Vedas* are a barbarous philosophy, destitute of all taste and progress. They are the offspring of cunning minds and muddy understandings in which all the decent drapery of life is torn off.

According to Ambedkar, Indian history and social evolution have been disfigured by false Hindu scriptures and unless rationality is not employed in interpreting them, it is difficult to search a unifying principle by which the whole society can be woven in one thread. The antique Hindu society has long stifled both reason and ambition; hence it should be cast aside to grant the individual free rein to seek one's own ends.

Ambedkar's attachment to intellectual truth has been as great as his curiosity and his faith in reason. He possessed a great instinct for criticism and evaluation. He evinced a passion for analysis and a hatred of woolly thinking. His instinct for criticism was inseparable from his great faith in rational discussion. In fact, what we owe to Ambedkar can be ascribed to his great regard for intellectual truth, his great clarity and steadiness of vision, his great instinct for criticism and his great enthusiasm for reason and rationality.

Ambedkar's love for logic and rationality was too immense. He regarded rationality as a superb instrument of aggression. He was the kind of controversialist who liked to bludgeon his opponents into complete submission and rationality to him, seemed the best available means of closing loopholes and silencing quibbles. Ambedkar's rationalistic approach to understand the problems of society and find their solutions is, therefore, endlessly fascinating.

Man

Ambedkar was a great humanist. Man was the centre of his thoughts. He considered that solving human problems with the help of reason is more important than religious beliefs. He exalted Man as much as he reduced Gods. Man was the inexhaustible theme of his ideology. Instead of the problems of cosmos and metaphysics, Ambedkar's ideology rotated around Man only. Man was a central fixed point in Ambedkar's thought. For him, a wondrous thing is Man – none more wondrous. The ancient Indian scriptures made Gods, kings, spirits and *Varna* system; Ambedkar alone made Man.

The right to think his own thoughts, the right to speak them publicly, the right to act according to conscience so far as the welfare of others allows, were for Ambedkar, the most precious of rights. His belief that a man's chief contribution to natural life is his personality developed to the highest degree, is perhaps his supreme gift to the generations that came after him. At the same time, he realized the importance of society, and he refused to abide by Hindu traditions that stifled society. Had Ambedkar not been interested in individual as well as society, his fascination would have been much less than it is today! His interest in Man and society was because of his passionate belief in reason, his scientific spirit, his fresh, critical outlook and his humanism. It is because of his attachment to Man and humanism that Ambedkar has continued to be the inspiration of the downtrodden and of so many succeeding generations.

For Ambedkar, Man was the focal point. The proper study of Indian society is Man, not God. Man should employ reason for breaking the shackles of bondage. He should avoid religious fanaticism and narrow caste loyalties. Man should evolve a true social order from his reason. Man should undertake all types of reforms – reforms of society, economics, laws and religion – and make for liberty, equality and fraternity. The only form of government suitable for the progress of man is the rational form of government, based on democratic and liberal values. It is this acutely critical spirit, combined with his lively faith in rationality that made Ambedkar a notable figure in the modern history of India.

Religion, politics and society were ruthlessly dissected by Ambedkar in order to discover if they were rational; if they promoted human progress, guaranteed individual rights and conferred justice. To recapitulate briefly, for Ambedkar, faith, ancient scriptures and supernatural things had reached their nadir; and the Man alone emerged triumphant. His ideology, never for a moment, lost sight of Man and rationality; and that is the reason for its relevance and restorative power.

Justice

According to Ambedkar, the ideology of justice is a compendious one and includes most of the other principles which have become the foundation of a moral order. Justice evokes ideas of equality, of proportion of 'compensation'. Justice is equity or fairness, or a society where equity prevails and in which everyone is treated equally. Equity signifies equality. Rules and regulations, right and righteousness are concerned with equality in value. All men are equal, all men are of the same essence and the common essence entitled them to the same fundamental rights and to equal liberty.

The factors that impede justice are deeply rooted in the Hindu caste system, of which Manu is the progenitor. The principles of gradation and rank, slavery, discrimination, social and religious inequalities and degradation of personality, embedded in Hindu social order, are in contravention of justice.

Justice, therefore, implies social equality. Privilege tilts the balance of social action in favour of its possessors. The more equal are the social rights of citizens, the more able they are to utilize their freedom. If liberty is to move to its appointed end it is important that there should be equality.

In the absence of economic security, social equality is not possible. Ambedkar wrote:

> A man may be free to enter any vocation he may choose ....Yet if he is deprived of security in employment he becomes a prey of mental and physical servitude incompatible with the very essence of liberty .... The perpetual fear of the morrow, its haunting sense of impending disaster, its fitful search for happiness and beauty which perpetually eludes, shows that without economic security, liberty is not worth having. Man may well be free and yet remain unable to realize the purposes of freedom.[2]

In addition to, for making justice a reality, knowledge must be made available to all. Mind must be trained to use its freedom. If knowledge is deprived, a man inevitably becomes a slave of those more fortunate than himself. Deprivation of knowledge is a denial of justice.

Justice must, in the long run, promote the sentiment of fraternity. Justice can fructify in a society where the sentiment of fraternity takes roots.

Justice is the cardinal principle in Ambedkar's ideology. Justice must satisfy the test of social utility and the test of individual justice. Justice must provide nourishment for ordinary human souls, comfort for ordinary human sorrow, and help for ordinary human weakness. In short, equality is the soul of justice. Justice can give a very polished performance if it reflects the true thoughts and feelings contained in equality and liberty. The principle of Justice forms the most important part of Ambedkar's ideology.

Philosophy and Religion

Ambedkar pointed out the difference between philosophy and religion. Philosophy is concerned with knowing truth. Religion is concerned with the love of truth. Philosophy is static. Religion is dynamic. These differences are merely two aspects of one and the same thing. Philosophy is static because it is connected only with knowing truth. Religion is dynamic because it is concerned with love of truth.

Unless religion is dynamic and begets in us the emotion of love for something, then it is better to be without any thing that we can call religion; for religion is perception of truth and if our perception of truth is not accompanied by our love for it then it will better not to be seen at all.

Philosophy should not remain transcendental. Such a philosophy has no influence on the way of life. Religion is politics and politics is brotherhood. Philosophy must become religion, that is, it must become a 'Working Ethic'. It must not remain mere metaphysics.

Ambedkar quoted with approval, the following words of Max Plowman:

> 'If religion were a metaphysic and nothing else, one thing is certain; it would never be the concern of the simple and humble men. To keep it wholly in the realm of metaphysic is to make nonsense of it. For belief in religion as in something not directly and vitally effective of politics is ultimately belief that is strictly speaking idiotic; because in the effective sense such a belief makes no difference, and in the world of time and space what 'makes no difference' does not exist'.[3]

It is for these reasons that Ambedkar regarded the philosophy of the *Upanishads* as ineffective. The *Upanishads* claim to expound that, 'by knowing which everything is known'. This quest for 'the absolute' is the basic weakness of the *Upanishads*. The treatises are full of absurd conceits, quaint fancies, and chaotic speculations. They keep man moving in the old rut. They are effete and antiquated; and their quest for wisdom is false. It is futile to look for wisdom in the musty parchments of metaphysical treatises. 'It is as if a caravan should travel across the desert to the shores of the Dead Sea in search of fresh water!'[4] There is nothing in *Upanishads* but an endless round of verbal jugglery there. One cannot understand life and its problems by reading *Upanishads*. The *Upanishad* philosophy had little or no influence on Hinduism as a social and political system. They turned out to be most ineffective and inconsequential piece of speculation with no effect on the moral and social order of the Hindus. The philosophy of *Upanishads* remained incomplete and therefore did not yield the fruit which it ought to have done. The great truth which the *Upanishads* said they had discovered and they asked man to follow this truth is, *Atman* and *Brahma* were one.

According to Ambedkar, the *Upanishads* became ineffective because its philosophers did not realize that to know truth was not enough. One must learn to love truth. A philosophy that does not love truth is a static one. Religion is dynamic because it is concerned with the love of truth.

This ideology of Ambedkar regarding the difference between the philosophy and religion must be kept in mind in order to understand his attack on the deficiencies of the *Upanishads*.

Critique of Customary Morality

Ambedkar is a critique of the customary morality of the Hindus. He said that a Hindu is social not moral in the strict sense of the term. A Hindu takes no responsibility for the ends he serves. He is a willing tool in the hands of his society. He is not a free agent. His notions of sin give remarkable proof of his unmoral character. It connotes the fall of man from a prescribed form of conduct. Sin, according to Hindu notion, is a disease of the soul. It means to be defiled, to become unclean, and purified by both – pilgrimage or sacrificial offering. But it is never the spiritual defilement which is associated with the harbouring of evil thoughts and purposes. This is the root meaning of customary morality.

Morality of the Hindu, therefore, is purely social. It means that the level of his morality is purely traditional and customary. Ambedkar pointed out two evils of customary morality. In the first place, there in no surety that it will always be charged with sincerity and purity of motive. For it is only when morality penetrates to the deepest springs of purpose and feeling in the individual, that pretense will cease to find a place in human behaviour. In the second place, customary morality is an anchor and a drag. It holds up the average man and holds back the man who forges ahead. Customary morality is only another name for moral stagnation. This is true of all cases where morality is only customary morality.

Another evil feature of customary morality is a matter of meritorious conduct. Ordinarily, the meritorious conduct is something which is good from the general or public point of view. But among the Hinduism, the meritorious conduct is not concerned with the worship of God or the general good of the community. Meritorious conduct in Hinduism is concerned with the giving of presents, of good and of honour to the Brahmins. Hindu ethics is worship of the superman.

On the account of the above reasons, Ambedkar believed, that customary morality of Hinduism is a drag on progress. No progress can be achieved in society so long as the hold of customary morality is not torn asunder. Instead of customary morality, Ambedkar pleaded modern morality based on rationality and the importance of Man. Customary morality circumscribes a Man; rational morality can alone liberate him.

The two core features in Ambedkar's ideology were: (i) the application of critical reason in passing judgments upon things and events and (ii) the criterion of judging right and wrong in the modern society is justice. Discarding the customary morality, Ambedkar's ideology laid emphasis on the canons of critical reason and justice.

Doctrine of Love and Wisdom

Ambedkar's ideology is also based on the twin principles of love and wisdom, derived from Buddhism. Buddha started his mission of reforming the society at the time when the Aryan community was steeped in the worst kind of 'debauchery: social, religious and spiritual'. Ambedkar wrote:

> 'Buddhism was a revolution. It was a great Revolution as the French Revolution. Though it began as a religious revolution, it became more than religious revolution. It became a social and political revolution'.[5]

Based on Buddhism, Ambedkar's ideology is the ideology of moral code, intended to regulate the thoughts and actions of men and women. It sets standard for a moral life for an individual to follow. It does not stop merely with setting an example by leading a life of purity. It is also meant to mould the character of the ordinary men and women in society. It upholds a form of baptism devised by Buddha. The baptism consisted in the convert to Buddhism undertaking to observe certain moral precepts laid down by Buddha. These precepts are known as *Pancha Sila* or the five precepts. They are – not to kill, not to steal, not to lie, not to be unchaste and not to drink intoxicants.

Like Buddha, Ambedkar was not satisfied with a man following the above precepts. He insisted upon encouraging others to follow them.

Ambedkar inculcated in his ideology, Buddha's practice of love as a virtue. Universal pity, sympathy for all suffering beings, goodwill to every form of sentient life is important ingredients of his ideology. As such, the two cardinal virtues of his ideology are love and wisdom. He quoted with approval, the following dictum of Buddha:

> As a mother at the risk of her life watches over her own child, her only child, so also let every one cultivate a boundless loving mind towards all beings. And let him cultivate goodwill towards, the entire world, a boundless (loving) mind above and below and across, unobstructed, without hatred, without enmity. This way of living is the best in the world.[6]

Ambedkar held to the doctrine of wisdom as firmly as he did to the doctrine of love. He asserted that morality begins with knowledge and ends with wisdom. He wished to transform and save the world. His method for the accomplishment of this end 'was the destruction of ignorance and the dissemination of knowledge as to the true values of life and the wise way to live'.

Like Buddha, Ambedkar did not arrogate to himself the power to save people. People must do that for themselves. And the way to save lay through knowledge. So much insistence did he place upon knowledge that he did not think that morality without knowledge was virtue.

In short, Ambedkar's ideology, derived from Buddhism, is a plea for both love and wisdom. A just social order should ignore completely and absolutely all advantages or disadvantages arising from birth, lineage, occupation, social status and sweep away all barriers and disabilities arising from the arbitrary rules of social impurity. Love, wisdom and righteousness are the true foundations of a just social order.

A Wide-ranging Ideology

Ambedkar's ideology is a wide-ranging one which throws cross-beams of light on the big social and political issues of human freedom, the grounds of rights and the means of their fulfilment, the basis of democracy, the individual and society, and the need of a new social order based on social justice. To millions of the depressed and downtrodden, his ideology is a glimmer of hope, because Ambedkar demolished, rather mercilessly, the infallibility of the *Vedas* and *Varna* system as they advocated inequalities and status by birth. His ideology aimed towards the creation of political, economic and social democracy on the principles of liberty, equality, fraternity and justice – in social, economic and political matters. The vision of his ideology was to establish a just, coherent and ideal society, free from exploitation and oppression, and pursuing the goal of fellow-feeling and brotherhood. The removal of social restraints imposed by caste-ridden antique society and the relentless march into social justice were the key features of Ambedkar's ideology.

Covered within his ideology, there lies all the theorizing about man and society, state and government, democracy and socialism, and social humanism and social justice. On one hand, Ambedkar destroyed the authority of ancient Indian scriptures; and on the other, he built his ideology on the western heritage of rationality, pragmatism, the dignity of Man and the liberal values. The classical humanism of ancient Greece, the values of the age of enlightenment, and the democratic values of the west, derived from J.S. Mill, Edmund Burke, John Dewey, Harold Laski and others, were blended together in a harmonious whole in Ambedkar's ideology. His insistence that individual personality has an ultimate value which must not be sacrificed to the claims of the exploiters of society was of great value. At the same time, the ultimate claims of individual personality has a relationship with the community as a whole and that Ambedkar had not forgotten. Strong infusion of the rationalistic, scientific spirit of intellectual curiosity and experience he gathered, has often reinforced his ideology of social humanism and social justice.

Ambedkar's ideology of social justice was a holistic one, which is enshrined in the preamble, fundamental rights and directive principles of the Indian Constitution. The ideology of social justice took within its sweep the objective of removing inequalities and affording equal opportunities to all citizens in social, economic and political affairs. His ideology of social justice was a vibrant and dynamic one; it was a search for a new model of socio-economic order. Social justice was also a crusade against the caste compartmentalization and a reliable path towards the creation of social democracy. Social justice, according to Ambedkar, is a radical, realist ideology, meant for the transformation of society through constitutional methods. Social justice is a pragmatic ideology to cure the social inequalities, injustice and other ailments of antique society.

Ambedkar is often characterized as a 'social rebel'. His ideology, therefore, is a revolt against the most glaring inequalities existing in the Hindu society, and the ghastly extent to which they were practicised by the caste Hindus. Casteism and the segregation of the untouchables that had continued for centuries are at variance with the ideology of Ambedkar. Ramachandra Guha writes:

'For members of the Scheduled Castes who had a glimmer of learning themselves, for those who had been to high school or travelled outside their home village, Ambedkar was both exemplar and icon, the man who had breached the upper-caste citadel and encouraged his fellows to do likewise'.[7]

To the untouchables, Ambedkar's ideology of social justice promised paradise on earth; to others it promised equality of opportunity; but to a limited section of caste Hindus, who did not relish it; it put them between the devil and the deep blue sea.

Whatever may be the criticism of Ambedkar's ideology, it was the representative of the age. Political ideology, like any other kind of thought, is fully understood only by relating it to the context of time, place and circumstances in which it occurred. Ambedkar's ideology was 'representative' of the age in the sense that he tried to remove the rotten garbage of the centuries that had piled up in the Hindu society. Instead of castes and classes and status by birth, Ambedkar in his ideology gave a pre-eminent place to Man. Man alone occupies the most central or dominant place in his ideology. Based on democratic values, social justice and fraternity, Ambedkar's ideology is monumental, especially the result of his years of devotional work.

Ambedkar's ideology has been a great mentor in the practical art of government. His one of the greatest ideological triumph can be seen in the drafting of the Indian Constitution. Indian Constitution is a comprehensive document, full of forward-looking ideology of secularism, independence of judiciary, abolition of untouchability, Fabianism, social justice, and other norms of the associated mode of life. His ideology of social justice is the most attractive diadem, embedded in our Constitution. The purpose of the State to Ambedkar appeared to be the same as to John Stuart Mill, who 'laid stress upon the idea that every individual should aim to promote the general happiness. Social well-being was the end of government, the fostering of virtue and intelligence was the test of its success'.[8]

Ambedkar's ideology sought to unite the vast country with its great diversity, many languages and creeds within a common bond of the constitutional justice on the great ideals of liberty, equality, fraternity and social justice. He showed an uncompromising respect for human dignity, an unquestioning commitment to equality and non-discrimination and an abiding concern for the poor and the weak. The ultimate aim of his ideology was the creation of a just social order.

Ambedkar was a pragmatic thinker. His pragmatic ideology – connected with real situations, practical problems and difficulties – was based on vision and action. He did not like the clever dodges of politicians or the tricks of the trade. He grasped the principles of State and politics only by the harder route of learning, conflict and experiencing humiliations. He was indeed a savant, possessing great knowledge and ability. He did not like the slick, simple notion or the short-circuit answer to meet the problems of the day. Such short-circuit methods or ideas, he regarded, as least fruitful and most frustratingly inadequate in practice. All in all, his pragmatic ideology was sensible and realistic. His wonderful intellectual subtlety, distinction and creativeness are visible in the field of pragmatic ideology.

His ideology, in short, was a wide-ranging one. It was an ideology of liberation, loaded in favour of Man. It was free from speculative theories. Its aim was the creation of a just social order. It was saturated with the principles of social justice. It was very strong in reason and rationality. It had exercised a remarkable influence on the framing of Indian Constitution. Its influence on the shaping of events had been tremendous. It is difficult to refute the relevance of his ideology in the Indian context. It was an ideology of vision and action, and each element nourishes the other.

Social and Political Truths

Ambedkar's ideological statements were full of social and political truths. What he said about social, economic and political democracy are self-evident truths. The ends pursued by men in society are many, as are the means by which they may choose to pursue them. In a plural society – where different men form into many different groups for pursuing many ends by many means – it is inevitable that not all ends will be compatible one with another, as inevitable as it is that some means will prove inadequate for attaining the proposed ends, and that some consequences will be those which none of the protagonists desired. In a variegated society in which aims and interests collide, conflicts occur; consensus is difficult as petty squabbles flourish. But it goes to the credit of Ambedkar that in a plural and variegated society, he uttered certain social and political truths which had their impact on the framers of the Constitution. The ends and means did not collide; they were accepted by the founding fathers. Ambedkar advocated that the end of the State is the realization of liberty, equality and fraternity through the constitutional means. He advocated political, economic and social democracy and showed the way how this trinity could be attained. He declared that the State must establish democracy, not only in semblance but in actuality. These, and some other social and political truths, given below cannot be categorized as irrelevant.

Ambedkar used to emphasize statements, and if need be, coin a new version of the same statement, so that the idea contained is easy to understand. A few instances can be quoted. Ambedkar said that 'inequality is the soul of Hinduism', that 'Hinduism is overwhelmed with the fear of pollution; it has not got the power to purify'; and that 'the Hindu social order is a ladder of castes placed one above the other together representing an ascending scale of hatred and a descending scale of contempt'. These social truths, Ambedkar uttered with emphasis in order to demonstrate that the Hindu social order is based on classes and not on individual and that it is a rigid one. Besides promoting the principle of graded inequality, its most striking feature is the worship of the superman. In this respect, Ambedkar said that the Hindu social order is nothing but Nietzsche's Gospel put in action. Nietzsche himself never claimed any originality for his theory of the superman. He borrowed it from *Manusmriti.* Ambedkar's social ideology expounded in *Philosophy of Hinduism*, and *Annihilation of Caste*, contains numerous similar assertions, demonstrating the social truths in an honest and direct way.

Similarly, Ambedkar expressed the political truths in such a sharp way, that the idea which he wished to convey could penetrate even into the thick skulls of his opponents. In his speeches, delivered in the Constituent Assembly[9] on 4 November 1948 and 25 November 1949,[10] Ambedkar uttered a number of political truths. He said that 'democracy in India is only a top-dressing on an Indian soil, which is essentially undemocratic'; that 'political democracy cannot last unless there lies at the base of it social democracy'; that 'real liberty of action exist only when exploitation has been annihilated'; that 'the downtrodden classes are tired of being governed, they are impatient to govern themselves'; that 'hero-worship is a sure road to degradation and to eventual dictatorship'; that 'it is futile to pass any judgment upon the Constitution without reference to the part which the people and their parties are likely to play'; that the anxiety is 'will Indians place the country above their creed or will they place creed above country'; that 'we must hold fast to constitutional methods of achieving our social and economic objectives'; that the 'unconstitutional methods are nothing but grammar of anarchy'; that 'on the 26 January 1950, we are going to enter into a life of contradictions ... how long shall we continue to live this life of contradictions?'; that 'the sooner we realize that we are not as yet 'a nation in the social and psychological sense of the word', the better for us'; that 'fraternity can be a fact only when there is a nation'; that 'without fraternity, equality and liberty will be no deeper than coats of paint'; that the 'constitutional morality is not a natural sentiment; it has to be cultivated'; and that 'if things go wrong under the new Constitution, the reason will not be that we had a bad Constitution. What we will have to say is, that Man was Vile'.

These, and similar other social and political truths uttered by Ambedkar form a significant part of his ideology of constitutionalism. The reliability of his constitutionalism has not been questioned.

Arun Shourie's Comments

Arun Shourie in his work *Worshipping False Gods*, is very critical of Ambedkar. He says that Ambedkar has been deified by a section of politicians who have 'lunged for casteist politics and so they have made icons of persons like Ambedkar'. In a derogatory tone Shourie writes:

> 'Indeed, no one is idolized these days the way he is. His statue is one of the largest in the parliament complex. His portrait in the Central Hall of Parliament is larger than life. The Bharat Ratna has been conferred on him posthumously, a national holiday has been declared in his honour. Postage stamps have been issued in his honour. Universities have been named after him. His statues – dressed in garish blue, holding a copy of the Constitution – have been put up in city after city: it is a fair guess that by now they far outnumber those of Gandhiji. Politicians, activists and other notables flock to these on several anniversaries of his .... He is hailed as the one who gave us the Constitution we now have .... He is hailed as the one who strove to lift the lower castes, indeed the dispossessed in general. Not just that, while Gandhiji and other Congress leaders – provided of course that they were Hindus, at least by birth – are held to have been responsible for the partition of the country, because of the propaganda surrounding his name Ambedkar is assumed to have been, and shown to have been one of the fighters for the country's freedom – in the recent television spots which have been put out by government to mark the 50th anniversary of the country's independence, Ambedkar's photographs has been shown between those of Bhagat Singh and Subhash Chandra Bose'![11]

Arun Shourie's above comments are meant to hurt Ambedkar; the latter was categorically against Bhakti cult or hero-worship in politics. Ambedkar had a great faith in constitutional democracy, both in form and in fact; and detested idolization or deification in politics. He regarded deification, nothing but populism. He was opposed to casteist approach in politics. If a section of politicians are engaged in deification of Ambedkar, this trend is nothing less than a disaster. Hence, there is nothing much in Arun Shourie's comments about Ambedkar.

Essential Conditions

Ambedkar's ideology of social justice that promises paradise on earth is difficult of realization, unless certain essential conditions are fulfilled. The conditions under which the doctrine of social justice might be expected to fit reality to an acceptable degree are many. Democracy thrives in social patterns that display certain characteristics and it might well be doubted whether there is any sense in asking how it would fare in India that lack those characteristics – or how the people of this country have shaped or would shape their characters in future.

The first condition is that the human material of politics – the people, who operate the party machines, are elected to serve in Parliament, rise to Cabinet office – should be of sufficiently high quality. This means more than that individual of adequate ability, virtue and moral character must exist in sufficient numbers. The adequacy of material is particularly important for the success of democratic government and fulfilling the ideal of social justice.

The second condition for the success of social justice is that the effective range of political decision should not be extended too far. To put this more concretely: the range does not only depend, for instance, on the kind and quality of matters that can be successfully handled by a government subject to the strain of an incessant struggle for its political life; it also depends, at any given time and place, on the quality of men who form that government and on the type of political machine and the pattern of public opinion they have to work with.

As a third condition, social justice and social democracy, in an era of globalization and privatization must be able to command, the services of a well-trained bureaucracy of good standing and tradition, endowed with a strong sense of duty and a no less strong *esprit de corps*. It is not enough that the bureaucracy should be efficient and competent to give advice. It must be responsive, accountable and strong enough to guide and, if shall be, to maintain their independence of thought. In order to be able to do, this it must be in a position to evolve principles of its own and sufficiently independent to assert them. It must be a power in its own right. It must be capable to usher in social transformation.

The fourth condition is that the tendency to eulogize political leaders and hero-worship must come to an end. Hero-worship is antithetical to the norms of a good democracy. Excessive hero-worship is a sure road to disaster. In addition to hero-worship, the caste-based leadership and caste-ridden thinking, a peculiar phenomenon of Indian politics, must be abandoned, because it leads to fragmentation of society. Fragmentation of people on caste lines is antagonistic to the principle of fraternity, that Ambedkar loved and advocated so much.

The fifth condition is democratic self-control. It means electorate and legislatures must be on an intellectual and moral level high enough to be proof against the offerings of the crook and the crank, or else men who are neither, will be driven into the ways of both. Politicians in Parliament must resist the temptation to upset or embarrass the government each time they could do so. No successful policy is possible if they do this. What Ambedkar spoke about the constitutional morality must be acquired both by the leaders as well as the electorates; otherwise the ideals of social justice as contained in our Constitution would be difficult of realization! The people of all classes must resolve to abide by the rules of the democratic game and this in turn implies that they are substantially agreed on the fundamentals of their institutional structure. At present these conditions fail to be fulfilled. The net result is a lot of fraction in our society. Parties are at loggerheads; to them their creed is more important than national interest. Casteist tendencies in social and political life are on the rise. Poverty and corruption are widespread. The social bases of democracy are weak. Policy implementation is weak and unsystematic. The tide of populism is rising.

And lastly, the formal structure of democracy – general elections, parties, and legislatures, Cabinets and Chief Minister/Prime Minister is there, but in fact their operations are loose and disjointed. India is maintaining the form of constitutional democracy but in actuality it is shifting towards populism. Unless the structures and processes of our government are not properly tuned; unless the various organs do not maintain equilibrium in theory and practice both, the ideal of social justice, deeply embedded in our Constitution, would not be able to deliver the desired results. But this does not mean that ideal of social justice is not relevant to the situation. If the above conditions are fulfilled social justice would be an alchemy, possessing mysterious powers to change the society. Social justice is the surpassing good and when this is established all the people will sing merrily.

Reservations

From his early childhood, Ambedkar dedicated himself to the upliftment of the scheduled castes among whom he was born. There were many temptations in his way; but he did not consider his own interests. Dedicating himself to the upliftment of the scheduled castes, he followed the adage which says that 'it is better to be narrow-minded if you wish to be enthusiastic about a cause which you wish to accomplish'. At the time of the framing of Indian Constitution, constitutional safeguards and reservations (in legislatures, services and educational institutions) were provided to the SCs and STs, but they were not to Ambedkar's 'satisfaction'. Later on, around 1990, the reservation policy was extended to OBCs. Though reservations for SCs and STs have been just and reasonable and even accepted by the society as a whole, but the extension of reservations to the OBCs whatever may be the arguments in its favour, have eroded Ambedkar's ideology of building a casteless society, because this provision has given a fillip to the consolidation of caste structures in India. It has generated 'a lot of politics, polemics, legal disputes, social divisions, violent protests and agitations and creamy layers and gloomy spectacles. Strong and articulate vested interests and advocacy groups have emerged both for and against reservations. More and more areas of claim and claimant categories are emerging on the scene'. As such, there is a need to review the reservation policy about the OBCs alone; and, if need be, to systematize it in such a way that caste compartmentalization and conflicts be reduced to a minimum.

Relevance

Ambedkar's ideology has been comprehensively discussed. It is a forward-looking ideology meant to replace the antique society by a modern one. It is indeed a quest towards the promised land.

Ambedkar's ideology speaks of the religion of antique society as against the religion of modern society. These two religions differ in the conceptions regarding the relations between God, Society and Man. In ancient society, men and their Gods formed a social and political as well as a religions whole. Religion was founded on kinship between the God and his worshippers. Modern society has eliminated God from its composition. It consists of men only. The God of the antique society was an exclusive God; it never conceived that God could be universal God. In antique society, God was the father of his people but the basis of this conception of fatherhood was deemed to be physical. In modern society, the idea of divine fatherhood has become entirely dissociated from the physical basis of natural fatherhood. In its place Man is conceived to be created in the image of God. In antique society, religion was a part of the citizen's public life, reduced to fixed forms and rituals, but in modern society, religion is above all a matter of individual conviction. In antique society, the idea of divine governance prevailed, but in modern society, it has ceased to occupy the central position. It is Man who occupies the central place. So Ambedkar in his ideology rejected the morality of the antique society and upheld the morality of the modern society.

Ambedkar denounced the cult of superman, expounded in *Manusmriti*. The superman is the core and heart of the philosophy of Hinduism. The gospel of superman teaches that what is right for the supermen is the only thing which is called morality. This superman is the class of Brahmins who occupy the highest position in the *Varna* system. This class is only interested in maintaining their privileges. Manu's supermen were not supermen by reason of their worth, but by reason of their birth. Their title of being supermen was not lost even if they lost their virtue. In Ambedkar's ideology, the cult of superman did not satisfy the test of justice or utility. Superman is the negation of the interest of common man. He is not interested in the society as a whole. His interest lies in a class and is concerned in sustaining and supporting the rights of a particular class. 'Hinduism is Superman's heaven and the common man's damnation'. Hence, according to Ambedkar, the cult of superman was detestable.

In addition to the cult of superman, Ambedkar was very critical of the Bhakti cult or the hero-worship in politics. The idea or charismatic leadership filled him with disgust. The hero-worship, or worshipping in a very enthusiastic way is highly dangerous to the democratic system as a whole. It may cripple the working of democratic structures and pave a way for the upsurge of dictatorial tendencies.

There was a virulent criticism of caste in Ambedkar's ideology. Caste devitalizes a man. It is a process of sterilization. Education, wealth, labour are all necessary for every individual if he is to reach a free and full manhood. Mere education without wealth and labour is barren. Wealth without education is brutal. Each is necessary to every one. They are necessary for the growth of a man.

In his ideology, Ambedkar exposed the hollowness of the Hindu social order which is reared on three principles – graded inequality, fixity of occupations for each class by heredity and the fixation of people within their respective classes. His ideology was a devastating attack upon the infallibility of the *Vedas*. In his rationalistic ideology all the old scriptures were false and fanaticism folly. Inequality was writ large upon the *Vedas*; liberty was the exclusive domain of caste Hindus, and fraternity was an illusion. The hope of justice in *Varna* system was a mirage.

Ambedkar's ideology has been expressed in concrete terms rather than in the abstract. He dismissed speculative, metaphysical and utopian theories. There were no romantic conceits in his ideology. The inadequacies of the metaphysical and theological doctrines were clearly expressed in his ideology of critical reason. Metaphysics, to Ambedkar, 'is like a blind man in a dark room, looking for a black cat which was not there'. And theology to him, 'is like a blind man in the dark room, looking for a black cat which was not there but the theologian declared to have found there'.

Ambedkar's ideology was not dogmatic, but a pragmatic one. It was based on utility, realism, love and wisdom. It was a quest for the realization of the ideals of liberty, equality, fraternity and social justice. It was specifically designed for social justice; and social justice, it may be said, appears like the exotic blooms of the orchid. It was concerned with the ending of all sorts of exploitation and oppression. The great merit of his ideology lay in its safeguarding of the individual and the abolition of untouchability. Neither there was a propensity for hatred nor to exaggerate anything in his ideology.

Ambedkar's ideology is relevant because in it Man and rationality occupy a central position. The focus of his ideology is upon Man and his welfare. The criterion or standard by which all things are to be judged is rationality. The application of critical reason, critical analysis and scientific temper to dissect religion, politics and society were fundamental in his ideology.

Ambedkar's ideology reflected vision and action. Both were embedded in the Indian Constitution. His ideology was a reassertion of the doctrine of constitutionalism in the Indian context. His constitutional ideology was rooted in democratic values, safeguarding of the rights of an individual and prescribing the means to enforce the rights. The Independence of judiciary is the hallmark of his ideology. By its power of judicial review, the judiciary plays the role of the guardian of the Constitution. Its power of judicial activism is meant to check the vagaries of the executive. One can, therefore safely draw the conclusion that his ideology is relevant for the building of a new, vibrant social order, exuberant in the dignity of an individual, and making him free from the fetters of ignorance, shame and humiliation. This is only one good ideology relevant to the situation, to resolve the contradictions and inequalities that prevail, and to usher in a healthy social order full of life and energy – indeed a very bright and strong one. This is the significance of Ambedkar's ideology. Ambedkar may justly be called as one of the great prophets of enlightenment and modernity in the annals of modern India.

Notes

1. V.P. Varma: *Modern Indian Political Thought* (Agra, Lakshmi Narain Agrawal, 1978), p. 5.
2. Dr. Babasaheb Ambedkar *Writings and Speeches*, Vol. 3, 1987, p. 39.
3. Ibid., p. 87.
4. Ibid., p. 86.
5. Ibid., p. 153.
6. Ibid., p. 187.
7. Ramachandra Guha: *India After Gandhi* (London, Picador, 2008), p. 379.
8. Mohammad Shabbir (ed): *Ambedkar on Law, Constitution and Social Justice* (Jaipur, Rawat Publications, 2005), p. 183.
9. CAD Official Report, Vol. VII, 1948, pp. 31–44.
10. CAD Official Report, Vol. X, 25 November 1949, pp. 972–989.
11. M.G. Chitkara: *Dr. Ambedkar and Social Justice* (New Delhi, APH Publishing Corporation, 2002), p. 190.
12. Mohammad Shabbir (ed), p. 189.

Bibliography

Primary Sources

Dr. Babasaheb Ambedkar Writings and Speeches, Government of Maharashtra, Bombay.

Vol. 1. (1979)

- *Castes in India (1916)*
- *Annihilation of Caste (1936)*
- *Maharashtra as a Linguistic Province (1948)*
- *Need for Checks and Balances (1953)*
- *Thought on Linguistic States (1955)*
- *Ranade, Gandhi and Jinnah (1943)*
- *Evidence before the South Borough Committee (1919)*
- *Federation versus Freedom (1939)*
- *Communal Deadlock and a Way to Solve It (1945)*
- *States and Minorities (1947)*
- *Small Holdings in India (1918)*
- *Mr. Russell and the Reconstruction of Society (1918)*

Vol. 2. (1982)

- *Dr. Ambedkar in Bombay Legislature (1927–1939)*
- *Dr. Ambedkar with the Simon Commission (1927–28)*
- *Dr. Ambedkar at the Round Table Conferences (1930–1939)*

Vol. 3. (1987)

- *Philosophy of Hinduism*

- *India and the Pre-requisites of Communism*
- *Revolution and Counter-Revolution*
- *Buddha or Karl Marx*

Vol. 4. (1987)

- *Riddles in Hinduism*

Vol. 5. (1989)

- *Essays on Untouchables and Untouchability*

Vol. 6. (1989)

- *The Problem of the Rupee (1923)*
- *Evolution of Provincial Finance in British India (1952)*

Vol. 7. (1990)

- *Who Were the Shudras?*
- *The Untouchables*

Vol. 8. (1990)

- *Pakistan or the Partition of India*

Vol. 9. (1990)

- *What Congress and Gandhi Have Done to the Untouchables*
- *Mr. Gandhi and the Emancipation of the Untouchables*

Vol. 10. (1991)

- *Dr. Ambedkar as Member of the Governor General's Executive Council, 1942–46*

Vol. 11. (1992)

- *The Buddha and His Dhamma*

Vol. 12. (1993)

- *Unpublished Writings; Ancient Indian Commerce; Notes on Laws; Waiting for a Visa, Miscellaneous Notes*, etc.

Vol. 13. (1994)

- *Dr. Ambedkar as the Principal Architect of the Constitution of India*

Vol. 14 (1994, Part–1)

- *Dr. Ambedkar and The Hindu Code Bill*

Vol. 14 (1995, Part–2)

- *Dr. Ambedkar and The Hindu Code Bill*

Vol. 15 (1997)

- *Dr. Ambedkar as Free India's First Law Minister and Member of Opposition in Indian Parliament (1947–1956).*

Vol. 17. (2003)

- *Dr. B.R. Ambedkar and his Egalitarian Revolution – Struggle for Human Rights. Events Starting from March 1927 to 17 November 1956 in the Chronological Order. (Part I)*
- *Dr. B.R. Ambedkar and his Egalitarian Revolution – Socio-Political and Religious Activities. Events Starting from November 1929 to 8 May 1956 in the Chronological Order. (Part II)*
- *Dr. B.R. Ambedkar and his Egalitarian Revolution – Speeches. Events Starting from 1 January to 20 November 1956 in the Chronological Order. (Part III)*

Vol. 21 (2006)

- *Dr. B.R. Ambedkar's Photo Album and Correspondence.*

Books by B.R. Ambedkar

Annihilation of Caste, Bheem Patrika Publications, Jalandhar, 1944.

Buddha or Karl Marx, Anand Sahitya Sadan, Aligarh, 1989.

Evolution of Provincial Finance in British India. P.S. King and Sons Ltd., London, 1925.

Federation versus Freedom, Gokhale Institute of Politics and Economics, R.K. Tatnis, Bombay, 1939.

Mr. Gandhi and the Emancipation of the Untouchables, Thacker and Co. Ltd., Bombay, 1943.

Gandhi and Gandhism, Bhim Patrika Publications, Jalandhar, 1970.

History of Indian Currency and Banking, Thacker & Co., Bombay, 1946.

Pakistan or Partition of India, Thacker and Co. Ltd., Bombay, 1946.

Ranade, Gandhi and Jinnah, Bheem Patrika Publications, Jalandhar, 1964.

States and Minorities, Thacker and Co. Ltd., Bombay, 1947.

States and Minorities, What Are Their Rights and How to Secure Them in the Constitution of Free India, Baba Saheb Ambedkar Memorial Society, Hyderabad, 1970.

State Socialism, Bheem Patrika Publications, Jalandhar, 1990.

The Untouchables: Who Were They and Why They Became Untouchables, Amrit Book Co., New Delhi, 1948.

The Problem of the Rupee: Its Origin and its Solution, P.S. King and Sons Ltd., London, 1923. Reprinted by Thacker & Co., Bombay, 1947, under the title *History of Indian Currency and Banking*.

Thoughts on Pakistan, Thacker and Co. Ltd., Bombay, 1941.

Thoughts on Linguistic States, published by B.R. Ambedkar, 26 Alipur Road, Civil Lines, Delhi, 1955.

The Buddha and His Dhamma, Siddharth College Publications, Bombay, 1957.

The Rise and Fall of Hindu Women, Bheem Patrika Publications, Jalandhar, 1980.

What Congress and Gandhi Have Done to the Untouchables, Thacker and Co. Ltd., Bombay 1945.

Who Were the Shudras? And How They Came to be Fourth Varna in Indo-Aryan Society, Thacker & Co. Ltd., Bombay, 1946.

Communal Deadlock and a Way to Solve it, Address on 6 May 1945, Bheem Patrika Publications, Jalandhar.

On Poona Pact, Bheem Patrika Publications, Jalandhar.

Speeches and Articles of Dr Ambedkar

Ambedkar's Presidential Address before All India Scheduled Caste Federation at Nagpur, April, 1942.

Ambedkar's Presidential Address at I Session of All India Depressed Classes Congress, 8 August 1930.

Ambedkar's Memorandum entitled 'The Cabinet Mission and the Untouchables', Ambedkar College, Mahad Librarian, 1962.

Annihilation of Caste: With a Reply to Mahatma Gandhi – Undelivered address before the Annual Conference of the Jat Pat Todak Mandal of Lahore, 1936.

'Castes in India: Their Genesis, Mechanism and Development' – a paper read by him before the Anthropology Seminar at Columbia University, New York, May 1916. Published in Indian Antiquary, Vol. XLI, May 1917.

Communal Deadlock and Way to Solve It – Address to the Annual Session of the All India Scheduled Castes Federation, Bombay, 1945.

Federation versus Freedom, address delivered on 29 January 1939 (Kala Memorial Lecture) at the Annual Function of the Gokhale Institute of Politics and Economics, Poona.

Future of Parliamentary Democracy, Speech on 28 October 1951 in DAV College, Jalandhar city.

Memorandum submitted to the Minorities Committee of RTC dated 12 November 1930 which obtained a scheme of political safeguards for the protection of depressed classes in the future Constitution of a self-governing India.

Memorandum placed before the Cabinet Mission, New Delhi, 5 April 1946.

Mr. Russell and Reconstruction of Society – a review article published in the *Journal of the Indian Economic Society,* Vol. I, 1918.

On Parliamentary Democracy – Speech delivered at Poona District Law Library, Poona, 1952.

Prospects of Parliamentary Democracy in India, Talk for B.B.C. London, 20 May 1956.

Ranade, Gandhi and Jinnah – Address on the 101th Birth Celebration of M.G. Ranade at Poona on 10 January 1943.

Small Holdings in India and their Remedies – an article published in the *Journal of the Indian Economic Society,* Vol. I, 1918.

Statement on Safeguard for Depressed Classes submitted to the Simon Commission on behalf of Bahishkrit Hitkarini Sabha on 29 May 1928 (by Ambedkar).

'The Buddha and the Future of His Religion', *The Maha Bodhi Journal,* Calcutta, Vol. 58, April–May 1950.

'The Rise and Fall of the Hindu Women', *The Maha Bodhi Journal,* Calcutta, June 1951.

Thus Spoke Ambedkar Vol. I, Selected Speeches compiled by Bhagwan Das, Buddhist Publishing House, Jalandhar, 1963.

Thus Spoke Ambedkar, Vol. II, Bhagwan Das, Buddhist Publishing House, Jalandhar, 1968.

Thus Spoke Ambedkar, Vol. III, Bhagwan Das, Ambedkar Sahithya Prakashan, Bangalore, 1979.

Thus Spoke Ambedkar, Vol. IV, Bhagwan Das, Ambedkar Sahithya Prakashan, Bangalore, 1979.

Why Conversion – Speech delivered in Marathi at the Mahar Parishad on 30–31 May 1936 in Bombay, Translated into English by Vasant Moon, Lokrajya, Bombay, 1981.

Secondary Sources

Ahir, D.C., *Buddhism and Ambedkar*, Ajay Prakashan, New Delhi, 1968.

——, *Dr. Ambedkar and Indian Constitution*, Buddha Vihara, Lucknow, 1972.

——, *Gandhi and Ambedkar*, Ajay Prakashan, New Delhi, 1969.

——, *The Legacy of Dr. Ambedkar*, B.R. Publishing Corporation, Delhi, 1990.

Ahluwalia, B.K. and Shashi Ahluwalia, (eds), *Dr. Ambedkar and Human Rights*, Vivek Publishing Company, Delhi, 1981.

Ahluwalia, Shashi, *Founder of Modern India*, Mandi Publication, New Delhi, 1986.

Appadurai, A., *The Substance of Politics*, Oxford University Press, Delhi, 1965.

Baisantry, D.K., *Dr. Ambedkar: A Pioneer of Labour Welfare*, Buddhist Publishing House, Jalandhar, 1990.

Bakshi, S.R. (ed), *Social Ideology of B.R. Ambedkar*, Deep & Deep Publication, New Delhi, 2001.

——, *Political Ideology of B.R. Ambedkar*, Deep & Deep Publications, New Delhi, 2002.

Balley, L.R. (ed), *Thoughts on Ambedkar*, Bheem Patrika Publications, Jalandhar, 1972.

——, *Thoughts on Ambedkar*, Bheem Patrika Publications, Jalandhar, 1972.

Banerjee, A.C., *Indian Constitutional Document*, Vol. III, A. Mukerjee & Co., Calcutta, 1949.

Banerjee, D.N., *Some Aspects of the Indian Constitution*, World Press Pvt. Ltd., Calcutta, 1962.

Barker, E., *Plato and His Predecessors*, London, 1952.

Basu, D.D., *Commentary on Constitution of India* (3rd edition), Calcutta, 1955.

Bharill, Chandra, *Social and Political Ideas of B.R. Ambedkar*, Aalekh Publishers, Jaipur, 1977.

Bharti, K.S., *Foundation of Ambedkar Thought*, Datta Son Publication, Nagpur, 1990.

Bose, Devbrata, *The Problems of Indian Society*, Popular Prakashan, Bombay, 1968.

Buhler, G., *The Laws of Manu*, Motilal Banarasidas, Delhi, 1964.

Carus, Paul, *The Gospel of Buddha*, National Book Trust, New Delhi, 1975.

Chandha, Yogesh, *Rediscovering Gandhi*, Arrow Books, London, 1980.

Chandra, Ramesh and Sangh Mitra, *Caste System in India*, Commonwealth Publishers, New Delhi, 2003.

——, *The Ambedkar Era*, Commonwealth Publishers, New Delhi, 2003.

Chitkara, M.G., *Dr. Ambedkar and Social Justice,* APH Publishing Corporation, New Delhi, 2002.

Constituent Assembly Debates I to XII, Lok Sabha Secretariat, New Delhi, 1985.

Curtis, Michael (ed), *The Great Political Theories*, Avon Book Division, New York, 1961.

Devam Shanti and C.M. Wagh, *Dr. Ambedkar and Conversion*, Dr. Ambedkar Publications Society, Hyderabad, 1965.

Dongre, M.K., *Economic Thoughts of Dr. B.R. Ambedkar,* Ambedkar Samaj Publication, Nagpur, 1974.

Eleanor, Zelliot, *Gandhi and Ambedkar*, Trailokya Boudh Mahasangh Sahayak Gana, Pune, 1983.

Forsyth and Keens-Soper (ed), *A Guide to the Political Classics*, Oxford University Press, Oxford, 1988.

Gauba, O.P., *Dimensions of Social Justice*, National Publishing House, New Delhi, 1983.

Ghosh, S.K., *Protection of Minorities and Scheduled Castes,* Ashish Publishing House, New Delhi, 1980.

Ghurye, G.S., *Caste and Class in India*, Popular Book Depot, Bombay, 1957.

Guha, Ramchandra, *India after Gandhi*, Picador, London, 2008.

——(ed), *Makers of Modern India*, Penguin Books India, New Delhi, 2010.

Gupta, D.C., *Indian National Movement and Constitutional Development*, Vikas Publishing House, Delhi, 1970.

Gupta, V.P. and Mohini Gupta (ed), *Makers of Modern India Series II, Dr. Ambedkar,* Ambe Books, Delhi, 1998.

Huberman, Leo, *Introduction to Socialism*, Progressive Book Depot, New Delhi, 1968.

Hutton, J.H., *Caste in India*, Oxford University Press, London, 1969.

Jaffrelot, Christophe, *Dr. Ambedkar and Untouchability,* Permanent Black, New Delhi, 2005.

Jatava, D.R., *Ambedkar: The Prime Mover,* ABD Publishers, Jaipur, 2004.

——, *B.R. Ambedkar: Study in Society and Politics,* National Publishing House, New Delhi, 1998.

——, *B.R. Ambedkar: A Vision of Man and Morals,* ABD Publishers, Jaipur, 1999.

——, *The Critics of Dr. Ambedkar,* Bhartiya Shoshit Jan Utthan Parishad, New Delhi, 1975.

——, *The Political Philosophy of Dr. B.R. Ambedkar,* Phoenix Publishing Agency, Agra, 1965.

——, *The Social Philosophy of Dr. B.R. Ambedkar,* Phoenix Publishing Agency, Agra, 1965.

Johari, J.C., *Comparative Politics,* Sterling Publishing, New Delhi, 1976.

Kamaji, Kshirsagar Ramchandra, *Political Thought of Dr. Babasaheb Ambedkar,* Intellectual Publishing House, New Delhi, 1992.

Keer, Dhananjay, *Dr. Ambedkar: Life and Mission,* Popular Prakashan, Bombay, 1971.

Khabade, Dinkar, *Dr. Ambedkar and Western Thinkers,* Usha Wagh, Sugava Prakashan, Pune, 1989.

Khairmody, C.B., *Bhimrao Ramji Ambedkar: A Biography,* Vol. I-IV, Bharat Bhushan Printing Press, Bombay, 1959.

Kuber, W.N., *Builders of Modern India,* B.R. Ambedkar Publications Division, Ministry of Information and Broadcasting, Delhi, 1987.

——, *Dr. Ambedkar: A Critical Study,* People's Publishing House, New Delhi, 1973.

Loknande, G.S., *Bhimrao Ramji Ambedkar: A Study in Social Democracy,* II Revised Edition, Intellectual Publishing House, New Delhi, 1982.

Lynch, Owen M., *The Politics of Untouchability,* National Publishing House, Delhi, 1974.

Majumdar, A.K. and Bhanwar Singh, *Ambedkar and Social Justice,* Radha Publications, New Delhi, 1997.

Mandal, S.N., *Dr. Ambedkar: His Thought and Observation,* National Publishing House, New Delhi, 2004.

Menon, V.P., *The Story of the Integration of Indian States*, Macmillan, New York, 1956.

——, *Transfer of Power in India*, Orient Longmans, Bombay, 1957.

Mouli, V. Chandra, *B.R. Ambedkar: Man and His Vision*, Sterling Publisher Pvt. Ltd., New Delhi, 1990.

Munshi, K.M., *Indian Constitutional Documents, Vol. I-II, Munshi Papers*, Bhartiya Vidya Bhawan, Bombay, 1967.

Narsu, P. Laxmi, *The Essence of Buddhism*, Thacker & Co., Bombay, 1948.

Nim, Hoti Lal (complied), *Thoughts on Dr. Ambedkar*, Siddharth Educational and Cultural Society, Agra, 1969.

Panikkar, K.M., *The Foundation of New India*, Allen and Unwin, London, 1963.

Rajasekharaih, A.M., *Social Philosophy of Dr. Ambedkar*, Dr. Ambedkar Memorial Trust, Hyderabad, 1987.

——, *B.R. Ambedkar: The Quest for Social Justice*, Uppal Publishing House, New Delhi, 1989.

——, *The Politics of Emancipation*, Sindhu Publications, Bombay, 1971.

Ranga, M.L. (ed), *B.R. Ambedkar: Life, Work and Relevance*, Manohar Publishers, New Delhi, 2000.

Rao, J.S. Narayan, A. Somasekhar, K. Audiseshaiah, *B.R. Ambedkar: His Relevance Today*, Gyan Publishing House, New Delhi, 2002.

Rathore, L.S., *Dr. Ambedkar: His Works and Key Concepts*, Keynote Address, National Post Graduate College, Lucknow.

——, *Formative Influence on B.R. Ambedkar*, Keynote Address, National Post Graduate College, Lucknow.

——, *Political and Social Philosophy of Dr. Ambedkar*, Keynote Address, National Post Graduate College, Lucknow, 26–27 May 2007.

Robin, Jeanette, *Dr. Ambedkar and His Movement*, Dr. Ambedkar Publication Society, Hyderabad, 1964.

Sangharakshita, Ven, *Ambedkar and Buddhism*, Windhorse Publications, Glasgow, England, 1986.

Shabbir, Mohammad, *Ambedkar on Law, Constitution and Social Justice*, Rawat Publications, Jaipur, 2005.

Sharma, Kusum, *Ambedkar and Indian Constitution*, Ashish Publishing House, New Delhi, 1997.

Sharma, S.R., *Life and Works of Dr. Ambedkar*, Jaipur, Book Enclave, 2006.

Sharma, Sanjay Prakash, *Dr. B.R. Ambedkar: A Crusader of Social Justice,* RBSA Publishers, Jaipur, 2003.

Shashi, S.S. (ed.), *Ambedkar and Social Justice*, Vol. 1, Ministry of Information and Broadcasting, Government of India, Patiala House, New Delhi,1992.

Shukla, J.J., *Dr. B.R. Ambedkar on Hinduism*, Globe Books & Periodicals, Ahmedabad.

Singh, Gian, *Dr. Ambedkar and Humanism*, Bheem Patrika Publication, Jalandhar, 1990.

Singh, Paramanand, *Equality, Reservation and Discrimination*, Deep & Deep Publication, New Delhi.

Singh, Sukhbir, *History of Political Thought*, Vol. I, Rastogi Publications, Meerut, 2006.

Smith, Donald E., *India as a Secular State*, Princeton University Press, London, 1963.

Srivivasan, N., *Democratic Government in India,* Asia Publishing House, Delhi, 1954.

Tattvabhushana, Sitamath, *The Philosophy of Brahmoism*, Higginbotham & Co., Madras, 1990.

Thompson, Edward, *Enlist India for Freedom*, Victor Gollanecz Ltd., London, 1940.

Thomson, David (ed), *Political Ideas*, Penguin Books, Middlesex, 1970.

Vakil, A.K., *Gandhi-Ambedkar Dispute: An Analytical Study*, Ashish Publishing House, New Delhi, 1991.

Varma, V.P., *Modern Indian Political Thought,* Lakshmi Narain Agarwal, Agra, 1978.

Wayper, C.L., *Political Thought*, B.I. Publications, New Delhi, 1974.

Index